My Way to Ornithology

HARRIS' SPARROW. Unsigned drawing by George Miksch Sutton.

MY WAY TO
Ornithology

Olin Sewall Pettingill, Jr.

Foreword by Gary D. Schnell

UNIVERSITY OF OKLAHOMA PRESS
NORMAN AND LONDON

For Polly-Ann and Mary-Ann

Text and jacket design by Bill Cason.

Library of Congress Cataloging-in-Publication Data

Pettingill, Olin Sewall, 1907–
    My way to ornithology / Olin Sewall Pettingill, Jr. ; foreword by
Gary D. Schnell.
    p.   cm.
    ISBN 0-8061-2409-1 (alk. paper)
    1. Pettingill, Olin Sewall, 1907–   . 2. Ornithologists—United
States—Biography.   I. Title.
    QL31.P48A3   1992
    598′092—dc20
    [B]   91-50869
                                                                         CIP

Three of the chapters in this book were previously published, entirely or in part: "Superintendent's Son" originally appeared as "The Boy on the Bicycle" in *Down East* magazine (May, 1982); "Sea Island Adventure" originally appeared as "Fog, Gulls, and a Revolver" in *Audubon* magazine (November, 1984); "Honeymoon on Cobb Island" originally appeared with the same title in the book *Discovery* (J. B. Lippincott Company: New York, 1961), and is used with the permission of its editor, John K. Terres.

The drawing of the Harris' Sparrow by the late George Miksch Sutton that appears in the frontispiece, from Josselyn Van Tyne and Andrew J. Berger, *Fundamentals of Ornithology*, Copyright © 1956, reprinted by permission of John Wiley and Sons, Inc.

All photographs of birds in the book are by Olin Sewall Pettingill, Jr. All other photographs are from the collection of Olin Sewall Pettingill, Jr.

The paper in this book meets the guidelines for permanence and durability of the Committee on Production Guidelines for Book Longevity of the Council on Library Resources, Inc. ⊗

Contents

Illustrations

Foreword

HAVING SPENT five summers during the 1960s at the University of Michigan Biological Station engaged informally or formally in studying ornithology, I was influenced in significant ways by the teaching, counseling, and general tutelage of Sewall Pettingill. Furthermore, his close personal and professional association with George Sutton, a colleague of mine for a number of years at the University of Oklahoma, provided one of several continuing links between Sewall and myself. When the manuscript for this book came to my attention, I was intrigued. While I was familiar with many of Sewall's accomplishments, I had only a sketchy knowledge of his early background. Furthermore, as I now have the advantages (and some disadvantages) of perspective due to time, Sewall's narrative brought me a convenient opportunity to reflect on circumstances, opportunities, and people who were important in my own development as a scientist.

In this book, Sewall Pettingill provides engaging accounts of his early experiences, particularly those important to his becoming a professional ornithologist. We are given a glimpse of the environment in which he was born and raised, as he recounts a series of events from the time of his childhood through appointment to his first permanent position as assistant professor at Carleton College in Northfield, Minnesota. In order to appreciate more fully his accounts and their significance in his development as a professional, it is helpful to look first at Sewall's accomplishments as an ornithologist following his appointment at Carleton.

From 1936 through 1953 Sewall Pettingill served as a faculty member at Carleton College, where he taught a number of courses, including ornithology. As recounted in the book,

Sewall spent the summer of 1932 as a student at the University of Michigan Biological Station near Cheboygan. He returned to the "bug camp" in 1938 to begin what would be thirty-five years of teaching summer ornithology field courses to over eight hundred students, a number of whom have become successful ornithologists or scholars in other fields.

In 1960, Sewall became director of the Laboratory of Ornithology at Cornell University, a position held until his retirement in 1973. The laboratory, which grew under his leadership, has performed an important role in American ornithology in emphasizing amateur as well as professional ornithology, and providing links between the two.

Sewall had an important effect as a teacher at Carleton and the biological station in Michigan, but his influence on students of birds has been much broader. While teaching ornithology at Carleton he developed a series of study assignments for students that formed the basis of *A Laboratory and Field Manual of Ornithology*, a book first published in 1939. The fifth edition, called *Ornithology in Laboratory and Field*, appeared in 1985. Over its fifty-year history, the manual has served hundreds of ornithology classes and thousands of students from several generations.

His bibliography, which consists of almost one hundred contributions, includes several other highly successful books. He was the first to develop the idea of a "bird-finding" book with *A Guide to Bird Finding East of the Mississippi* in 1951; it was followed in 1953 by a companion volume on western birding spots. Sewall gathered relevant data from the scientific literature and marshaled over six hundred people from coast to coast who contributed first-hand knowledge of good birding spots; information was provided by state on physiographic regions, natural areas, and principal ornithological attractions. The works, revised and updated as second editions in 1977 and 1981, respectively, are regularly consulted by ornithologists and bird watchers, and have been emulated by numerous authors. As a regular contributor to *Audubon* magazine from 1957 to 1968, Sewall reached a wide audience with his columns on bird-finding. He also served as editor of *The Bird Watchers' America*, a 1965 volume that included accounts from over forty authorities on special areas for birds in

North America. All of these contributions reflect his continuing interest in popularizing the study of birds.

Sewall's editorial and organizational skills were particularly useful when he served as editor-in-chief of *The Audubon Illustrated Handbook of American Birds* (1968). He was editor of the section on birds in *Biological Abstracts* from 1942 to 1953 and review editor of *The Wilson Bulletin* from 1959 to 1969. He assembled information on birds of prey for the *World Book Encyclopedia*, and wrote the section on birds in the revised edition of *Collier's Encyclopedia*. Sewall acted as a consultant for books in the series Our Living World of Nature and for *The American Heritage Dictionary of the English Language*. At the Cornell Laboratory of Ornithology, Sewall initiated and edited *The Living Bird*, an annual that contained articles of notable interest to both amateurs and professionals. The laboratory also published the widely distributed *Seminars in Ornithology, A Home Study Course in Bird Biology* (1972), for which he served as editor.

His photographic and other studies have led to Sewall's involvement in a number of expeditions. Along with George Sutton, he organized a 1941 trip to Tamaulipas. In 1945, he took leave from Carleton for a year to conduct a study of whooping cranes sponsored by the National Audubon Society and the U.S. Fish and Wildlife Service. The birds were followed from the Gulf Coast to their nesting areas in Canada and back. Sewall took other extended trips to Iceland (1958), Midway Atoll (1963), New Zealand (1965), Argentina (1969), and the Falkland Islands (1953–54, 1971–72). He also served as a lecturer and naturalist on tours of the Antarctic (1970, 1971, 1978).

In this book, we see signs of his growing interest in filming. Sewall is a talented photographer and has made major contributions through these endeavors. From over forty miles of exposed film, he produced fourteen films for lecture tours and nine educational films for Coronet Instructional Media. Four Walt Disney nature productions include significant portions of his footage.

Sewall probably was at his best as a teacher and entertainer while lecturing and showing his films. When the National Audubon Society began its highly popular Audubon

Screen Tours in 1943, Sewall was one of the first participants, typically accompanied by his wife, Eleanor. In those times before the widespread availability of nature films on television, the lecturer gave live dialogue while showing a motion picture. Sewall presented thousands of lectures throughout the United States, Canada, Great Britain, Bermuda, the Bahamas, and a number of Caribbean islands. The presentations, attended by more than half a million people, were educational for the general public and a major stimulus for many of us who went on to become professionals.

Sewall has also made significant contributions to societies devoted to the study of birds. Starting in 1937 he served as secretary, vice-president, and then president of the Wilson Ornithological Society. In addition, he was secretary of the American Ornithologists' Union and president of the Maine Audubon Society. For almost twenty years, he was a member of the board of directors of the National Audubon Society.

Sewall is one of the better known figures in ornithology and his contributions have been formally recognized. In 1962, the Detroit Audubon Society gave him a special award "in recognition and appreciation of his distinguished contributions to the field of ornithology and conservation." He received the Arthur A. Allen Award from Cornell in 1974 for distinguished service to ornithology. The Ludlow Griscom Award of the American Birding Association was presented to him in 1982 for "outstanding contributions to excellence in field ornithology," and Sewall was the 1985 recipient of the Eugene Eisenmann Medal from the Linnaean Society of New York, for "excellence in ornithology and encouragement of the amateur." He has honorary degrees from Bowdoin College (1956), Colby College (1979), and the University of Maine (1982).

In *My Way to Ornithology*, the reader sees the beginnings of a number of Sewall's interests that ultimately led to his becoming an ornithologist. He provides an integrated account of early events and experiences that, in retrospect, can be identified as important in his later development. We see how special skills were acquired that would serve him well throughout his career. The book provides a record of the personal experiences of a successful ornithologist, especially those that affected his choice of profession and his ability to learn and pursue it.

What were some of the influences that proved important? For one, Sewall had a supportive home environment. His parents and other relatives provided him with considerable encouragement. Also, at an early age, he met Eleanor, who was highly supportive as a friend, wife, coworker, and companion throughout much of his career. From early on, considerable time was spent in the country, often on his grandparents' farm. Sewall conveys pleasant memories of his stays on the family farm, even including the inevitable hard work. Also, growing up on the grounds of the Western Maine Sanatorium for tuberculosis patients, where his father served as superintendent, was much like living on a farm. Exposure to the out-of-doors was a day-to-day part of his adolescent life. Furthermore, he participated in more elaborate sojourns on organized camping and hiking trips. In boyhood experiences that Sewall recounts in the book, there are hints of his upcoming involvement with birds, but certainly nothing dramatic. In fact, it is clear that early on Sewall tended to ignore bird life, with the exception of his being intrigued by chickens and their habits.

We see birds becoming more of a focus when Sewall goes off to college. He was stimulated by certain books, by his interactions with dedicated teachers, and later by fellow students. A summer of living full time as a biologist at the University of Michigan Biological Station crystallized his interest in becoming an ornithologist. We see how a staunch bond with George Sutton began to form in graduate school, even before Sewall and George roomed together in the Fuertes's house. It was not long before they were joint participants in field research projects. The ties that developed between the Pettingills and George Sutton were also strong on a personal level, as evidenced by the fact that George was best man at the Pettingill wedding and godfather of their two daughters. As Sewall wrote to me in 1971, soon after my arrival at the University of Oklahoma as a new faculty member and curator of birds, "There is no person more a part of my family and more loved by us all than George Sutton."

Many of the professional activities and opportunities Sewall pursued involved writing and public speaking. In addition to presentations directed to his scientific peers, Sewall often was engaged in conveying information about birds to interested groups of amateurs and other nonprofessionals. His experience with the student newspaper and other publications as a writer and editor proved invaluable. Through student participation in these activities, Sewall acquired basic skills, such as typing and copy editing, that served him well as a student and later as a practicing professional. Often he undoubtedly found writing to be a "struggle" (as most of us do), yet Sewall wrote effectively. He developed a knack for conveying in simple yet effective form the interesting facts and conclusions reached by research specialists. Furthermore, his acting experience proved invaluable when entertaining and educating an audience. He became quite a showman, developing the skills to communicate effectively with general audiences.

Social functions have been an integral component in Sewall's professional activities, whether he was hosting a function as director of the Laboratory of Ornithology, on the screen-tour circuit, or holding an informal gathering for students at the biological station. It is not surprising that Eleanor and Sewall had excellent social skills; they had frequent opportunities to hone them during the years at home and in college. Fraternity life offered a ready social outlet for Sewall, and also provided a setting that fostered the development of self-confidence and leadership qualities. His fraternity years represented an important formative period for him, during which time the opinions of peers were judged to be particularly important.

Along with social skills, organizational abilities can be critical to a professional biologist and administrator, whether in carrying out regular activities or in mounting an expedition. This is particularly true if, like Sewall, you cart along a wide variety of photographic paraphernalia as you head for faraway places. Organizing a group of fraternity brothers or a cadre of student cub reporters is no easy task, which one quickly learns as a fraternity president or the associate editor of a student newspaper. Experience in such positions can often be as

valuable as that gained through more formal academic arrangements. Also, after having been involved in planning for
relatively elaborate camping and mountain-climbing trips as a
youth, Sewall had some understanding of what was required
to prepare for expeditions like the one to Hudson Bay. As
anyone who has undertaken international fieldwork knows,
the challenges should not be underestimated.

Many people do not realize the amount of work and pressure (often self-imposed) associated with the presentation of
even a short scientific paper. Sewall gives us an interesting
account of himself as a young scientist preparing to give a talk
at a national scientific meeting and of the onerous task of preparing the high-quality lantern slides to be used. Certainly,
the 35-mm colored slides of today are much less trouble for
the preparer; however, they lack the personal touch of the
hand-painted transparencies of the 1920s and early 1930s.

My Way to Ornithology tells us a bit about what it was like
to be an ornithologist in the period prior to World War II. For
instance, collecting specimens was an important and custom-
ary activity of teachers and researchers studying birds, particularly because adequate field identification guides did not
exist. Many of us as undergraduate and graduate students in
later years continued to benefit through using Sewall's excellent bird collection.

The account provides us with a personal look at Sewall.
For instance, there is no glossing over of the fact that he did
not apply himself in high school and was a very marginal academic performer. Years later, it never occurred to me as a
young and not-too-stellar student sitting in one of his ornithology classes that Sewall would have been anything other
than a model academician. An incident at the biological station sticks in my mind. Along with several others, I was surprised—almost shocked—at grading time that this professor,
whom we perceived as a stern mentor, gave considerable
benefit of the doubt to a bright student who, during a good
portion of the summer, placed a considerably higher priority
on social adjusting and late-night, early-morning beach parties than on his studies. It puzzled me at the time; this response did not fit with the image I had of Sewall as a no-
nonsense taskmaster. In fact, he must have had much more

empathy for those of us with lapses in our academic records than I had heretofore suspected.

I think you will find Sewall's account instructive, and my guess is that you will be entertained as well. Many of us have some similar stories to tell, but Sewall has one up on us, being in a way preadapted. He formed the early habit of keeping a daily log or diary; thus, he "remembers" details about important personal events that, for the rest of us, have long since faded from memory. This intriguing account will help us all to understand better how a field biologist is formed.

GARY D. SCHNELL

Norman, Oklahoma

My Way to Ornithology

CHAPTER 1 / *Preliminaries*

HIGH ON A HILL in Belgrade, Maine, sits a former farm home, now a handsome summer residence. Scarcely a summer has passed when I haven't driven up the hill with family or friends, not to see the home, however handsomely it is maintained, but to show off the view. West below the hill and three miles distant, Long Pond parallels it, and beyond that westward lies a receding succession of hills ending with New Hampshire's White Mountains on the horizon. Although nearby Vienna Mountain rudely blocks the view northwestward, more hills recede east of it with Great Pond in the foreground.

This home on the hill, early in the century, was the center of a four-hundred-acre farm owned by my maternal grandparents. There I was born and, during the years of my early boyhood, spent some of the happiest days of my life.

My grandparents, Oscar and Viola Groves, had formerly lived in Augusta, Maine, where Oscar was an upholsterer by trade, though he always dreamed of owning and operating a farm. Much as Viola, who enjoyed the social life in Maine's capital city, disliked the prospective isolation of a farm, she would acquiesce after the turn of the century when Oscar found the farm of his dreams high on that Belgrade hill. There was one problem: he needed more money to buy the farm than he had saved. At this point one of Viola's sisters, Millie, already a prosperous dressmaker on Commonwealth Avenue in Boston, took out a mortgage on the farm. So there they moved. By now their one and only child, a daughter Marion, had graduated from high school in Augusta and in the fall of 1901 undertook advanced studies in piano at Kents Hill School—then called Maine Wesleyan Seminary and Female College—in the town of Readfield not far away.

Among the other students arriving at Kents Hill in the fall of 1901 was Olin Sewall Pettingill from the nearby town of Wayne. He played the violin and gave solo performances in the course of the year; and he played football. Although the son of a farmer, he let it be known at the outset that farming was not for him. He had befriended and admired a Wayne physician whose career he vowed to emulate, and he made no secret of being at Kents Hill for the primary purpose of educating himself for entrance to the Maine Medical School at Bowdoin College in Brunswick.

Olin graduated from Kents Hill in June of 1903 and entered Maine Medical School that fall. By then he had fallen in love with Marion Groves, who completed her studies the same year and joined her parents in Belgrade to teach school locally. Olin's father died in 1904 and his mother earlier. Soon Olin and Marion announced their engagement. He was lean, about six feet tall, with dark complexion and sharp features; she was short, nearly five feet, and plump. (Olin's father, on meeting her, teased him later about her looking like a pillow with a string tied around the middle.) Was it their mutual love of music that had attracted them to each other? Perhaps. In any case, it was Kents Hill that had brought them together. They were married on December 12, 1906, and to them I was born on October 30, 1907. I was to be their only child and was called Sewall, my middle name.

About a month before I was born, Olin had started his last year of medical school, serving as intern at the Maine General Hospital in Portland, while Marion stayed with her parents in Belgrade. Olin was not long an intern before he came down with typhoid fever and went to Belgrade to recuperate; he had recovered by the time I appeared. Soon the three of us were off to Portland where we lived in an apartment until the eventful day in June, 1909, when Father became a Doctor of Medicine.

By then there was no question in Father's mind as to what he would do: establish general practice in Livermore Falls, a few miles north of Wayne, where an aging practitioner had encouraged Father to become his replacement. There my parents acquired a huge house, renovated two front rooms for office and waiting room, purchased all essential equipment and furnishings, and put outside the front door a big black sign with gold lettering, "Olin S. Pettingill, M.D." But alas! Barely four months passed before disaster struck. Father broke down with tuberculosis—commonly called consumption then. TB later. What to do? He had no choice: go to the Maine Sanatorium in Hebron, many miles westward, and "take the cure"—which might require many weeks or months, possibly longer. Devastated by this misfortune, Father left for Hebron; Mother stored the furnishings, closed the house and took down the sign, and with me, now three years old, resumed residence with her parents in Belgrade. The year was 1910.

The cure for TB in the early part of this century required open air, plenty of it, year-round. The Maine Sanatorium, designed for this purpose, was appropriately on Greenwood Mountain (elevation 2,300 feet) to take full advantage of the clear, dry atmosphere. Patients were expected to sit outdoors at all times and sleep on porches, roofed but otherwise open in any season including winter. Faithful to the treatment, Father recovered in a few months, now with a new objective. Having overcome TB, he would henceforth devote his medical career to its cure and prevention. For the next five years Mother and I followed him to successive posts in three out-of-state sanatoriums.

First, in 1911, he became resident physician at Stony Wold Sanatorium on Lake Kushaqua in New York's Adirondacks. Then four years old, I have no sharp recollection of our months there. In her letters home to Belgrade, Mother spoke about being quartered in the "main building" and quoted Father as saying that it was "like living in an old-ladies home."

Relief from the confines of Stony Wold came in 1912 when Father was appointed assistant physician at Rutland State Sanatorium near Worcester, Massachusetts. He had to reside in the administration building so as to be on call. Mother and I lived in the village of Rutland, renting one tiny house and later another, both within easy walking distance for Father during evenings or on weekends when not on call. Mother did all the housework and kept me outside whenever the weather was tolerable. There were no neighborhood children my age for playmates. For amusement, I had a tent in which I occupied myself with all sorts of cast-off paraphernalia.

By the fall of 1913 I had reached school age, but not without a crisis. A few days before Mother was to escort me to the local school for admission, I began to lose hair in tufts, revealing circular red spots on my scalp. From some mysterious source, probably from the barber, I had caught ringworm. My head had to be shaved and regularly treated with a sticky ointment. I had to wear a cap all the time, night and day. Regardless, to school I went with special permission to wear my cap inside. The curiosity of my schoolmates for any such privilege was insatiable until, after much inducement by them and despite my reluctance, I temporarily removed the cap. One inspection by them was quite enough. I remember little else about the beginning of my formal education except for this personal embarrassment.

While at the Rutland Sanatorium, Father won many admirers and friends. One was a patient, Oscar F. Adler, a talented artist on his way to recovery. He would become an intimate friend of my family in the years ahead and an important influence in my own life. Somewhat casually, Father asked him if he would paint us a little picture—of anything. Hardly a month had passed before Mr. Adler presented us with a twenty- by twenty-eight-inch oil of cows recumbent under trees against the background of a sunny pasture. For the oil and the frame Mr. Adler selected for it, Father insisted on paying him. Although a small sum, it was really more than he could afford but it became our cherished possession. Wherever we lived thereafter, the Adler painting was always hung where it could not be overlooked.

Our third move came in the fall of 1914 when Father was appointed assistant superintendent at Rhode Island State Sanatorium isolated near Wallum Lake, surrounded by a vast pine forest, just south of the Massachusetts line. Now we were in a new situation, living in the administration building paralleled closely on one side by the women's ward, the other by the men's. Both had two stories. Our apartment on the second floor had one good view from the front, and we ate in the staff dining room.

I was seven and should have been in school but there was no school in the entire area. It was up to Mother to teach me, which she did in the apartment, acquiring a little desk, blackboard, and all necessary books. She established school hours and held me to them—or at least she tried. According to letters of exasperation to her parents, I was an exhausting pupil, unable to concentrate, forever counting the minutes until she would take me out for a walk to look for birds and wildflowers, although I had no special interest in them.

There were no children my age anywhere near. At first I was allowed to play with the superintendent's two daughters, much younger than I and exceedingly shy, who lived in a house separate from the sanatorial complex. Unfortunately, I was too rough, overly boisterous, and—worst of all—used "naughty" words. Before long I was sternly told to keep away.

Mother obtained her first piano and, accompanied by Father with his violin, often played after supper for their own enjoyment or for anyone else who wished to drop in. Father's principal recreation that winter was sailing an iceboat up and down Wallum Lake. As spring approached, he developed "car fever"; we sorely needed some means of escaping isolation. After totaling family accounts, Father decided we could manage to buy a car, a new Ford. Indelible in my memory is my first sight of that shiny vehicle, the very latest model with a windshield which, at its base in front, sloped to the hood instead of meeting it at a right angle—the very earliest in streamlining! That spring we barely missed a day going somewhere. Mother became as proficient in the driver's seat as Father even though, short as she was, she had to bolster herself with a pillow at her back in order to reach the three pedals with her feet.

During my early years I went often to Belgrade. I was forever hounding my parents about wanting to go and impatiently awaited the dates for departing. Simply stated, I craved the excitement of the farm, the horses and cows, "my" dog Jack, the chickens, the seasonal activities, and the fields, orchards, pastures, and woods in which to roam at will. I have no idea of the amount of time I spent on the farm, only that I never missed a summer and at least a week or two in practically every fall, winter, and spring of being a "farm boy."

CHAPTER 2 / *Farm Boy*

MY REACHING BELGRADE was always by train. After I was five in 1912, I went alone—Mother, Aunt Millie, or some family friend escorting me to the North Station in Boston, putting me aboard a parlor car with a lunch and instructions to the conductor as to my destination. I was sure to have enough money to treat myself to a box of Bangor Taffy—a delectable always sold on the Boston and Maine Railroad—and another box for Grandfather, who adored sweets.

Awaiting me by prearrangement on the platform at Belgrade Depot was Grandfather, ready with a bear hug as I stepped out with the help of the conductor. My baggage collected, we walked to Grandfather's buggy (or sleigh in winter), tied up at the general store and far enough away so that his horse Nellie would not be frightened by the train's commotion. Soon we were off for the three miles to the farm. The trek up and down hills seemed to me interminable until we ascended the last and longest; over its brow was home.

Grandmother, having been sitting by the living room window watching for us, was already in the stable by the time we drew in. Descending from the buggy, I welcomed her kisses and a big hug. Meanwhile dog Jack was bouncing up and down beside me for some share of attention.

My grandparents' home was large and commodious. Long, two-storied, and gabled with dormer windows, its first floor consisted of a big kitchen at the east end, entering into a dining room with windows on both north and south sides, then my grandparents' bedroom off the northwest corner of the dining room, a south-facing living room off the southwest corner, and finally, at the west end of the house, a parlor and a hallway to the front door and the stairs with overhead balcony.

Upstairs were four bedrooms leading off from either front or back hallways. My room with a dormer window was above the living room. From the back hallway steep stairs—practically a ladder—led down to the dining room and the south entrance to the front porch. The cellar was dirt-floored, with bins for winter storage of vegetables, and housed the cistern for collecting rain water from the roof, then to be hand-pumped into the kitchen sink for washing, never for drinking.

Extending east from the kitchen, via a "back kitchen," was a long shed for the cream separator, the supply of stove wood, and a luxury of sorts—an *indoor* privy. The shed was connected to the stable for the three horses, Nellie, Ned, and Lion (each with a stall), assorted wagons and sleighs, and Grandfather's workshop. Overhead was the hay mow, with chutes for hay into each of the horse stalls. Below the main floor was the pigsty. Unlike on many Maine farms, the barn for the cattle with their required lofts of hay was separated within a short walking distance from the house and stable, as were the henhouse, the icehouse, and the wellhouse from which, by long-handled pump, came all the drinking water for the livestock as well as for ourselves.

At the time, I never realized how little, if any, attention had been given to positioning the house and locating its windows to reap full advantage of the remarkable view. Not until years later, when I saw how new country homes were planned, built, and windowed specially for taking in their picturesque surroundings, did the realization occur to me. My father, who spent his boyhood on a farm high on a hill in Wayne, Maine, had a sensible explanation: "We worked outdoors with a marvelous view all day, sometimes from dawn until dusk. Our house was for meals, sleeping, and comfort."

To me, the Belgrade house was the ultimate in comfort, if not luxury. All floors, except in the kitchen, were carpeted. Much of the furniture had been upholstered by Grandfather during his Augusta days. I remember the chaise longue in the living room and the elegant fabrics on the chairs and divan in the parlor, a room usually closed off with the shades drawn; it was opened only on special occasions as when Grandmother hosted a meeting of the Ladies Aide, a charitable group. Some of the other things that never ceased to impress me: the massive, square, dining room table of oak, with its eight matching chairs, and the floor-to-ceiling sideboard with fancy pitchers, glassware, and a huge silver chafing dish; the mahogany tables and chairs in the living room and parlor; the grandfather clock in the front hall; the handsomely gold-framed pictures, including some on easels, on the balcony above the stairs; and most of all, Grandmother's pride and joy, a ceiling-high cabinet consisting of a twelve-place set of blue-wreathed dinnerware, a farewell gift from friends and neighbors in Augusta when she and Grandfather left for Belgrade. Every time I arrived at the farm I went over the house to see if everything was as wonderful as I remembered it from the last time.

Heating was by wood stoves in the kitchen and living room, by coal-fired stove in the dining room. No electricity. No radio, of course. Interior lighting was by kerosene lamps in the house, kerosene lanterns elsewhere. The sole modern convenience was a telephone, at best a party line.

Grandfather and Grandmother Groves were practically my second parents. Grandfather was of average height, thick-set and strong, and balding with iron-gray locks he let grow long. He never wore glasses. He spoke emphatically and decisively, but rarely used profanity. "Not by a damnsight" was his most extreme response to matters displeasing him. Outside the house he chewed tobacco, much to Grandmother's disgust, though she never objected to his cigar-smoking inside. Grandmother was of the same height, neither plump nor fleshy, her gray hair was pugged in back, and she wore rimless glasses. Always with a pleasant expression, she usually spoke in a soft voice and loved to laugh. She rarely sat still, always finding something to do. A very congenial person who enjoyed conversation, she became hard of hearing soon after moving to the farm and, much to her annoyance, had to use an ear horn and ask people to speak loudly. Although she and Grandfather often had heated arguments, he shouting to make her hear, at no time were they ever cross with me. Frequently, they would warn me not to do this or that, my own safety in mind, but I don't recall ever being disciplined. In their view, it seemed, I could do no wrong.

Independence was Grandfather's hallmark. From the very

beginning at the farm he did all the work—the daily chores, the seasonal jobs, the upkeep of the buildings—seldom with hired hands. Now and then Grandmother helped with the haying, gardening, and picking apples, and my parents assisted when they were visiting. His only time away from the farm was when he served on a jury in Portland. A bachelor neighbor did the farm work at the time. Grandfather's strength, endurance, and remarkable health never failed him and at no time was he confined for as much as a day in bed.

In any season, his daily routine began before breakfast with milking, sometimes as many as a dozen cows. In winter, he began before dawn. In summer, after milking, he first drove the cows to pasture before breakfast. Afterwards came chores such as running the cream separator, feeding the horses in the stable as well as cleaning out their stalls and the cattle tie-ups in the barn. By then it was midmorning, time to go out to the roadside mailbox for the daily card from the U.S. Weather Bureau, giving the weather forecast, and both *The Kennebec Journal* and *The Boston Herald* which he took into the house for briefly scanning the headlines. Soon he was outside to go ahead with whatever seasonal work he had scheduled. He returned for a hearty dinner at noon, followed by perhaps a catnap in his favorite living room chair; and again he was outside for the same scheduled work until milking at about five, summer or winter. Before supper, not as hearty, he put on his slippers and thereafter resorted to his favorite chair for thoroughly reading the newspapers. At the point of his retiring between nine and ten, he filled his mouth with peppermints from the chafing dish on the dining room sideboard on his way to the bedroom.

I had no playmates as there were no children my age in the neighborhood, but never for a moment did I ever feel lonesome. Jack was my companion, always trusting and friendly, ready to greet neighbors or strangers by bouncing forward, tail wagging, never barking. Jack was the worst of watchdogs. He simply never suspected any human being to be capable of treachery.

I was told that Jack was a border collie, although he was small for a collie with a short muzzle. He was richly furred black, save for a fully white waistcoat, orange-brown on his face and legs, and white paws. The farm was his bailiwick inside and out. Entering the house, his procedure was to inspect his dish below the kitchen sink for possible edibles-in-waiting, then to rest either on his favorite rug near the stove in the dining room or in his hideaway—a dark recess under the elevated head of the chaise longue, which projected from a corner of the living room. Outside, his loafing spot was the back stoop, the principal entranceway to the shed and house, overlooking both stable and barn as well as miles of countryside. There he waited for participation in any upcoming farming activities.

Of all the farm work, nothing apparently delighted him more in the warmer months than bringing in the cows for milking. With no urging, he joined Grandfather for the trek down the big steep hill to the west pasture where the cows were already waiting near the barred gate. After Grandfather let the bars down, Jack herded the cows through and kept them moving to the barn. If any animal stopped or got out of line, Jack responded to Grandfather's "sic 'em" with a nip at the animal's legs or face, enforced with a bark or two, perhaps with a few growls, should the cow be slow to heed. In the early morning, Jack was on the stoop waiting to return the cows to pasture.

As I grew older and was allowed to wander at will over the farm, Jack accompanied me. He enjoyed treeing squirrels and chasing woodchucks into stonewalls or back into their burrows, but his efforts were halfhearted for he was in no sense a game dog. Eventually I had a four-wheeled cart in which, with a little harness made by Grandfather, Jack hauled in produce from the garden or anything else I thought worth moving. Jack, although reasonably tolerant of this chore, acted subdued, demeaned, and had to be led.

Our evenings after supper were spent in the living room around a circular table supporting our illumination, a huge nickel-based kerosene lamp with a white global shade. Grandfather, stretched out in his favorite chair, read avidly, first the newspapers, then perhaps more pages of a biography of some recently notable person, or a little of Charles Dickens, of whom he was a great fan. He was an admirer of Shakespeare and could quote him at length. Grandmother, in her rocker close to the table, sometimes read, but more often, in her lap or on the table, wrote in her diary for the day or penned one of her numerous letters, or worked on the household and farming accounts which Grandfather chose to ignore. If queried about some monetary item while deep in his reading, his response was gruff—and rarely very helpful.

I sat at the end of the chaise longue nearest the table, sometimes looking through books or magazines, perhaps drawing something. Eventually I was old enough to read the "Bedtime Stories" by Thornton W. Burgess that had begun in *The Boston Herald,* each with an appealing drawing by Harrison Cady. They couldn't have come at a more influential time in my life. If I hadn't read them right after Grandfather scanned the paper's headlines in the morning, I did in the evening.

The evenings after supper I always looked forward to and liked. What I disliked was the approaching moment when it was time for me to go upstairs to bed. On the second floor facing south, my bedroom had only one window, a dormer, with sashes loose in the frame. When the wind blew hard, the window rattled, making me imagine giraffes poking it with their snouts. The plastered ceiling, owing to roof leaks at an earlier time, was stained with brown streaks and circles, forming all sorts of weird shapes. I hated one that suggested some humanoid monster with a horrible leer. After I complained about it again and again, Grandmother stood on my bed and struck it repeatedly with a flyswatter to prove it was lifeless.

The bedroom was without heat. In winter, my big double bed had soft flannel sheets covered with thick, light puffs. Grandmother's routine, after supper, was putting a hot soapstone, wrapped in a towel, between the sheets near the side of the bed where I would sleep. By the time I went to bed, it was cozy.

Knowing that I disliked total darkness after going to bed, Grandmother left a lamp burning at the foot of the stairs. Rarely did I stay awake long enough to see the lamp taken away. Following the custom of these times, kids were usually put to bed early and so was I, long before my grandparents retired. While this was tolerable in winter, I despised being sent off to bed at other times of the year when the days were long and it was still light for play.

With no electricity, the one luxury my grandparents had was the telephone on the wall of the dining room. It served at least a half dozen families. It was cranked by hand and heard by every party. One ring was for "central," two long rings were for us, two-long-rings-one-short for somebody else, and so on. Grandmother, hard of hearing, rarely heard the phone. Not Grandfather! He heard all the rings and knew who they were for. When he heard rings that interested him, to the phone he went "to rubber" by carefully lifting the receiver and putting his hand over the mouthpiece. For Grandmother and me, absolute silence was imperative. If the call was for us, Grandfather fully expected to hear clicks, indicating that receivers were coming off their hooks. There was no such thing as a private conversation. Whatever was said would become common knowledge in the neighborhood.

The three-mile trip to the Depot for supplies was routine in any season. In winter, the town kept the road passable to sleds and sleighs by pressing down the snow under a huge wooden roller drawn by four horses. With Nellie pulling our sleigh, off we went, Grandfather bundled up in a buffalo coat, I in a mackinaw with a couple of sweaters beneath. A big buffalo robe over our legs provided all the warmth needed. In spring, at thawing time, the trip was by Nellie-drawn buggy, one seat for two and uncovered. There were spots where Nellie wallowed in the mud as she pulled the buggy through slush halfway up to the wheel hubs.

At the general store, I sometimes became annoyed and impatient with Grandfather who, after buying all the supplies, stood around and gossiped with friends. This was one of his few chances for catching up on the latest doings, aside from rubbering on the phone at home.

Nellie, having gone over the route so many times, knew where the watering troughs were and turned to them of her own accord. After drinking all she wanted, she was inclined to stand for a rest until prompted to get along. On our return, she knew when she was climbing the last hill. No plodding now, she was all for getting home. Once over the brow of the hill in view of the farm, she burst into a trot to the stable. Aware that hay or grain would be forthcoming, she could barely stand still while being unharnessed, so anxious was she to make a beeline for her stall. Once there, she stomped and whinnied until fed.

After so many trips to the Depot, I became used to the farms we passed and knew who occupied them. Occasionally, if one of the farmers was outside, Grandfather stopped to pass the time of day. I remember being impressed by a few abandoned farms we passed, the buildings in disrepair. Some were already just cellars where houses had been, their granite foundations bordered by a few clumps of lilacs and, in summer, by flowering goldenglow. In our earlier trips we passed a house practically falling down, its windowpanes gone and rags stuffed in their places, but still occupied by a young family, obviously impoverished. The kids were dirty, their clothes in tatters. What I didn't realize then was that one-family farms were waning, as they had been before the turn of the century. I simply assumed that their fate was due to bad luck or laziness and thought no more about it.

Both of my grandparents were staunch Republicans, like most residents of Belgrade. Among the very few Democrats was one family whose head was one of the stalwarts of his party in the district. To hear him discussed at meals or at any other time, I envisioned him as grotesque, possibly the devil incarnate, replete with horns, until the day when he was pointed out to me on a visit to the Depot. As far as I could discern, he was as ordinarily normal and pleasant as everyone else with whom Grandfather hobnobbed.

Partisan politics were always on my grandparents' minds. Although Grandfather attended town meetings where he made himself heard, he was never a candidate for office. I cannot forget how upset my grandparents were when Theodore Roosevelt—"Teddy," whom they greatly admired—bolted the Republican party with his Bull Moose campaign, thereby splitting the party and bringing about the election of Woodrow Wilson, a Democrat, as president. (Grandfather stayed with his party, making no bones about it.) From then on *that Wilson* was the cause of everything wrong locally, nationally, and internationally.

There were always seasonal jobs. In late summer, apples had to be picked and sorted, the good ones for barreling and shipment, the poorer ones for pressing into cider. Grandmother and I participated to the extent of picking apples from the lower branches and gathering those which had fallen. Early fall was the time to harvest potatoes and other vegetables, wheelbarrowing them to the house, then taking them down to the cellar to their respective bins. As winter approached, Grandfather put specially made banking boards against the north and west foundations of the house, then covered them with fir and spruce boughs to hold the snow for insulation. Winter meant more rugged activities: trips to Long Pond, on the sled drawn by Ned and Lion, to cut ice into blocks, lift them out and slide them aboard, haul them to the double-walled icehouse, and finally push them up a ramp into the icehouse where they were lined up, covered with sawdust for insulation during the coming summer, and thus readied for the next layer on top which would come another day. There were trips with the same team into the nearby woods to haul up four-foot, hardwood logs from trees which Grandfather had previously felled and cut up himself. Piled near the house, the logs would later be cut to stove size by two men with a horse-drawn, motorized sawing machine. At odd times in the weeks ahead, Grandfather would split the wood, leave it to dry, and eventually pile it in the shed.

With the first signs of spring, when the air had the smell of the softening earth, it was time for Grandfather to break road to his sap camp at the far end of the pasture where big maples edged the woods along Long Pond. Ned and Lion pulled the sled carrying shovels and such necessary tools as bitstock and bits, and new gallon cans with screwed-on caps. We reached the camp as it had been left a year ago. No thing of beauty, it was just a half-gabled shed and slab-sided with two doors, two openings below the roof, and no windows. As we opened the doors, they creaked in protest. Inside lay a huge, oblong iron basin, upside down, and resting on a brick oven of similar shape. A dozen or more pails, fitted together, were tipped over on a shelf where there was also a wooden-lidded box full of metal sap spiles, each with a hook.

The first day was preparation. We turned over the basin,

brushing out the cobwebs, and placed it on the open-topped oven. The pails and spiles we wiped clean. Then we were off, I carrying pails and spiles, Grandfather bitstock and bits. At the first maple of suitably large girth, he selected a spot at waist height on the tree's south (warmer) side, drilled a hole deep enough for the spile, tapped the spile in, and hung a pail on it. Such was the procedure at maple after maple until all the pails were hung. If we stayed long enough, we saw the first drops of water-clear sap. It had a faintly sweet taste, I found, though I had to spit out the finely ground bits of wood—the result of drilling the hole—coming with the first drops.

The next day, provided it was sunny and warm enough for the sap to run, we were back early, built a roaring fire under the basin and poured in the pails of sap which soon boiled, sending up clouds of steam through the openings in the roof. All the time we were busy gathering and chopping up dried wood in the vicinity to keep the fire roaring and the steam rising until the sap became syrupy. This we emptied into some of the new cans brought for the purpose and headed homeward with the results of the day's work. It was Grandmother's job to boil down the sap further on the kitchen stove.

Boiling down sap for maple syrup or maple sugar required about ten days, weather permitting. They were pleasurable days and the products were for family use, not income.

Another seasonal job I recall vividly was haying, which began after the first of July, amid the constant prospect of thunderstorms. After Grandfather had mown a field—Ned and Lion hauling the machine while he maneuvered them around rock piles and ledges—the hay had to dry for several days. Then, provided there was no rain in the offing, he or Grandmother hitched Nellie to the two-wheeled rake for collecting the hay into long parallel rows stretching from one end of the field to the other. Soon thereafter, Grandfather, with pitchfork in hand, broke up the rows into tumbles ready for loading. Now came my role along with Grandmother's: we had to drive Ned and Lion with the hayrack to the field and proceed to spread out and tread on the tumbles of hay which Grandfather pitched to us. This was fun for me, even though hot in the glaring sun, as was the ride on the brimming load to stable or barn, with the reward of a cold drink of water from the pump. There were times, however, when we barely got the last load into the barn before a thunderstorm, coming toward us from the west, arrived in full fury.

Nothing did my grandparents dread more than the midsummer thunderstorms with the possibility of their buildings, exposed on so high a hill, being struck and set on fire by lightning. There was no fire department to call on. Their barn and stable, stuffed with new hay, were veritable tinderboxes. At least their barn was not connected to the house and stable, as on many Maine farms, so they might not lose all their buildings if one caught fire. Why did they not have lightning rods? Many Belgrade buildings had these on their roof ridges—often fancy with large white or otherwise colorful balls at the tops, sometimes with a weather vane below—wired to the ground. Whether lightning rods ever proved effective, I never knew, but Grandfather flatly refused to have them.

In midsummer one year, we were terrified by two thunderstorms, a week apart. The weather was unusually hot and sultry. Haying was over, the barn and stable mows full to capacity. For several days prior to the first storm there had been thundershowers in the afternoons, none violent. Then came the late afternoon when the whole western sky darkened; the air was deathly still. By this time the cows had been milked. At first we heard rumbles but before long they increased to a steady roar. By supper time it was practically dark, and the whole western sky was illuminated by almost continuous flashes. Hurrying through the meal, we were soon on the front steps to watch.

We could see the approaching storm line—a gray, curtain-like cloud from north to south—yet there was no driving wind, no evidence of rain, just blinding streaks of lightning between cloud line and earth. Steadily the storm approached. Finally, a slight breeze and several too-near bolts of lightning drove us inside. Within moments we were under bombardment. Looking out of the windows, we could clearly see the landscape for miles around as there was little rain or mist. This was no ordinary storm! Far to the west we saw, between flashes, the sky glowing red from a fire. Then a set of buildings across from Long Pond was burning. We kept hurrying about the house to get views from all windows. To the northwest, on the flank of Vienna Mountain, there were buildings on fire. From all directions there were evidences of fires. Nearby flashes of lightning made our phone tinkle. With only a mild let-up, the storm kept lingering, not spending its fury until long after midnight. We had counted fourteen fires.

The whole evening seemed interminable. Although there were periods when lightning was less intense, suggesting that the storm had passed, we were in constant expectation of being struck. The next morning the telephone line was alive with neighbors telling of their reactions. Some had harnessed their horses and loaded wagons with some of their most cherished possessions.

The sultry weather continued for a week, followed by the second storm, practically a repeat of the first in time of night, duration, and fury. Again we passed a terrifying evening, during which we counted twelve fires. Miraculously, no buildings on our hill were struck during either storm.

The henhouse, with its two dozen or so Plymouth Rock hens and one rooster, was the center of much of my attention. During cold and rainy weather, I spent more time in it than anywhere else, sitting on a box just inside the door to watch activities. They were never dull.

It didn't take me long to realize that no two hens looked alike and that no two hens showed the same disposition. Furthermore, the more I watched, the more I became aware of some sort of social scale. Some hens were forever pecking others, which didn't peck back but, in turn, pecked others, and there were one or two hens which never pecked at all. When I threw corn on the floor, certain individuals immediately took to the center of the handout while others had to be satisfied with the fringe. If they so much as tried to work toward the center, they were soundly pecked and driven back, apparently belonging to the lower end of the scale. When I drove all the hens off the corn and then sat back to watch, they again converged on the food in the same order as before.

Watching the hens going to roost was amusing—there were so many trials and errors. First, each bird looked up for a vacant space, hesitated, and then flew up, sometimes making the space, sometimes not and falling off, or trying to stay up by holding on with her chin, clinging with her feet, while flapping her wings. On reaching the roost, one hen often pushed off another, thereby causing the whole roost to wobble and making the hens already installed on it flap their wings and teeter lest they all fall off.

The social scale even applied when going to roost. The "best" parts of the roost, nearest the wall at the far end, were taken by the very same hens that had taken center stage when I distributed the corn. The hens at the lower end of the scale, having stayed late to pick the remaining corn, flew up to whatever spaces were left. If they side-stepped close to the birds already on the roost, they were pecked and dislodged, and had to fly up again. As darkness set in, I couldn't resist moving some of the hens with the best of the roost and replacing them with some of the hens with the worst. As for the rooster, he was already on the part of the roost he preferred and never challenged the hens.

Winter mornings in the henhouse were lively. Some of the hens "sang"; others entered next boxes to lay. When a hen emerged from the nest, after laying her egg, she began cackling. This set off a cacophony of cackles among the other hens. Even the rooster contributed a few *cockle-doodle-dos.*

When in the mood, the rooster did a little scratching in the floor litter. Finding a buried kernel of corn, he called up his harem. If one hen seemed especially interested, he quickly circled her, one wing down in her direction, then mounted her, provided she was agreeable. After the act, both birds shook their feathers and flapped their wings. End of episode.

My grandparents couldn't understand why I spent so much time in the henhouse. They didn't know, nor I either, that I was developing a lasting attachment to chickens and, furthermore, gaining an acquaintance with bird behavior that would be valuable to me later in studying birds, notably those species which performed in leks where a social hierarchy was well known.

I must have been born with an inherent liking for all creatures in feathers. How else can I explain my special attraction to hens and the hours I spent watching them? Every moment they gave me so much enjoyment that I decided I would be a chicken farmer or poultryman by profession. I kept this no secret from my grandparents and parents.

There was no indication in my years as a farm boy that I would ever become an ornithologist. Only my mother, who visited often and once lived with us for several months while she taught school locally, knew a few of the common birds and pointed them out to me. One day, when I must have been about four years old, she led me into a field where, parting a clump of red clover, she showed me my first bird nest. In it four naked, newly hatched nestlings lifted their heads, gaping. They were bobolinks. That my first nest ever seen should be of this species was most prophetic, for many years later my students and I would spend summers studying bobolinks in Michigan and I would go to Argentina for the specific purpose of observing bobolinks on their wintering grounds.

All of us at the farm, except Mother, paid little attention to birds. We had no books for identifying them. The hawks we saw were all "chicken" hawks; the handsome bird in the big trees around the house was the "golden robin" (northern oriole); and the bird singing so sweetly at twilight in the woods below the hill was the "lonesome bird" (hermit thrush).

The Burgess "Bedtime Stories," when they started in *The Boston Herald*, stimulated my interest in natural history. Not only did they stir me in their narrative form, but they gave further meaning to the fields and forests, as well as some of the common wild creatures I already knew. Burgess's characters were real with catchy names, such as Johnny Chuck and Sammy Jay, and he made the natural world romantic with his Merry Little Breezes, Rough Brother North Wind, Mistress Moon, the Black Shadows, and the Old Briar-patch. I looked forward to each daily installment and painstakingly cut out the stories and made scrapbooks of them.

In the late summer of 1915, while my parents and I were still living in Rhode Island, came truly exciting news. The Maine Sanatorium, where Father had been a patient, had been taken over by the state as the Western Maine Sanatorium, and Father was appointed its first superintendent. With unbounded joy, we went back to Maine. Yes, this time to live!

FEEDING CHICKENS, 1909. At my grandparents' farm at Belgrade.

FAMILY PORTRAIT, 1912

DRESSED UP FOR A PORTRAIT SITTING, 1918

Miss Plumstead at the Greenwood Mountain School, 1919.

In My Eighth-Grade Class, Middleton Center School, 1921. In front row, the author at far left, Lawrence Kinney at far right, and Harry Berry in middle. In middle row, Eleanor is the girl at right. In back row, Miss Manning stands at right.

Grandmother Groves

GRANDFATHER GROVES

AUNT MILLIE

Aunt Mame and Uncle Luther

AUNTIE BROWN

CHAPTER 3 / *Superintendent's Son*

I WAS EIGHT years old when we arrived in our new Ford at the Western Maine Sanatorium on Greenwood Mountain in October, 1915. What a delightful location, just as Father had described from his sojourn as a patient there. The institution took full advantage of the clear, dry atmosphere while providing a broad view of the western mountainous landscape.

The sanatorium was virtually self-contained. There were three (later four) separate "cottages" of wood construction for over one hundred patients, and a four-story administration building of brick, cement, and steel for medical and business offices, dining, recreation, and staff housing. Our apartment was on the third floor; from its west windows, which overlooked Hebron Academy, Mount Washington loomed on the horizon, near enough for us to make out the Summit House on a sparkling winter's day. Besides its own power plant for heat and electricity and a pumping station for spring water, the sanatorium owned and operated a huge farm with barn, pasture, and fields of hay for cattle and horses, a creamery and piggery, gardens, orchards, rich woodland, and homes for farm personnel. Father, having been brought up on a farm, had declared he would never be a farmer. Now, with a farm under his jurisdiction, he often remarked wryly when a problem there needed his attention, "Here am I, back on the farm."

The cottages, green-shingled with white trim, were especially designed for outdoor living in all seasons in all vagaries of weather. During the day patients sat or lounged on the verandas, in winter heavily clothed and wrapped in blankets. Back from each veranda under a roof, they slept in wards where the high south side was always open, except in storms when it could be closed by sliding doors. Obviously, the cottages were neither designed nor intended for advanced cases of TB. (Such cases were treated at the Central Maine Sanatorium in Fairfield.) Thus, in aspect, Western Maine Sanatorium more closely resembled a health resort than a place for sick people.

Patients walked to their meals, exercised after long rest periods, and enjoyed a wide selection of recreational opportunities. Generally discouraged when they arrived at the sanatorium—as though their lives and careers were ruined forever—they soon found their attitude changed by Father and his staff, including nurses who had also recovered from TB, with words to the effect: "Cheer up, you'll get well just as we did. It will take time. Just do as we advise and you'll be leaving here before you know it."

Thinking back about my years there, I seem to have had the best of all possible worlds. As the superintendent's son and only staff child, I was showered with attention and privileges. Aside from the cottages and medical offices, which Father ordered off limits to me, I was free to roam and play anywhere and to be *in*, one way or another, on important happenings. The sanatorium's farm always attracted me because I could count on some activity—for instance, milking when the machinery clacked and huffed, relieving from the cows what Grandfather had to accomplish with his hands. So did the power plant, where I soon considered myself an authority on operations, chiefly how the enormous electricity generators had to be lubricated regularly.

If Father worried lest I contract TB, I was aware of it only to the extent that he tapped my chest now and then, sometimes listening with a stethoscope while asking me to cough. He insisted that he and I sleep outdoors. Hence, one of his first innovations after taking over the sanatorium was to screen the third-floor porch on the south side of the administration building and there put beds in which we slept. In winter, we donned flannel nightshirts, each one piece with an attached hood plus leg extensions to include our feet. Under layers of blankets we were cozy enough and never surprised to find snow filtered over our beds when we awoke in the morning. Male members of the staff, some of them doctors, slept on the porch. Whether they were coerced, encouraged, or simply felt that they should because their boss did, I never knew.

We dined on the second floor, in a room for the doctors, their spouses, and guests, next to the main dining hall for patients, nurses, and clerical staff. Father ruled that the food must be the same as was served in the main dining hall—and it was. From the farm came the milk and cream (pasteurized, of course), garden produce, and apples. From the outside came the rest of the food. Some of it I hated. No doubt all the food served was thoroughly nutritious—I had no basis for contending otherwise—but to this day I can never face oatmeal cooked to a deathly gray, balls of mashed potato under a blanket of brown gravy, slices of brown beef, soupy yellow custards, puddings with tapioca ("frog's eyes"), or sliced peaches ("goldfish") without an urge to balk.

Dining as I did at the parental table had special advantages. I was privy to impending events, or sudden emergencies in the power plant, on the farm, or somewhere else in the institutional complex, and would be one of the first spectators. I sat with guests, usually engaged in medicine or public health, occasionally in other endeavors.

A big event twice a year was the meeting of the board of trustees, preceded by a bustle of preparations; everything everywhere, it seemed, had to be picked up, cleaned up, and polished up. Breakfast in our dining room before the trustees arrived was fraught with suspense, Father on edge, Mother concerned about how she was to keep the wives amused. Evening dinner, the trustees gone, was sometimes euphoric, sometimes a letdown, depending on how favorably or unfavorably the governing body had acted upon Father's proposed projects. On occasion the governor and other state officials announced plans to visit the sanatorium, causing a stir. I remember anticipating the appearance of newly elected Governor Carl E. Milliken. Could he possibly be, I wondered, the handsome man his campaign posters had portrayed? Not only did he live up to his billing, he let me shake his hand, my first contact with anyone so exalted.

My formal education, beginning in 1915, was in a one-room schoolhouse in Hebron over a mile away. I usually walked or bicycled with lunchpail, except in bad weather, or if delayed, when I was transported in the family car by Mother. Yes, my mother, a *woman*, behind the wheel of a car—a sight that never ceased to astonish my schoolmates.

After 1916, the sanatorium began accepting children about my age who had been exposed to TB and required preventive care. For them, Father had an abandoned shack converted into a one-room school, open air to the extent of having the south and east sides readily opened to the elements by hinged windows. Regular school desks were installed facing the north or front end of the room, which was equipped with teacher's desk, blackboards, and an all-important wood-burning stove, the only source of heat. I was never happier. Right here at the sanatorium I would have playmates for the first time anywhere, and they would be my schoolmates too, as Father had consented to my attending.

Called the Greenwood Mountain School and certified by the state, the school was all business from the time it opened in September until it closed in June. On wintry days, we came warmly dressed and sat in woolen bags, getting out of them to step forward to the front of the room for recitations—the procedure in any season. Should there be severely cold days when the stove failed to give out enough heat for us to sit in comfort, let alone to write, the school convened in the assembly hall of the administration building. That there should be no school, because of weather, was unthinkable.

The teacher during the first two years was Miss Bettie Marden. When she left to teach in Massachusetts, Miss Frances Plumstead replaced her. Both were born in Maine; both were ex-patients with great vitality. They were outwardly stern, tolerating no nonsense. When tested at the outset of the year by some sort of misbehavior—for example, a prank taking place in the back of the room while a recitation was under way up front—down the aisle they strode to give the perpetrator a dressing down, and, if need be, a few tugs on the collar, or at worst, a few resounding slaps from a ruler on the open palm. Their authority and respect established, their inner warmth and intellectual vitality soon came through to us all.

To both teachers I owed my everlasting gratitude in later years because they loved nature and helped open the way to my professional interests. Miss Marden had an engaging talent for reading to us. Our reward for a good day's work was to hear a few pages from a book, invariably with a natural history slant. Two of the books she read were Gene Stratton-Porter's *A Girl of the Limberlost* and *Freckles*, although she discreetly avoided passages she said were "too intimate."

Miss Plumstead liked birds especially and took us on spring bird walks over the sanatorium farmlands and down into the deep, rich woods on the south slope of Greenwood Mountain. She taught us the value of keeping annual spring lists: putting down the name of each bird species when first seen with the date, thereby acquiring a record for comparison the following spring. I bound my lists and on the cover of the first one I pasted a picture of a bobolink.

I enjoyed listing the species of birds that I identified on my own walks each spring—playing a solo listing game of sorts—to see if I could improve the length of the list each year. Aside from consulting with Miss Plumstead, my principal source of identification was Mother's much-used copy of Chester A. Reed's *Bird Guide: Land Birds East of the Rockies from Parrots to Bluebirds.* Pocket-size, with one species pictured in color per page, it was only slightly helpful and a far cry from the superb identification guides available many years later. Nevertheless, I will give full credit to Reed's guide for opening up to me for the first time the vast array of birds to see, if I traveled afar—green jays, vermilion and scissor-tailed flycatchers, pyrrhuloxias, painted buntings, among others. I dreamed of seeing them all, as I eventually did, except for the first bird in the book, the Carolina paroquet, which was already extinct, and the ivory-billed woodpecker, which was nearly so.

I continued reading Thornton Burgess's syndicated bedtime stories but, by now, he was also publishing little books about each of his wildlife personalities. Consequently, whenever my parents insisted that I accompany them on a shopping spree in the nearby city of Lewiston, I acquiesced with the promise that I could go into the big department store for the latest Burgess book.

In 1919, when I was twelve and still an avid reader of Burgess's stories, I was given one of the most exciting books in my early life, *The Burgess Bird Book for Children*. A year later I received *The Burgess Animal Book for Children*, new and equally exciting, covering the more common mammals. In both, Burgess brought together the principal characters in his bedtime stories, and others besides, with brief descriptions of their ways of life. What particularly thrilled me about the books were the illustrations, all in full color. They were not drawings in the style of Harrison Cady's, but were painted birds and mammals, absolutely lifelike. It would be many years before I would know how to pronounce the name of the artist, Louis Agassiz Fuertes, or appreciate the fact that my reaction to his watercolor paintings mirrored that of naturalists the world over. Later I would live in the house that he once occupied.

Soon after the appearance of the two Burgess books, I stopped reading his stories as I had outgrown them. Thanks to Miss Plumstead's encouragement, I became a junior member of the National Association of Audubon Societies (later the National Audubon Society) and began to sport the association's lapel button with a robin on it. I also took out a subscription to *Bird-Lore*, the association's bimonthly magazine.

As it was in its plant operations, the sanatorium was self-contained for its recreational and social activities. Whether Valentine's Day or St. Patrick's Day, Easter or Halloween, or any other day for special recognition, the dining hall was decorated with streamers, table runners and centerpieces, and paper napkins appropriate for the occasion. On Christmas Eve, Father played Santa Claus, arriving at the assembly hall in a horse-drawn sleigh, its tinkling bells audible to the audience inside. Moments later, in he ran with a bulging sack slung over his shoulder. In it were presents (actually jokes) which he then proceeded to pull out and distribute, along with citations applicable to the quirks or foibles of the recipients.

Saturday nights meant entertainment. Sometimes magicians, monologuists, or musicians were engaged. If not, there were movies. Besides the feature picture, there was a short subject such as the capers of Charlie Chaplin or the awful predicaments of Pearl White.

Twice a year, Father invited Oscar Adler, the artist, whose acquaintance we had made while he was a patient at the

Rutland Sanatorium in Massachusetts, to visit us. Although cured, he was small in stature, thin, and physically frail, and occasionally the victim of excruciatingly painful migraine headaches. When feeling well, he always sat at our table and had a way of sparking conversations with quips, humorous anecdotes, and sometimes imitations of a well-known personality at the sanatorium or elsewhere. All of us addressed him as Mr. Adler, except Father who called him "Plute" because Mr. Adler believed Pluto Water, a mineral water, helped to deter his headaches and he kept bottles of it in his room.

Father's invitations to Mr. Adler were not entirely for social reasons. He was expected to coach a play. For this, he had the essential energy, drive, and flair for drama to make actors out of doctors, nurses, laboratory technicians, stenographers—anyone he could muster. If a play called for a juvenile, I got the role, but it was incidental to my fun and education in watching rehearsals during which, with skill compounded with boundless patience, he brought out unsuspected talents in the least auspicious beginners. After the play was given on a Saturday night, it was repeated later in grange halls in neighboring towns.

I found taking part in some of the plays truly exciting. Never before had I been on a stage in front of an audience and actually performed; never before had I experienced the profound satisfaction that comes from an enthusiastic audience reaction. In the back of my mind entered the conviction that I liked acting and, henceforth, I would never turn down an opportunity to perform before an audience in one way or another.

When Mr. Adler was with us in warm weather and the sky effects suited him, he set out with paintbox, palette, and a canvas stretched on a wooden frame with an easel for support, to paint in oil a particular landscape that appealed to him. If not in school, very often I tagged along to watch his procedure. Day after day, provided the sky was "right," he returned to the same spot. Before the canvas on its easel was a six-foot path, already well worn, over which he stepped back after each brush stroke to compare his effort with what he was reproducing. More often than not, what he saw displeased him; whereupon he wiped out the stroke and tried again. All the time I was unaware that I was gaining an introduction to the intricacies of artwork, the discerning eye and the skill with brush required in painting a landscape or any other subject. This would enhance my appreciation of bird portraiture in the years to come.

During one of Mr. Adler's visits, my parents prevailed upon him to paint my portrait. I was, therefore, literally commanded to don a stiff ("Buster Brown") collar with bow tie, wear a jacket and stand still for at least an hour each day—and look pleasant. As the moments of each session dragged on, while I thought of all the goings-on outside which I was missing, anything like a pleasant expression became impossible. Mr. Adler's pleadings that I "brighten up" were futile. The portrait in oil, finished at last with Mr. Adler's apologies, was soon framed and hung conspicuously wherever my parents lived thereafter. For me, a quick glance at that dour kid on the wall was all that I could bear. Whenever asked if *that* was a picture of me, I would nod affirmatively and change the subject forthwith.

In my early years I never lived or stayed near bodies of water except briefly at Lake Kushaqua in the Adirondacks and Wallum Lake in Rhode Island. In Belgrade, and now on Greenwood Mountain, I was just a hill kid. This lack of familiarity with bodies of water dawned on Father when, along with Grandfather Groves, he took me fishing from a rowboat on Long Pond at Belgrade. I was ten years of age, yet scared to death. Every time the boat rocked, I clung to its sides, fearful that I would fall overboard. The submerged boulders we passed over were threatening monsters. "Enough of this," Father must have said to himself. Hence, the following summer, in 1918, he insisted on enrolling me at Camp Morgan for Boys on Lake Maranacook near Wayne. Much as I protested the idea—missing my sojourn on the Belgrade farm—the summer became an important one in my life.

Away from both sanatorium and family farm, I experienced the first pangs of homesickness, but they didn't last long for I was subjected to a rigorous daily regime under the guidance of counselors. Chief among them was Fred Roderique, a friend of my parents, who kept a sharp eye on my progress. I learned to swim, row a boat, paddle a canoe, and manage a sailboat. There were two highlights of my summer under Fred's guidance. One was a three-day canoe trip with kids of my age along a chain of lakes where we fished as we proceeded and then camped each night, learning how to build fires and cook, and later hearing Fred's stories as we sat around the fires afterwards before retiring to our tents. The other was a climbing excursion up Tumbledown Mountain near Weld, Maine, far enough away to require camping the nights before and after the climb near its base. Every moment that summer broadened my horizons—heretofore only those visible from high hills. Mountain-climbing and being on the water in any craft, for whatever purpose, would soon become sources of great satisfaction to me.

As a youngster from his family farm on Morrison Heights in Wayne, Father had looked down on Lake Androscoggin (then called Wayne Pond) where he had fun boating and fishing at every opportunity. While at the Western Maine Sanatorium, he purchased land on the east shore of the Lake and, in 1920, contracted with a local friend, who was both carpenter and builder, to put up a "camp" (actually a two-story cottage) on the property. Further inducing Father's choice of the site, besides its being in his home town, was that his sister and brother-in-law, Mary and Luther Norris, my Aunt Mame and Uncle Luther, owned a farm only a mile or so away. Although he was a farmer, Uncle Luther's heart was never in farming. Politics and especially hunting and guiding sportsmen were his joy. The fact that, with good reason, we would henceforth come to Wayne for weekends and vacations could not have pleased my aunt and uncle more. Father, Mother, and I slept for the first time in our new camp toward the end of the summer in 1920. We would enjoy our camp at one time or another every summer thereafter.

Owing to its isolation, the Western Maine Sanatorium was hardly affected by the First World War. Newspapers bore the tidings, good or bad. In our dining room was a wall map of Europe on which, with pins, the day-to-day progress of the Western Front was marked. Occasionally came a notification of someone's relative killed in action, which it became Father's burden to deliver. When the 'flu epidemic swept the country toward the end of the war, Father quarantined the sanatorium. No visitors were allowed; nobody could leave; we were isolated as never before. I was too young to realize fully the grave concern of the medical staff lest the 'flu reach the patients. Fortunately, precautionary measures succeeded.

After the war and the 'flu epidemic, Father was visited from time to time—mysteriously, it seemed to me—by three men bearing architectural drawings and seeking his advice on a TB sanatorium to be built by Essex County in northeastern Massachusetts; it would be the ultimate for coping with the disease. Construction would begin as soon as postwar conditions stabilized.

Probably Father knew, or at least guessed, why he was being consulted: he would be invited to open the institution and become its superintendent. But the thought of leaving Maine, especially now that we had a camp in Wayne some twenty-five miles away for weekends and vacations, appealed neither to him nor to Mother. The three men were the county commissioners, confident that Father was the right man for the job. They offered him the post. He accepted but only on condition that we have a home of our own. Not in the least bit disconcerted, the commissioners told my parents to indicate just what they wanted and spare no details. My parents complied with specifications they thought so exorbitant as to discourage the commissioners. Not at all!

It happened that on the extensive grounds acquired for the Essex Sanatorium in the town of Middleton, was a handsome eighteenth-century mansion with six rooms, each with a fireplace. This the commissioners agreed to modernize completely to my parents' satisfaction, with four additional rooms (one for recreation), private quarters for a live-in maid, a sun porch, and a screened-in porch over which was a sleeping porch. Mother was delegated to select the wallpaper, all new furnishings, and the carpets. Salaries for the maid and caretaker and costs of all food supplies would be paid by the sanatorium.

I was heartbroken. The Western Maine Sanatorium had been my boyhood home for over five years. The trails that led down into the woods always yielded for my bird lists something new or unexpected in any season. My parents attempted to offer consolation: besides living in a huge house with a room of my own and a sleeping porch to which I had become accustomed, I could have chicken coops and raise all the poultry I could manage.

Inevitably the day came, in early April of 1921, when we drove away in our Buick from the front steps of the administration building where all the staff and all our friends, including my classmates in the eighth grade, had gathered to wish us well and wave good-bye.

CHAPTER 4 / *Teenager*

WE MOVED into our new home in Middleton, Massachusetts, on the same day we had left Maine, April 5, 1921. There was every prospect, so I thought, of my inspecting, next day, the new Essex Sanatorium—that institution which had so ruthlessly uprooted my existence—and putting off the dreaded day when I had to enter a school new to me. But Mother had already enrolled me and insisted that I go to school next morning and get the ordeal over with. Besides, the teacher was expecting me.

The school I was destined to attend was the Middleton Center School (for grade students only) in the middle of town about two miles away. To get there, I had to take the trolley, which I reluctantly did the next morning, lunchpail in hand.

I had fully intended to enter the school as inconspicuously as possible, somehow to melt into the eighth grade. Unfortunately, I did not take an early enough trolley and was woefully late. School had long since begun by the time I arrived; the schoolyard was deserted. The dingy yellow, two-story school building looked uninviting, an array of bicycles leaning indifferently against it. A partially opened window let out sounds, somewhat muffled, of activities within. There were two entrances, one for boys, the other for girls. How would I know which one was for me? Taking a firmer grip on my lunchpail, I approached one entrance, pulled open the door, and slipped through into a huge corridor. Doors to the rooms were closed, so I was still unnoticed. The corridor reeked with a musty odor, almost stifling. The edges of the floor were strewn with rubbers and lunchpails; hooks on the walls supported all sorts of coats and jackets and, I was relieved to see, caps for boys. I was in the right corridor. But the caps were not my size; too small. Caps my size must be on the second floor. So I climbed stairs that creaked with my every step, my apprehension mounting.

The second floor corridor was a duplication of the first except that the wearing apparel was of larger size. I now had a choice of two doors. Adding my jacket, cap, and lunchpail to the accumulation, I selected the door nearest which the caps were the size of mine, took a deep breath and knocked. Heavy, short-spaced footsteps approached on the other side. The door whisked open and I faced Miss Caroline C. Manning, my new teacher. A plump, middle-aged woman no taller than I in my fourteen-year-old frame, she peered at me momentarily through large dark-rimmed glasses, then smiled warmly and said, "Oh yes, come in; we were looking for you."

All my hopes of an inconspicuous entrance vanished. Over Miss Manning's shoulder I saw several rows of staring faces which, so I found out, belonged to the seventh as well as the eighth grades. I followed Miss Manning like a lamb for what seemed a mile across the front of the room to a vacant seat in the second row on the eighth-grade side of the room, and slid quickly into it, hoping thereby to slip into anonymity. Yet there was no chance of escaping prominence for I was, from that moment on, "the new kid."

At my desk I sensed many eyes behind me just staring. Also, I could sense many unspoken questions along with the staring eyes. What kind of a guy was I? Could I fight? Was I interested in girls? Was I stuck up? Was I smart? Probably the unhappiest kid in the room, besides myself, was the boy at the desk in front of me who was fairly aching for chances to turn around and stare at me.

"Eleanor, please get Sewall a history book and show him where we are working. You can get his other books later." Upon this admonition from Miss Manning, a girl in the front seat of the row next to the eighth-grade door instantly left the room. I glanced toward her, too late to see her face but not too late to notice magnificent curls cascading over her shoulders. While my history work awaited Eleanor's return, I awaited a glimpse of the other side of Eleanor.

When Eleanor came back with my book, I looked at her, then down at my desk, hardly believing I had seen such bright blue eyes along with such a friendly, understanding smile. At my desk she opened the book with efficiency, pointed out the pages necessary, and returned to her desk.

School work was resumed. While my grade was quizzed by Miss Manning, I pretended keen interest, all the while thanking heaven that I would not be called on today. I marveled at how well Eleanor knew the subject; in fact, she seemed a repository of information. What manner of girl was she anyhow? I forgot the stares at me by staring at her.

Soon it was the seventh grade's turn to recite while we were commanded to study the next day's history lesson. As Miss Manning went to the other side of the room, Eleanor stepped to the blackboard to erase all the writing. At the conclusion of the seventh grade's recitation, Eleanor stepped up to the front of the room and pressed several buttons, causing signals to buzz throughout the building. She had declared recess. I could see that Eleanor was indispensable as Miss Manning's helper.

During the brief recess, Eleanor fetched the remainder of the books I needed, together with other essentials such as paper, ruler, and notebooks. Miss Manning gave me some advice on how to catch up on missed work—a discouraging prospect indeed—and left a heap of material on my desk. Eleanor, who had been heeding Miss Manning's procedures from a short distance away, then came over with some suggestions for a few shortcuts. Bless her, the prospects of catching up were no longer as discouraging.

At noon recess I grabbed my lunchpail and headed for the school yard where the boys had gathered. Leaning against the fence, I stuffed my sandwiches down my reluctant gullet while surrounded by gawking kids of all ages. They asked me where I was from and why I was there. I felt like a chicken in a strange coop. And knowing chickens, I realized my mettle would sooner or later be tested and my position in the social order determined. As the buzzer sounded for the return inside, I guardedly asked one of the eighth grade-boys: "What's the name of the girl who helps Miss Manning so much?" His reply: "Eleanor Rice."

At long last my first day at Middleton school came to an end. It was no less painful a day of adjustment than those following. Whereas I had been a self-imposed leader in the Greenwood Mountain School from its beginning, I was now an intruder—an awkward thirteenth in a class of twelve boys and girls whose social bonds were already knit. Then, too, I had to endure the suffocating confinement of a closed-in school room and the daily rides on a dusty trolley. Yet the readjustments I made, finding the social bond among twelve kids not as impenetrable as it had first seemed and the school room not as dismal. And there was Eleanor, who had a special talent for handling social situations and soon made the sun shine for me unlike any other girl I had ever known.

My first week of school over, I had a chance to inspect the Essex Sanatorium for over two hundred patients, not yet opened. It was utterly different from the sanatorium we had left in Maine, consisting of one long unit in soft gray stucco with artificial stone trimming. The three-story administration building, the central structure constructed in colonial style with a cupola, led by corridors east and west to two-storied wards, one ward for each sex. Only two buildings stood apart, the nurses' home on the west and the power plant below on the southern slope. Our house was south of the sanatorial complex near the highway and trolley line.

The Essex Sanatorium was opened formally on May 26, 1921, amid much fanfare. Prominent officials from all over the county, as well as the state, attended. As many as fifty patients would be admitted immediately and more applications for admission were arriving steadily. Father's staff included his superintendent of nurses and several others whom he had hired from the Western Maine Sanatorium.

I realized that I would never feel as attached to this sanatorium as to the one at Greenwood Mountain. Not only would I be living away from it and going to school elsewhere, but I already had a new chicken coop near our home. Soon I was in business with a Rhode Island Red rooster and three hens. Within a short while I would have another larger coop and more Rhode Island Red hens.

My school work soon became far more pleasant than I expected. My twelve classmates accepted me and several, among them Eleanor, helped to get me in stride with all studies. Miss Manning began making up the program for our graduation, assigning us different roles, chiefly performances, and rehearsing some of us for choral contributions. A long program was surely in store. Two classmates, Lawrence Kinney and Harry Berry, I liked especially well, although their personal interests were tinkering with radios and old automobiles, interests that were far from mine. More often than not after school, I took the next trolley home to take care of my "poultry farm." Graduation was June 23 in the Middleton Town Hall.

The very next day, I boarded the train for Maine. At the invitation of the new superintendent of Western Maine Sanatorium, I was privileged to graduate with my class there. Thus, I graduated from two grammar schools in the same year, perhaps a record of sorts. Part of that summer I spent with my grandparents in Belgrade, the rest with my parents at Lake Androscoggin in Wayne. Our caretaker, Emery, took care of my chickens as he always would in the future when I was away.

However distraught we may have been to leave Maine, the move greatly pleased Aunt Millie. She had long since closed her dressmaking establishment on Commonwealth Avenue in Boston and had married George Myron Whitman, a retired milliner, who had also operated on Commonwealth Avenue. They now resided in West Medford, a Boston suburb not far from us. Uncle Myron, or "Uncle Bill" as we usually called him, was short, balding, huge enough around the waist to be roly-poly, and invariably well groomed. In contrast to Aunt Millie, who was rather sober, quite proper, and easily shocked, Uncle Bill was the opposite, forever ready with a quip. He liked to kid and could burst into laughter at the slightest provocation. He was the life of the party more than anyone else I had ever known.

My chicken business prospered. I soon acquired over two dozen hens, kept daily records of eggs laid, and accounted for money spent in maintaining the flock. I sold some of the eggs to the sanatorium, others to Aunt Millie. Later I added some bantams, ducks, and geese. In 1924, at the Essex County Fair in Topsfield, I exhibited the best of my feathered collection, winning six prizes, two of them firsts. Proud as I was of my ribbons, I had already forsaken my dream of becoming a poultryman and gradually sold or gave away my collection after 1924.

I had always lived in one way or another amidst the medical profession. Father truly loved it and never once regretted becoming an M.D. I think he hoped—may even have expected—that I would choose the profession. Without giving the matter much serious thought, and without any pressure whatsoever from Father, I simply presumed that I would go into medicine, although in the back of my mind I really wanted to study birds for a living, to be an ornithologist. To enter medical school, I would first need a high school education, then go to and graduate from a college.

There was only one college I wanted to attend: Bowdoin. Many of Father's friends, medical and nonmedical, were loyal Bowdoinites and with them I went to alumni meetings. While at Greenwood Mountain, we had sleighed to Hebron Academy in midwinter to hear Donald B. MacMillan lecture on his exploits in the far North Country and tell of Admiral Robert E. Peary's efforts to reach the North Pole. Both were Bowdoin alumni. One recent winter in Middleton, newspapers carried items on the invasion of snowy owls in New England, reported by Alfred O. Gross of the Bowdoin faculty. Bowdoin championed the North Country, already appealing to me. Bowdoin had an authority on birds, an ornithologist. Where else but Bowdoin? Little did I imagine then the significant role Dr. Gross and Bowdoin would play in the development of my way to ornithology.

I was home from Maine by early September, 1921, to start high school. Since Middleton lacked one, the nearest was Holten High School in Danvers, a few miles east of us, reached by the same trolley line that had previously borne me in the opposite direction. Most of my Middleton classmates, including Harry Berry, went elsewhere to school, but aboard each morning were Lawrence Kinney, with whom I often sat, and Eleanor Rice, who was usually with a group of girls. Seldom, after coming aboard, did I fail to scan the occupants to see if Eleanor, her curls now gone and hair bobbed, was among them. Before we reached our destination, Danvers Square, a few blocks from the school, more students had come aboard.

After school, as I had at the Middleton school, I hurried to take the next trolley home. No loafing around for me. I had chickens to care for and other things I liked to do alone.

The scholastic record of my four years in high school was poor as I had to enroll in stiff courses required for entering Bowdoin. Report cards to my parents bore such statements as "Sewall is not applying himself." Eleanor, who took the same courses for entering Wheaton College in Norton, Massachusetts, had a better record. My problem was indeed one of application; I had more exciting thoughts on my mind, particularly Eleanor.

Never before had a girl so attracted me. Eleanor, I would soon learn, was fourteen months younger than I, and lived with her aunt in a fine white house with a veranda overlooking the Middleton Congregational Church just across the street. Her mother, Mary Ann, had died when she was a baby. Consequently, her mother's sister Elva, Mrs. Benjamin F. Brown—Aunt Elva or "Auntie Brown" as we called her in the years to come—became her surrogate mother. A gracious gray-haired lady, slightly round-shouldered, firm in discipline and with a ready sense of humor, Auntie Brown was always delightful company in any social situation. Eleanor's father, Walter B. Rice, lonely ever since the death of his only wife, owned and operated a hardware store in a nearby town and lived by himself in an adjacent apartment. I saw very little of him, except when he visited at Auntie Brown's to spend time with his daughter or attended special events involving her.

Life with my parents in Middleton contrasted sharply with that at Greenwood Mountain. Once settled in our sumptuous home, with appropriate furnishings in colonial style selected by Mother, we could now dine as a family alone, served by our maid, Velma. At supper Father reported on events at the sanatorium, often seeking Mother's advice on a personnel matter with which he must eventually cope. Any personal question of my own which I raised for advice, even though it was minor by comparison, was never ignored.

After supper in the colder months, the usual routine was relaxation in the living room, Father with a cigar and settled back in his favorite Morris chair, Mother in a rocking chair, knitting or reading. Soon uneasy myself, I either went to my room upstairs, if there was school work needing attention, or to the cellar where we had a darkroom with facilities for developing, printing, and enlarging photographs. I always retired to my bed on the sleeping porch, Father in his on the opposite side. With hinged windows that could be adjusted to suit the season, we no longer had to bundle up for sleeping as we did on the open porch at Greenwood Mountain.

In the warmer months, with long sunlit evenings, Father and I broke the after-supper routine by playing croquet on the front lawn. Two doctors from the sanatorium were on hand to join us. We played with heavy mallets, holding their short handles in one hand as we bent over the balls for taking careful aim. Father was an expert at the game, better than I or the doctors. Occasionally, the competition was so intense and prolonged that the final game lasted into the dusk, and we had to use flashlights to pinpoint the wickets and stakes. I can honestly say that I liked croquet better than any other outdoor game in my life.

Our family routine was frequently broken, however. For lunch or dinner, we entertained staff from the sanatorium as well as numerous friends from neighboring towns. Houseguests who stayed overnight or longer were readily accommodated since we had two extra rooms with baths. One of our first houseguests was our longtime friend Oscar Adler, invited to coach a play as he had several times at Greenwood Mountain. Always pleasurable company, he would be with us twice a year in the future for coaching more plays. Now that my activities were elsewhere than at the sanatorium, I saw only his final productions, rarely the rehearsals.

As time went on, Father and Mother became increasingly involved in affairs outside the sanatorium, Father in medical societies, local and national, and in the Danvers Rotary Club, Mother in various women's clubs in Middleton and Danvers and the Massachusetts Maine Daughters in Boston. Mother and Miss Manning supervised the Middleton Girl Scouts. Both women were short, plump and, when in scout uniforms, looked like twins. Never forgotten by Father, and occasionally retold by him to Mother's annoyance, was a Memorial Day parade in Danvers when, as the two women drew up the rear of the marching Middleton scouts, Father heard a spectator shouting at them from the sidewalk, "Here comes the heavy artillery!"

Father was a Civil War buff, motivated by his father who had served in the Eleventh Maine Infantry Volunteers and kept a diary. (Later from it, Father published his father's *Memoirs of the Civil War* in 1966.) In early May of 1922, Father seized the opportunity to visit some of the battlefields in his father's story, after first attending the annual meeting of the National Tuberculosis Association in Washington, D.C. He invited me to accompany him, getting me excused from school. While he was involved with five days of meetings, I could see the capital city on my own, which I did partly by bus but mostly on foot.

Unfortunately, I wore new ankle-high shoes and soon had blisters on both heels. Regardless of the discomfort, there was scarcely a government building, museum, or art gallery I missed. I joined a tour of the Capitol where I saw Vice-President Calvin Coolidge presiding over the Senate. What enthralled me most was the National Zoo, where I spent more time than anywhere else, watching activities in the aviaries and the behavior of waterfowl on the ponds. There would come a day, I hoped, when I would see some of these species in their natural habitats.

On the fifth day of the meeting, association members were received at the White House. All members, and I with them, lined up to shake hands with President Warren G. Harding. Probably because I was a youngster, the president gave me more than passing attention; to this day I recall his handsome face, smile, and particularly his soft handshake.

The next day Father, accompanied by a medical friend who was similarly informed on the Civil War, and I entrained for Richmond, Virginia, hired a Ford, and set out for what remained of the battlefields around Petersburg. By prearrangement, we were guided by Captain Carter R. Bishop, who had served in the army of the Confederacy as a very young man. Courteous, soft-spoken, and knowledgeable, he could not have been more helpful. A friendship with Father was struck up, which would result in correspondence and a visit later from him in Middleton. Admittedly my attention to the battlefields was frequently diverted by the birds in the area—my first views of cardinals, mockingbirds, tufted titmice, and other southern species.

On two occasions the sanatorium staged winter carnivals, both in early February, on an iced-over pond southeast of the power plant. To the first in 1922, as well as the second in 1924, figure skaters and speed skaters were induced to come from the arena in Boston and perform. A hockey game and a band concert added to the entertainment. As far as I was concerned, the second carnival surpassed the first because among the invited participants was Arthur T. Walden. With his dog team from Wonalancet, New Hampshire, he gave sled rides to young and old over the snowy countryside. Walden, outgoing and talkative, was our breakfast guest along with his famous lead dog, Chinook, sitting obediently on his haunches near us and actually scanning our table since his massive head was higher. Before departing, Walden invited us to Wonalancet for some trips with his dog teams. With no hesitation, Father and I accepted, although Mother politely declined as she had already had a fine ride the day before. And so on March 14, 1924, Father and I got into our cold-weather togs and were driven by the sanatorium chauffeur to Portsmouth, New Hampshire, where we entrained to Mount Whittier and were met by automobile, reaching the Walden home by sundown. The next day, clear and sparkling after a light snowfall, we were taken in the morning by two teams, Chinook leading Walden's, to the top of Mount Katherine.

Back at the Walden home after lunch, we packed food for supper and breakfast and loaded it along with robes and sleeping bags on two sleds, and were off for several miles to a campsite in a woodsy setting. There we built a lean-to of spruce boughs and, in front, started a roaring fire. After a fine meal cooked over coals came the best part of the evening: the storytelling by Walden of his early years of "dog-punching" in the Yukon. By this time all the sled dogs, released and fed, were each curled up deep in the snow and asleep except for Chinook, who stayed with his master. Before long we were all in our sleeping bags, feet toward the fire, which was kept alive all night by one or more of the men. Then came a hearty breakfast and the ride to the Walden home by noon.

Mr. and Mrs. Walden could not have been more hospitable and would not accept any remuneration, even as we bade them good-bye after lunch. It would be four years later, in 1928, that Walden, along with Chinook and several dog teams with drivers, would join the First Byrd Antarctic Expedition.

I have little recollection of my classes and teachers during my first year in high school. Eleanor and I took the same courses in the same rooms. She was sharp in algebra, sharper than I ever would be in anything mathematical, which gave me an excuse for stopping with her in a corridor to get help on some complexity.

The recollection of my classes and teachers in the next three years is similarly vague with one exception: the class each year in English taught by Frances G. Wadleigh. She was tall, gaunt, with a long, narrow face exaggerated by hair drawn tightly back in a low pug. However homely she may have been, her homeliness yielded to her warmth of character, her sense of humor, and above all her sensitiveness to her students' concerns. She was a teacher in the truest sense.

Miss Wadleigh clearly revealed her love of good literature. She cited books that I should read and encouraged me to write compositions emulating their style. She took time in class and out to criticize my efforts, showing me where I could improve by varying sentence structure, avoiding wordiness, and expressing myself in a concise manner. So inspired was I that I wrote five pieces for the literary section of *The Holten*, the school magazine. Reading these pieces today makes me cringe at their naivete, but at the time I so enjoyed writing them, and took such pride in seeing them in print, that I indicated my intention to become a writer. On reading these pieces, Aunt Millie, much impressed and unbeknownst to me, changed her will, leaving me half of her estate (the other half to Mother, which would eventually revert to me) in order that its income might give me an independent means of support for my ambition.

My sophomore year outside of school work was singularly eventful. With our Middleton friends, Eleanor and I attended dancing school in Salem. We joined the Middleton Grange and the Congregational Church. Then came the Sophomore Hop on May 18, 1923, giving me the opportunity to muster my courage and ask Eleanor to go with me. She accepted unhesitatingly, much to my elation. As the occasion approached, together we decided with whom we should exchange dances and made up our program accordingly. I never had a happier evening and was jealous of every male who danced with my first date. Our dancing lessons served us well; we matched to perfection and were sorrowful when the time came for the band to play "Good Night Ladies."

For our memorable evening, I had picked up Eleanor by trolley and taken her home by the same means. (I could not use the Buick because I would not have a driving license until I was sixteen in October.) Afterwards, having escorted Eleanor up to Auntie Brown's front door and opened it, I put my arm around her and said good night with a kiss, a meaningful one. Her response was, "Oh, you silly" and, gently tapping my cheek, she stepped inside and closed the door. My trolley ride home was on cloud nine. I had triumphed! Eleanor was "my girl" now and forever; woe unto anyone who would take her away from me. Our departures thereafter from Auntie Brown's were ever more lingering with Eleanor's responses as meaningful as mine. We had fallen in love.

At age sixteen, I had reached maximum height, just under six feet. I had no desire to participate in contact sports but I was always a rooting bystander at home football games. The extent of my sporting involvement was in golf when my family joined the Salem Country Club. There I took lessons, learning the essentials in golfing, but I lacked something—perhaps the necessary physical coordination or the patience to improve it. Nevertheless I stuck with golf, using it later to meet the sports requirement in college.

Travel was a matter for greater enthusiasm, however. I was not long in realizing that Eleanor was a kindred spirit in thinking about and planning for adventures to far places. Knowing that Miss Wadleigh was from New Hampshire and had spoken glowingly of the White Mountains, why not ask her to lead us in climbing them? Lawrence Kinney and Harry

Berry were keen about joining us. Miss Wadleigh, we found, needed no inducing; indeed she welcomed the prospect.

I was full of excitement. At Belgrade, I had gazed many times at the Presidential Range from afar and later, at Greenwood Mountain, from much closer. Remembering how much I had enjoyed the scramble up Tumbledown Mountain during my summer at Camp Morgan, I wanted the challenge of tackling bigger mountains including Mount Washington, the highest peak in New England. We gathered at Miss Wadleigh's apartment to plan our itinerary and discuss the necessary clothing and camping gear for the expedition, which was to take place as soon as school had closed in 1924. My parents drove the four of us to Miss Wadleigh's home in Union, New Hampshire, and would pick us up there seven days later. In Miss Wadleigh's car, we started at once to the western foot of the White Mountains where we camped for the night in Crawford Notch.

Early the next morning our ascent began up the Edmands Trail through dense woods that seemed interminable. At last, we were above timberline and eventually reached the Lake of the Clouds where, in the neighboring hut of the Appalachian Mountain Club, we spent the night. We continued up to the Summit House on Mount Washington for the second night. On the third day, we followed the trails north from Mount Washington, almost entirely above timberline, except for crossing wooded cols, leading to the summits of Mount Adams and then Mount Madison. We camped for the night in a stone hut snug in a col between the two mountains. By nightfall on the fourth day, we had returned to the Summit House. After our descent the next day to Miss Wadleigh's car and camping again in Crawford Notch, we spent our final day touring the Franconia area. We walked up the Flume and admired the Old Man of the Mountains (Great Stone Face), lofty above Profile Lake, then returned to Union where my parents picked us up as scheduled.

The trip proved Eleanor as hardy as I for strenuous excursions, which included camping, and equally ecstatic about what we saw—the tantalizingly few vistas from the Edmands Trail as we plodded impatiently up the forested slopes; the

views from above timberline overlooking a receding contin-
uum of mountains; the gorgeous sunset from Mount Washington where we spent the second night; and the intense
lightning of a thunderstorm raging below us from the same
summit where we spent the fourth night. During this introduction to the White Mountains at age seventeen, I still did
not know enough about birds to regret missing the opportunities in mountain situations for seeing or hearing species
which would have been new to me. I was totally unaware of
the zonal distribution of birds.

Holidays, always at home, were especially festive with the
regular presence of Aunt Millie and Uncle Bill. On Thanksgiving Day, after a big dinner, Uncle Bill, Father, and I customarily listened by radio to the traditional Cornell University–University of Pennsylvania football game.

Father's health continued unimpaired. He gained weight,
even became conspicuously large around the waist. Nevertheless, he continued worrying about "breaking down," remembering his misfortune at the beginning of his medical career. If
he had as much as a simple cold, he took to bed, not on the
sleeping porch but inside. Mother, who enjoyed good health
all her life, scoffed at Father's concerns, making light of them.

As at Greenwood Mountain, Father was much concerned
about my maintaining my health, giving me a generous al-
lowance and never once encouraging me to take on jobs of
any sort for "pocket money." He insisted that my summer
vacations should be spent leisurely in Wayne, along with
Mother, on Lake Androscoggin, and in Belgrade on short visits with my grandparents. He joined us occasionally on weekends and for his summer vacations.

Upon arriving in Wayne, we first called on Aunt Mame
and Uncle Luther and made tentative plans for their coming
down to our camp for meals. We took for granted that we
would gather Saturday nights at the Androscoggin Yacht Club
for baked bean suppers. Uncle Luther was always looking forward to fishing with Father during his upcoming stays.

In Wayne, since we had a rowboat with an outboard
motor, I spent much of my time on the lake fishing, looking
for loon nests early in the summer, checking up on a family

of bald eagles nesting on an island, or just rowing alone along the shore. I came to know the three-mile-long lake like a book, exploring practically every inch of shoreline and locating all rocks barely submerged offshore, which my motor might strike. If there were thunderstorms threatening, I made sure to make it back to camp with time to spare. Although I knew the different bird species in the camp's immediate vicinity, somehow I lacked the inducements to look for their nests.

I continued subscribing to *Bird-Lore*, which I faithfully read, and bought a copy of *Bird-Life* by Frank M. Chapman to aid me in bird identification and to answer questions I had about bird habits. Lacking, however, was Miss Frances Plumstead's stimulation as there was not a soul I had met, after leaving Greenwood Mountain, who knew or cared the least bit about birds. But my interest in birds persisted nonetheless, as did my interest in Thornton Burgess.

By 1924, Burgess had become a popular figure, lecturing to thousands of children and packing auditoriums up and down the East Coast. One day I made a special trip into Boston to see his slide show in Tremont Temple, jammed with youngsters. I had become interested in Burgess the man as well as Burgess the writer. About this time, with radio coming into its own, I learned that station WBZ in Springfield, Massachusetts, had arranged with Burgess to organize the "Radio Nature League." The program was an open-meeting forum to which people—either live or by correspondence—contributed observations or asked questions. Noted naturalists were invited to speak. The program reached people in the Northeast in all walks of life and of all ages.

I must have my own radio—a crystal set, I decided—so that I could listen to the programs; but I knew nothing about the radio's intricacies, least of all how to put one together. My solution: I prevailed upon my good friend Lawrence Kinney to come to my rescue. With his help I built a set, equipped with a marvelous invention, a loudspeaker. No more headphones! I became a regular listener to the programs.

Outside of school hours during my last three years, especially after I had my driver's license at sixteen in the fall of 1923 and could borrow the family car, it seems in retrospect that my life was a whirl of activities: dates with Eleanor, either at Auntie Brown's "to study" or go to the movies; attending school dances; parties at homes of classmates.

Now that I had a license to drive, complications arose about the use of the family car when Father and/or Mother wanted to use it the same evening I did. (Father had access to the sanatorium's car during the day.) The solution came unexpectedly in my senior year when Father, without any urging from me, decided that I must have my own car. It should be a sports car—entirely his idea. So into Boston we went to find one. Alas, the few we looked over were unreasonable in cost as well as in maintenance. By no means discouraged, we would have one built that could accommodate two people. Acquiring a Ford Model T chassis, we took it into Boston where we had built on it a sports-car body, complete with windshield and a canvas top which could be folded back when desired. I painted the body bright red and we dubbed it "the bug." While not the most comfortable car and unlike any other vehicle I had ever seen, it gave me new independence, together with a degree of dubious distinction in the neighborhood. Eleanor said she adored it and I believe she spoke the truth.

I was not long in discovering that the bug's chassis was older than Father and I thought; parts of it were always giving out. Again I called on Lawrence Kinney for help. As proficient in maintaining cars as he was with radios, he showed how to line brakes, and repair or replace this part or that. From his education in mechanical problems, I was able to cope with many a future hold-up, be it at home, on the road, or in Maine.

Every year in midwinter it was traditional for Holten High School seniors to stage a play. My fourth year having come, I tried out for it, as did Eleanor who shared my liking for showmanship. Both of us won parts. Among the nine in the cast I was the college professor, Eleanor the languishing dilettante. The play meant tedious rehearsals after class hours. The coach, so casual—so different from Oscar Adler's meticulous attention to positioning on the stage, action, and enunciation—made me wonder if the play would ever come off as I thought it should. We performed it in a local theater since our high school had no suitable stage. My parents, Uncle Bill, Aunt

Millie, Auntie Brown, and Eleanor's father dutifully attended. Later Father wrote in his diary: "Sewall starred, very enjoyable entertainment."

Earning high school grades good enough for entering Bowdoin worried me. I took some entrance examinations at the end of my junior year, more later in my senior year; in both efforts I never knew the results. On May 1, 1925, I drove to Brunswick to register at Bowdoin and attend some classes, gaining an idea of what lay in store for me. Eleanor and I graduated from Holten High School on June 25, neither of us with any distinction. As far as I was concerned, the graduation exercises and speeches were perfunctory. The best part in our termination of high school was the graduation reception the following evening when the whole family, including Aunt Millie and Uncle Bill, Auntie Brown, and Mr. Rice, were on hand. All showed pride in our reaching this point in our lives.

Our 1925 summer in Wayne followed after the local Fourth of July celebrations including bonfires and fireworks in Salem. I drove to Wayne in my bug, my parents in their car. A week or so later Eleanor and Auntie Brown joined us at camp. This was their first visit. It was high time that I introduced Eleanor to Maine, considering that she had heard so much about it. Besides giving her the grand tour of Lake Androscoggin and showing her how to fish—she had never before baited a hook or removed a fish from one—I gave her a boat ride on Dead River, the flat-water stream connecting the lake with the river bearing the same name. We drove to Greenwood Mountain so that I could give her an idea of where I had lived over five years. And we spent a whole day with my grandparents in Belgrade. I showed her all the buildings, inside and out. In the barn, we climbed to the scaffolds above the mows and jumped down into the freshly stored hay. Although Eleanor had met my grandparents on their brief visits with us in Middleton, now they had a chance to perceive my girl informally, and I readily sensed their full approval.

CHAPTER 5 / *Year at Kents Hill*

WHEN EXACTLY after graduation from high school "the sky fell in on me," I have no record. Simply stated, I had failed some examinations for entering Bowdoin College and was refused admission in the fall. Eleanor had been admitted to Wheaton College in Norton, Massachusetts. I was in despair. What must I do? My only recourse, my parents decided, was to attend Kents Hill School—then officially called Maine Wesleyan Seminary and Women's College but informally Kents Hill Seminary—for a year of work that would help me meet Bowdoin's requirements the following year. Kents Hill had about 160 boarding students.

On September 8, 1925, my parents drove me to the train, which would deliver me to Readfield Depot where transportation awaited students going to Kents Hill. Situated high on a hill with a wide view of the Maine landscape north and west, the school consisted mainly of a dormitory, two buildings for classes and assorted activities, the principal's residence, and a farm.

The dormitory, Sampson Hall, accommodated students on its upper three floors, partitioned off to reserve one side for girls, the other for boys. The main floor had reception and recreation rooms. Below were the dining room and kitchen. Most of the faculty resided in Sampson Hall, an instructor in charge of each partitioned-off floor. As for the two buildings for classes, the smaller, Ricker Hall, had three stories with rooms for musical instruction, a recital hall, library, and store. A gymnasium was in the basement. The larger building, Bearce Hall, four stories tall, featured a white cupola with a gold-colored top. Inside, besides classrooms, was a chapel—an all-purpose facility for assemblies, musical and dramatic productions, or any special events as well as movies on Wednesday nights and sometimes social gatherings on Saturday nights—and administrative offices including one for the principal, T. W. Watkins.

I was assigned a northwest corner room on the second floor of Sampson Hall. There, to my astonishment and dismay, I met my roommate, who had been in my class at the Danvers high school. We had disliked each other for sundry reasons and I could foresee no chance of any emerging friendship.

During the first days, I was afflicted with homesickness compounded by my bitter disappointment in not being at Bowdoin. When free of classes, I took long walks by myself, sometimes sitting down and studying in a field on the west side of the school, beyond which, a couple of distant western hills away and out of sight, was my beloved Belgrade farm and grandparents. Inside the dormitory, I spent much time in my room studying until, in a room across the corridor from mine, I befriended Albert H. Lindsay and James S. Lunn. They became my confidants with whom I could express my feelings and from whom I could receive advice and encouragement. I was soon in regular correspondence with Eleanor, whose letters were always cheerful. To my surprise, after three weeks or so, my Danvers roommate withdrew suddenly from school for reasons I never knew and his place was taken by another student. After the first few days, I started giving attention to various school activities. I went to football games and enjoyed the Wednesday night movies in the chapel.

To Father, in a letter dated October 10, came the following from Principal Watkins: "We enclose Sewall's report for the first four weeks of school. It is quite a distinction for a boy to make the Honor Roll the first four weeks in school and doubly so when he is carrying such a heavy load . . . I do not need to tell you that he is establishing a reputation for character and personality fully as good as his studies." Soon after Father received the letter, he and Uncle Bill drove my bug (I couldn't imagine those two big men in it!) to Wayne, five miles away. Since students were not allowed to have cars at the school, at least I would have near access to mine when I wanted it.

By the end of October, I had begun to feel adjusted to Kents Hill, making friends, and was doing well scholastically as Principal Watkins's letter had attested.

Then came the evening of November 8.

I was alone in my room and readying for bed, undressed as far as my "union suit," when there was a knock at the door. Opening it, I was confronted by a blanket held up and spread out in front of me by one person with others standing behind him. Instantly the blanket was thrown over me. Wrapped in it, I was carried downstairs and out into the November chill, headed, I realized, for the cattle barn. Beneath it, I was tossed out of the blanket onto a heap of fresh cow manure and commanded to crawl in it, face down. (Having been a farm boy, I knew precisely what I was in for!) Once I had obeyed, a gruff shout came from the leader of my abductors: "That will teach you for squealing on Whitey"—the nickname for the instructor in charge of my floor. With that accusation ringing in my ears, my abductors departed, leaving me alone in the darkness.

I could see well enough where I was, and hastily made my way barefoot to the shower on my dormitory floor, disposed of my filthy union suit in the wastebasket, washed thoroughly, and beat it to my room. (Needless to say, the shower room bore the smell of the cattle barn well into the next day.) My roommate was not waiting, nor had he been in the room before I was carried away. I presume he had been tipped off on the upcoming abduction.

No sooner had I gotten into my room than Jim Lunn burst out of his room across the way and confronted the leader of the affair (who happened to occupy the room next to mine), castigating him in no uncertain terms for the whole performance. Blows were nearly struck. But I was too perplexed to listen, wondering *what* was the reason for the nasty business in the first place and *what* I should do because I felt humiliated and was becoming enraged.

At first I decided to dress, put on my overcoat, and walk out of the place to Wayne, pick up my bug, and drive home. Soon common sense prevailed. I would go to bed, which I did, and appear at breakfast as if nothing had happened. Admittedly, I had trouble sleeping because of the accusation of "squealing" on Whitey. About what? I was not in his classes. Our relationship had always been congenial. He was, however, more congenial with others on my floor, some of them football players more his age than mine.

Eventually I learned that Principal Watkins had reprimanded Whitey for a misdemeanor, which had come to his attention from some source. I, son of Kents Hill alumni and presumed self-appointed guardian of the school's morals, was the suspected informer.

In the dining room after breakfast, the principal called together all the boys he knew had been responsible for perpetrating the previous night's events, gave them a stern dressing down, and put them on a week's probation. Directly afterwards he apologized to me, as did several of the boys who had participated in my trip to the cattle barn.

It soon dawned on me that the whole unsavory affair resulted from how I was viewed in the eyes of my contemporaries. The only child in my whole family, I had had "everything my way." I was admired, trusted, believed in; I could do no wrong. Never a mixer, I was quite satisfied with a few close friends and content to be doing things by myself. Here at Kents Hill, away from the home environment and together day and night with a host of young people my age, I had made the mistake of not mixing enough. Often solemn, sometimes taciturn, my attitude was easily interpreted as perhaps snobbish or disapproving, thereby arousing suspicion. I must, I said to myself, be more outgoing, more social.

For the Wednesday night movies, I dated Vira Nickerson, classmate, who was loquacious, quick to comment on the lighter side of our associates, and fun to be with. From the outset, however, I let her know that my girl was in Wheaton College, and I also let Eleanor know the name of the girl I was dating. There was to be no two-timing. Besides movies, I dated Vira for socials on Saturday night in the chapel, which usually included square dancing. I stipulate "square dancing" because coupled dancing—for example, foxtrotting—was not permitted in staunchly Methodist-supported Kents Hill. Always amusing, nevertheless, was how a square dance, such as the Virginia Reel, often broke into a foxtrot until a faculty member had the music stopped.

After the Christmas recess, with Kents Hill now in the depths of winter, I acquired skis and ski poles, as did several other boys, for fully appreciating the outdoors when it was not too blustery. Otherwise during the winter, except for movies on Wednesday nights, Saturday night socials, and occasional basketball games, we spent an inordinate amount of time playing bridge or just holding bull sessions. The school lacked any sort of daily program to keep students active outside of class work.

Never one to shun the chance to perform on the stage, as proven in my days before Kents Hill, I tried out for the senior play, Booth Tarkington's *Clarence*, scheduled for March 6, and was given a minor part. Frequent rehearsals began in late January. More skillfully coached than my senior play in Danvers, it went off without a hitch before an entirely local audience.

Soon after returning from the Christmas recess, I became closely acquainted with Woodbury S. Adams, who roomed on the floor above me. In him—the son of a judge in Portsmouth, New Hampshire—I found a companion who was more maturely adjusted socially than any person my age I had yet known. One weekend I took him with me to Belgrade to stay with my grandparents, whose hearts he won by his genuine interest in their way of life. On another weekend, I took him to Wayne. While there, besides charming Aunt Mame and Uncle Luther, he went with me to the local grange for a bean supper. This he relished and afterwards had a fine time dancing with numerous girls he had never seen before.

In my correspondence with Eleanor, I had written at length about Woody. Since she had invited me to Wheaton's spring prom in April, she urged me at the same time to bring him too, as well as Lawrence Kinney from Middleton, and she would set up dates for both. This she accomplished with resulting success as both were delighted with their dates. On our way to and from Wheaton, Woody and I stopped over with my parents, who never failed thereafter to inquire about Woody—he was that unforgettable.

By a happy coincidence, Eleanor's spring recess from Wheaton and mine from Kents Hill were at the same time, giving us a few precious days together in Middleton. During this time together we continued with the idea I had mentioned in letters to her that, after our school year had ended in June, we climb Katahdin, Maine's highest mountain, a northern outpost of the Appalachians rising from the wilderness in the northern part of the state. And, furthermore, that we ask Miss Wadleigh to go with us. Just as I expected, Eleanor was ready for another adventure such as we had had climbing the White Mountains in 1924. We found Miss Wadleigh eager to go, as were Miss Maude Murphy and Miss Mary Swift, two grade-school teachers her age who shared her apartment. None of them had as much as seen Katahdin. Harry Berry and Lawrence Kinney would join us as they had in 1924, and so would two others: Elizabeth Penny, former classmate at Holten High School, and Lawrence Tedford, a former classmate in Middleton Center School. Plans were consequently set, although fulfilling them seemed years ahead rather than only four months away.

At no time during the year did I as much as look at birds, much less think about them. Not surprising really, as nobody else thought about or paid attention to birds. Anything approaching the subject of natural history was never mentioned in science classes. Spring bird walks were unheard of.

With the 102nd Commencement approaching on June 10–14, preparations accelerated for the numerous events during those five days. I was among eight students selected to compete on the first day in the Reuben B. Dunn Annual Prize Speaking Contest. I chose Poe's "The Raven" and days before began memorizing it, sometimes going out in the woods alone to recite it aloud. (Many times the trees must have reverberated with "Quoth the Raven, 'Nevermore!'") Happily, I won the then-coveted prize to the elation of my relatives, all present from Belgrade, Wayne, Middleton, and West Medford.

Graduation exercises were in nearby Torsey Memorial Church in the morning of June 14. Thus came to an end my year at Kents Hill, with continued regret in having missed a year at Bowdoin, yet with a strengthened feeling of self-assurance. I was now more fully prepared for college than I would have been a year before.

In a way I considered the Katahdin climb, which Eleanor and I had so meticulously planned, as a celebration of my graduation from Kents Hill. On June 26, eight of us (Lawrence Kinney could not go at the last minute for family reasons) headed for Maine, Eleanor and I in the bug, the others in two cars. After spending the first night at our camp in Wayne, we drove to the beginning of the tote road, then accessible only to horse-drawn buckboards, which led to the southwest base of Katahdin. We stopped for the night at the beginning of the tote road where we would leave our cars, and camped near them for the night. During the night it rained. By morning the sky had cleared, as we hiked in on the tote road for eight miles to our chosen headquarters, York's Twin Pine Camps. On reaching them, before us loomed across a little lake the magnificent great mountain, our challenge on the morrow. Eleanor and I had time in the early evening to catch some trout from a nearby dam of the Sourdnahunk Stream.

During the evening we decided we should hire a guide; consequently, we engaged one. Early the next morning, with him sharing some of our duffel and taking the lead, we tackled the Hunt Trail up the mountain. We had not gone far when Miss Murphy found the effort too strenuous. Harry returned with her to the camps, later catching up with us. Meanwhile our guide was far ahead, out of sight. This became the case all too often thereafter. Perhaps he considered himself not a guide but a pack horse. Before long we were referring to him as "With or Without."

The Hunt Trail, though not particularly arduous, required considerable exertion as we worked up through dense spruce forest. In a short time I developed a recurring thirst which I quenched at every spring or rivulet. (Forever after, when terribly thirsty, I have always thought of my "Katahdin thirst.") We made the tableland above timberline before noon. The sky was clear, save for a few fluffy clouds. Stretching from below us in all directions, except northward, was wilderness Maine with countless lakes, all sizes and shapes, mirroring the sky as far as the eye could see. Since the summit of Katahdin constitutes several miles of tableland or plateau, our well-marked trail led us easily northward to a slight rise, Katahdin's highest point (later to be called Baxter Peak) at 5,267 feet. There With or Without was awaiting us, and there we lunched.

Adhering to our itinerary, we descended soon after on the

Cathedral Trail to Chimney Pond, about two thousand feet below us on Katahdin's northeast side, in the Great Basin. By the time we arrived, With or Without had chosen our campsite beside Chimney Pond at the timberline. The setting—spectacular is the word to describe it—was walled, except on the north, by precipitous cliffs of striated granite. As in the White Mountains, I paid little attention to birds, much as I was interested in them. Had I known them better, for instance, I would have taken time to look for water pipits on the tableland, the sole breeding site of the species in Maine. Even so, I could not miss the common ravens performing their aerial maneuvers along the face of the cliffs above Chimney Pond.

Our return to York's Camps the next day was via the famed Knife Edge. To reach it we first had to tackle the trail up Pamola Peak, towering above us from the northeast edge of the basin. Climbing it required much scrambling over and around ledges. Then from Pamola back to the tableland came the mile-long Knife Edge. Walking it was like straddling the ridgepole of a gigantic barn, its slopes on either side dropping steeply fifteen hundred to two thousand feet to the talus at the timberline. Surefootedness was paramount; a stumble could mean a serious plunge. Had there been a strong wind, rather than a mild breeze favoring us, I shuddered at the thought of what the trek would have been like. Sensibly, we stopped often to sit down, rest, and marvel at our situation and the views it offered. But not With or Without; he simply kept moving. He stopped at the tableland to see if we had made the Knife Edge, then he was gone. By the time we had come down the Hunt Trail and arrived at York's Camps by late afternoon, all of us bone weary, With or Without was waiting for us—to be paid.

In the years to come, I would climb Katahdin again, more knowledgeable about birds than in 1926; and I would have opportunity to admire the great lone mountain at a distance from all directions, one side so greatly unlike another. But my preferred side, as it is for many people, is the one we first saw from the southwest. So impressed was I with the southwest side of Katahdin that one of my photographs of it later embellished the book plate in my personal library.

CHAPTER 6 / *Bowdoin Freshman*

THE 1926 SUMMER following my so-called Katahdin celebration was a pleasant one for me. I spent much of it with Mother at our camp on Lake Androscoggin in Wayne. Eleanor and Auntie Brown visited us, as did Aunt Millie and Uncle Bill, and I spent a day or two now and then with my grandparents in Belgrade.

As summer waned, I had to spend much more time than usual in Middleton—studying. Looming in September were two entrance examinations I must take to enter Bowdoin College, one in plane geometry, the other in Roman history. (I still lacked one and a half out of fourteen and a half points to fulfill entrance requirements.) To feel secure in my necessary knowledge of both subjects, I acquired a tutor, a summer-vacationing school teacher in Danvers, who would guide my reviews. I really needed her discipline to keep me on track amidst the multitude of tempting distractions.

There was always the Salem Country Club beckoning. Sometimes Eleanor went with me to play tennis, but more often I went for golf, ever hoping to improve my game. I played frequently with Father, occasionally with Mother and others. My partner one day was Clark Sears, who lived near Danvers and would be a junior at Bowdoin. I liked him at once. After telling me that he belonged to the Psi Upsilon Fraternity, he invited me to stay in his room at the fraternity house until I had my room in a dormitory.

My determination to enter Bowdoin had never wavered. In May I had driven in my bug from Kents Hill to Brunswick for a Bowdoin subfreshmen weekend. I attended Saturday classes and stayed overnight in one of the fraternity houses—obtaining a "feel" of the college—but I still knew very little about the *real* Bowdoin other than its particular reputation, which so greatly appealed to me.

Founded in 1794, Bowdoin was a men's college, would remain so until 1971 when it admitted women. Enrollment totaled about 550, the majority of students being from Maine and Massachusetts, and degrees of B.A. and B.S. were offered. Attendance was required at all classes, although a few cuts were allowed. The same was true at chapel, which held daily services in the early morning before classes and at vespers.

The chapel itself, the most striking building on the campus with its twin, 120-foot towers, was arranged inside like an English chapel, having a wide central aisle from entrance to dais, flanked on both sides with ranges of aisle-facing benches in four sections. The first section, nearest the entrance, was for freshmen, the next for sophomores, and so on.

Bowdoin was primarily a fraternity college, about ninety per cent of the student body belonging to one or another of eleven fraternities, all but one of which were chapters in national Greek letter societies. Each fraternity (never referred to as a "frat") owned and maintained its own house including kitchen, with an employed staff, and dining room facilities. For a reduction in board, one of the upperclassmen acted as steward and two other upperclassmen waited on tables. All janitorial services, such as polishing floors, washing windows, and shoveling the entrance walks clear of snow, were performed by freshmen. Most juniors and seniors roomed in the houses, freshmen and sophomores in the four dormitories on the campus. Students not belonging to fraternities roomed in the dormitories and took their meals in private homes or restaurants until the Moulton Union was built and became available to them in 1929.

Over the years Bowdoin had generated numerous traditions. No student passed another on the campus without saying "Hi." For applause or approval in classroom or chapel, or at any other inside gathering, students "wooded"—stamped their feet on the floor. Freshmen were required to wear specially designed caps, substituting in winter specially designed tams. As soon as freshmen had arrived on campus and registered, they were "rushed" by the fraternities for pledging, if they had not been pledged previously. Initiation into the fraternities took place in early November. Three times a year there were house parties: before Christmas, in midwinter following the conclusion of the first semester, and in May—"Ivy Time"—near the conclusion of the second. For these occasions, each lasting two days, the rooms in the fraternities were turned over to the invited women and chaperons, the men bunking in dormitories or elsewhere.

At last the day came in September, 1926, for me to enter Bowdoin. My parents drove me to our Wayne camp. The next day, September 20, Father took me to Brunswick (an hour's drive from Wayne), and waited until I had completed my examination in Roman history. The day following, he and I went to Brunswick for Freshman Day when Lieutenant Donald B. MacMillan spoke to us. On the third day, my parents drove me to Brunswick, leaving me to take the examination in plane geometry and departing for home. That night in accordance with Clark Sears's earlier invitation, I dined at the Psi Upsilon house and slept in his room. Before the evening was over I had pledged Psi U and was wearing its lapel button.

Six other freshmen had pledged Psi U. Thus, there were seven of us in what we called our delegation. Right away we were summoned by several upperclass Psi U's—a committee of sorts—who proceeded to put us in our place. No more glad-handing: we were underlings, faced as I knew with all manner of harassment ("hazing") in the four weeks to come. We were told to sit together in the dining room; given cleaning jobs around the house. I was called Olie, never Sewall, whether I liked it or not. Later on I would respond to yet another name, The Deacon, supposedly for my sober expression and sometimes stern, low voice in making comments, serious or facetious.

We were quizzed on the athletic sport we had elected and what extracurricular activity we would undertake. I said my elected sport was golf and that I would try out for a staff position on *The Bowdoin Orient*, the college's weekly newspaper. This meant starting at once as a cub reporter in hopes of becoming an associate editor by the end of the year; in this choice I could foresee opportunities to improve my writing.

No time did I lose in playing golf on the Brunswick course. Compared to the Salem Country Club's with its neatly mown fairways and manicured greens, it was more like a pasture. On my second day out, most unexpectedly I played with the president of Bowdoin College, Kenneth C. M. Sills, and two professors. We played fourteen holes; I came out one point ahead.

The Psi U house, on Main Street opposite the campus, was of all wooden construction, attractively green-shingled with white trim. The large living room and adjoining dining room with connecting kitchen occupied the main floor. Above the dining room was the chapter hall, a large room with vaulted ceiling. This was the Kappa chapter's sanctum sanctorum, accessible only to members. Except for the chapter hall, the upper two floors comprised student rooms, some large enough to accommodate two men—in one case three, in a third-floor room called "the Nursery." A couple of rooms were too small for beds; thus the occupants slept on the third floor in one long room dubbed "the Rampasture."

On the morning of September 23, I learned that I had passed geometry but not Roman history. Nevertheless, I was permitted to register on condition that I make up the half-point by taking another examination in June or September. I never felt more relieved—the make-up examination seemed years ahead. I registered for a B.A. degree, signing up for the prescribed courses in English, Latin, French, and Government. Again, I stayed for the night in Clark Sears's room.

Classes were already under way on September 24, Friday, but I found the time to buy my freshman cap, obtain my dormitory room, purchase furniture for it, and meet my roommate—a congenial fellow pledged to another fraternity—and slept in my room for the first time. On Saturday I entrained for home to pack my trunk, pick up my portable typewriter, and returned by the same means, arriving late Sunday night.

Almost immediately the *Orient* staff summoned all freshmen wanting to be cub reporters. We were given a wide variety of instructions. Besides reporting on weekly events, we should obtain interviews with professors about their special projects on campus and off, meet and talk with guest speakers for newsworthy comments, and later give the gist of what they said from the platform. My initial effort, a report on President Sills's speech in the chapel, appeared in the issue of October 13. Thereafter, scarcely an issue published was without one or more items from me. I was fast gaining valuable writing experience.

All too soon "Hell Week" at the Psi U house was upon us, organized by tradition to make us as miserable as possible whenever on the property. Among the fifteen written instructions addressed to us, in my case titled "Boob Pettingill": enter by the side door; show up only at meals and occupy the same seat in the dining room; never smile; when leaving right after dinner, bid good-night to every member, using his *full* name.

At the dinners, all members showed up with hand-hewed wooden paddles, ready for action. For the first dinner my delegation had to drink a toast—of diluted ink, we learned later. Then at the dinner and the ones to follow, we in turn were commanded to perform in front of the room's fireplace: to recite at top speed the twenty-five chapters in the Psi Upsilon Fraternity in the order of their enrollment; sing something; tell a story. Inevitably the performer flubbed or was shouted down, resulting in his having to make the rounds of the dining room, bend over and get a wallop from each member, if so inclined. (I had memorized the chapter roll as in 1926 so thoroughly that I can reel it off to this day!) Told to sing at one of the first dinners, I chose, while keeping a deadpan expression, "I'm Only a Bird in a Gilded Cage" and broke up everybody. Instead of my getting paddled, my delegation did, unable to keep their faces straight. Now aware of my repertoire of old-timers, I was told each subsequent night to sing another such as "I Want a Girl Just Like the Girl that Married Dear Old Dad." My delegation hated me!

The worst of Hell Week was yet to come. After our next to last dinner, we were blindfolded and driven several miles south of town, loaded into rowboats, and left on an island in the Androscoggin River. At dawn, we discovered that the island was near one shore, separated from us by water shallow enough for us to wade to it. We plodded in soggy pants and footwear back to Brunswick, arriving about 8:00 A.M.

On the last night, after the dinner performances, we were put through a relay sack race on our hands and knees, up and down stairs, and paddled as never before. When it was over—none of us won—we were marshalled in two lines opposite each other, leading out from the living room fireplace. Between the lines our soon-to-be-brothers walked solemnly in single file to the fire and threw on their paddles. Then the president, his back to the now-roaring fire, delivered a little speech about what sports we had been, how proud he was of us—all very sweet. Hell Week was over. Not quite! We were needed to go on certain errands for the initiation the next night.

Pete (Harold M.) Ridlon and I were sent out on a long country road, armed with a crude map that would direct us to a farm where we were to pick and bring back a goat. Although knowing full well this was a hoax (why a goat and for what purpose?), off we went, flashlights in hand. I thought I had an appropriate vocabulary of cuss words for all this foolishness, but Pete's was far superior to mine. Reaching the farm, we awakened the farmer, who had unkind words for our disturbing his sleep. Back at the Psi U House by 4:00 A.M., after walking some eleven miles, we were put in solitary confinement for our failure to return with a goat and would have nothing to eat until after initiation the next evening. I passed what may have been one of the longest days of my life.

At day's end, we delegates were blindfolded and led into the chapter hall where our blindfolds were removed. We were then escorted between the brothers, all in robes of garnet and gold (the fraternity's colors), and lined up standing in a row before the dais on which the president, wearing a crown designating his exalted office, proceeded with the ritual. First he declaimed the fraternity's high standards and great objectives, then he stepped down and to each of us in turn asked for our pledge of everlasting loyalty, and congratulated us with the fraternity's grip. The ceremony was thereupon concluded when all the brothers filed by us, stopping before each of us to extend the grip with congratulations.

A full banquet downstairs followed, not too soon for me as I had just about passed the point of starvation. Not until the after-banquet speeches were under way was I conscious of the clothes I had been wearing steadily for two days and two nights. Happily, back at the dormitory I was hastily out of them, showered, and in bed for a sound sleep. I slept too long!

By the time I awoke, my parents had arrived for it was Alumni Day, November 6. After the big noon luncheon in the gym, we attended the Bowdoin College– University of Maine football game, always the climactic event of the football season.

All through the semester so far—studying for classes, golfing, *Orient* reporting, fraternity hazing, attending every local movie (I was an ardent movie fan), and giving undue attention to other activities—I nevertheless found the time to keep up a steady correspondence with Eleanor at Wheaton College in Norton, Massachusetts. As mid-November approached, she was excited about my coming to her Sophomore Hop on November 13. I must have a tuxedo. So I took the train from Brunswick the day before and was met by my ever-obliging parents. Borrowing their Cadillac early the next morning, I hastened to Boston where I bought my tux and got fitted into it, and drove at high speed to Norton. I missed the dinner but not the colorful dance afterwards. There was time the following morning to attend chapel and see more of the campus than I had the year before. Eleanor and I invited two other couples to join us for a luncheon at the Mansfield Inn. Bringing them back to the campus and kissing Eleanor farewell, with my gratitude for such a wonderful time, I headed for Middleton where Father rushed me to the train for Brunswick.

As excited as Eleanor was about my coming to her Sophomore Hop, she was more excited about my having her come to our Christmas house party. She knew all about the reputation of Bowdoin's gala parties from some of her Wheaton friends who had attended them.

Two weeks before the party, scheduled for December 21, we freshmen were put to work polishing floors and doing numerous clean-up jobs, upstairs and down. We had set up a Christmas tree in the living room and decorated it, in preparation for our own Christmas celebration, the week before. All of us, house members as well as my delegation, contributed presents appropriate for the recipients—mostly jokes with comments, sometimes insulting but nonetheless hilarious.

Late in the afternoon of December 21, the Brunswick railroad station was swarming with Bowdoinites impatiently waiting for the five-thirty train to pull in from Boston with their dates from Wellesley, Smith, and other women's colleges including, of course, Wheaton. The train's arrival caused a frenzy of milling about, screaming and yelling names as none of us knew from which of the several cars the girls might emerge. Although it seemed an age, couples were soon together. Once Eleanor and I had joyfully embraced, I grabbed her suitcase and we joined the long procession of couples to the fraternity houses.

After some confusion at the Psi U house in getting our dates to their rooms and having them meet the chaperon—a mother of one of the brothers—dinner followed. Everyone was on edge as well as hungry. Meanwhile our four-piece band arrived, reminding all of us that we must hurry to dress formally, our dates going upstairs and we to our rooms elsewhere.

Never had Eleanor and I had a merrier evening dancing together and with others. Although the band ceased playing at 2:00 A.M., no one was in a hurry to leave; we lolled about on lounges in the living room. Our consciences eventually broke us up; I was back in my dormitory about three-thirty.

I appeared at the house the next morning at ten and killed another hour waiting for Eleanor to come down for the quickest breakfast ever. There was barely time to show her much of the campus before we returned to lunch. That afternoon we went to the Cumberland Theater downtown for three plays staged by the Masque and Gown, Bowdoin's dramatic society. Unforgettable was the second play, *The Swan Song*, with a moving performance by Albert E. Ecke, a senior, who would soon become a professional actor, known as Albert Van Dekker on the American stage and screen, later on British television.

The second night, beginning with a formal dance at the house, featured the college dance in the gym to the music of a twelve-piece jazz band. How long Eleanor and I danced there, I fail to remember. What I do remember was breaking away after midnight and dancing once, usually by phonograph, in each of the ten fraternity houses, ending at the Psi U house, and parting at 6:00 A.M.

The next morning Eleanor was packed and ready for breakfast at ten. We were aboard the train near noon on our way home to Middleton for the Christmas holidays, Mother and Auntie Brown meeting us. Remarkably, Eleanor and I had energy enough left that evening to visit briefly with Miss Wadleigh in Danvers.

In Brunswick, to wind up my first semester, came an eventful evening on January 12, 1927, when at long last I met Dr. Alfred O. Gross. I had an excuse as an *Orient* reporter to interview him about the New England Ruffed Grouse Investigation of which he was in charge. Knocking on his home door, I was invited in by a man shorter than I, bespectacled, with a ready greeting and firm handshake. I announced who I was, why I had come. We were soon comfortably seated in his living room, he on the divan, pipe in mouth. Here, I said to myself, is the true college professor, in modest, unpressed attire, easy in manner, and fluent in conversation sparked now and then with a flash of humor.

Having obtained the information I needed on the Ruffed Grouse Investigation, I found the time to state my personal interest in birds and how I wanted to study them. Dr. Gross's face lighted up as if to say, "Here is a young man after my own heart." He lost no time in expounding on the rewards of ornithology as a profession, how it had already led him, and would lead him again, to far places for contributions to knowledge. Indeed, he was leaving in the coming summer to study birds in Central and South America the following semester. The evening was getting late when Mrs. Gross appeared from upstairs, feeling no doubt that our meeting should be broken up. Edna Gross was, like her husband, an outgoing person, jolly, and as hospitable as one would expect of a professor's wife. Both she and her husband wanted me always to feel welcome at their home. On my way back to the dormitory, I fairly tingled at the thought of making ornithology my career.

Alfred Otto Gross was to become an important influence in my life. He had grown up as a farm boy in Illinois, graduated from the University of Illinois, and earned his Ph.D. at Harvard. His research, centering on marine invertebrates, had taken him to Bermuda where his interest switched to studying white-tailed tropicbirds. While in Bermuda, he met

Edna, whom he married two years later. In 1912, he became an instructor in the Maine Medical School, Brunswick, teaching comparative anatomy and embryology. After the closing of the school in 1920, he joined the Bowdoin faculty, teaching the same subjects and becoming full professor in 1922. A few years later he introduced a semester's course in ornithology. Following his first bird study in Bermuda, he produced many more significant life-history studies of birds, a few well after his retirement in 1953. During his most productive years at Bowdoin, more than one large western university tried to induce him to join its faculty, but Dr. Gross was adamant; he would stay at Bowdoin. His association with the college would last sixty years.

Despite Dr. Gross's reputation beyond the campus, on the campus he was not a prominent figure. If I mentioned his name at the Psi U house, I was met with incomprehension. "Dr. Gross, who's he?" was typical of the response from anyone not taking biology courses. This was understandable. On his class days, Dr. Gross hastened directly to the science building, climbing the three flights of stairs to his office and adjacent laboratories where, before and after classes, he was available to students for consultation; then he hurried home to his book-lined study with typewriter and desk, the latter cluttered with manuscripts in one stage or another of production. He rarely left his study to attend campus activities.

My midyear examinations pending, with a free weekend to spare beforehand, I decided to spend it preparing for them in Belgrade while at the same time enjoying my grandparents. On Friday, Grandfather met me at the Depot in his horse-drawn sleigh for a slushy ride to the farm. Grandmother was at the living room window watching for our arrival. By the next morning, a fierce northeast blizzard with winds at gale force whipped snow around the farm and over the hilltop. We could hear the wind roaring over the top of the living room chimney and sometimes saw the flames in the fireplace flicker from the downdraft. But we were snug in the sturdy old house, my grandparents reading and I studying.

Grandfather Groves was now milking only one cow, had one horse and a few chickens. For him and Grandmother, time for living on the farm was shortening. I was determined to relish every moment of this weekend, although by late Sunday I became apprehensive about returning to Brunswick on the morrow. Fortunately by then the storm began abating. In the morning, Grandfather hitched his reliable Nellie to a big sled and we reached the Depot in time for the train.

Returning to Bowdoin in February for the second semester, I registered for a continuation in the same courses. In addition, I registered for Advanced Public Speaking which included "exercises in extemporaneous speaking and delivery of various types of public address." This proved most fortunate for me in the weeks to come.

I skipped the Midwinter Hop and undertook more intensive work than ever in reporting for the *Orient*. In the immediate offing was the coming of William L. Finley to deliver the Mayhew Lecture, a lectureship founded in 1923 specifically "to provide lectures on bird life," though not to exclude other aspects of natural history. Dr. Gross gave me publicity material about Finley in advance of his coming on March 5.

Finley, from Oregon, titled his program "Camera Hunting in the Northland." He filled the local theater to capacity, his reputation as one of the leading wildlife lecturers of the day having preceded him. Prepared as I was for excellent motion pictures, I never expected to become enthralled by Finley's presentation, his precise timing of words to action on the screen, his lively sense of humor, and his flair for the dramatic as he built up his audience to climactic scenes. I was impressed, deeply so, for I admired good showmanship.

Much as I liked to participate in plays and platform presentations, furthest from my thoughts then was lecturing as Finley did, as it involved cinematography, about which I knew next to nothing. Besides, how could I afford the equipment and film to begin with? (Finley showed five thousand feet, selected from his twenty thousand feet of 35-mm film.) Nevertheless, I decided then and there: I must some day produce my own films and strive to lecture with them as Finley did.

The best I could do presently was to acquire a 16-mm home movie camera and a projector. Although the camera lacked telephoto lenses suitable for wildlife photography, at least it would give me experience in filming human activities as well as learning how to follow through on actions. I saw the equipment I wanted in Boston while on my upcoming spring vacation. Father was shocked at the cost, but I soon persuaded him of its worth to me and the pleasure it would give us all. Thus I had my equipment by summer. The results from it provided much amusement to family and friends who had never seen themselves in motion pictures.

Worries about passing my four courses were nagging me. Not one of the courses had I found in the least bit stimulating. The teaching was boresome; preparing for hour examinations was pure drudgery and the results poor. Considering all the distractions over the last four and a half months—freshmen duties and Hell Week at my fraternity, my regular reporting for the *Orient*, taking vacations and weekends away, the irresistible drawing power of local movies, and the Christmas house party—the wonder is that I succeeded in passing the midyear examinations.

In his New England Ruffed Grouse Investigation, Dr. Gross needed specimens of the species in order to determine their parasites and possible diseases. He wrote to Thornton Burgess of the "Radio Nature League" in Springfield, Massachusetts. Would Burgess let it be known on the air that he would welcome grouse shot by hunters or found dead? Burgess broadcast the request, explaining the reasons. The result: Dr. Gross received some two thousand specimens. Meanwhile, through correspondence with Burgess and their ensuing meetings, Burgess and Dr. Gross developed a close friendship.

One of the early outcomes of their relationship was an invitation to Burgess from Dr. Gross to give the second Mayhew Lecture of the academic year, scheduled on the campus after the spring recess, April 8. Burgess's lecture, simply titled "Bird Life" and illustrated by many glass lantern slides, was highly informative, though lacking Finley's verve as well as proving unsuited to the intellectual level of a college audience. I reported on the lecture but omitted any such evaluation.

Just before going home for the spring recess, I received the gratifying notice of my election as one of the associate editors of the *Orient*. Up to this point as a cub reporter I had received encouragement from Edward F. Dana, a sophomore in my fraternity, who was then associate editor. I learned, mean-while, that he was fond of birds, knew the common species; we had a mutual interest. With my election as an associate editor, Ed was elected one of the two managing editors. We would soon become close friends.

During the spring recess, Dr. Gross had been on Martha's Vineyard, a large island off the coast of Massachusetts, cen-susing the heath hen, the eastern race of the greater prairie chicken. Where this bird had once inhabited the scrub oak plains of the northeast mainland, now it was confined to the scrub oaks of Martha's Vineyard. Dr. Gross's first census in 1923 had yielded only twenty-eight heath hens. Since then, his counts revealed the number steadily dwindling to near ex-tinction. While interviewing him on the subject for the *Ori-ent*, I asked: "If I were to go to Martha's Vineyard during my spring recess next year, would I have a chance of seeing heath hens?" His reply was encouraging. Thornton Burgess also wanted to see the birds, and if possible film them. Dr. Gross would make arrangements for both of us.

After the spring recess, Dr. Gross had been following progress in a ruffed grouse nest in a woods outside Bruns-wick and one day invited me to accompany him. He would show me how he measured and weighed the eggs. A demon-stration for me in ornithological procedures! In our drive back to Brunswick he told me he was taking sabbatical leave next semester, to depart in June first to Panama, where Thornton Burgess would be with him on Barro Colorado Island in the Canal Zone, and then to Ecuador. He advised me to major in biology and take the one-year introductory course in zoology under Dr. Manton Copeland, and after he returned I could enroll in his ornithology course for the second semester. The prospect excited me.

With my responsibilities as associate editor of the *Orient*, it seemed that I spent more time than before the spring recess in reporting, especially on cultural programs. In late May, New England's famed poet, Robert Frost, was a Bowdoin guest. Besides holding a prearranged conference with stu-dents, he made one public appearance on the campus to read some of his many poems. During his stay I greatly valued my opportunity to interview this quiet-spoken, self-effacing man.

The three-day Ivy Activities, traditionally in charge of the junior class, began on May 25. Having borrowed the family Cadillac, I picked up Eleanor at the railroad station in time for supper and a change of clothes for the dance at our house and a few others. The following day we enjoyed an outing on Small Point, centered at a cottage belonging to the parents of one of my fraternity brothers. In the evening, we attended a production by the Masque and Gown, followed by an informal dance at the house. The last day featured the Ivy Day exercises in the afternoon—a prayer by the class chaplain, a poem by the class poet, oration by the class orator, presentation of gifts by the class president—and concluded with the planting of the ivy accompanied by the singing of the class ode. Directly after, the seniors attended their last chapel and, following the service, marched out slowly, led by the class marshall. Terminating the day was the big dance in the gym. My only regret was that I had exchanged Eleanor for so many dances that we had too few of them together. Ivy Activities over, I drove Eleanor to Portland the next day, May 28, for her train.

The four courses I had continued in the second semester were no more stimulating than in the first. The course in public speaking, however, I found inspirational and at the conclusion I won the Hiland Lockwood Fairbanks Prize "for excellence" in the course.

But my upcoming summer's vacation had a cloud hanging over it. I had to study Roman history to pass the postponed examination on the subject when I returned to Bowdoin in September. Before leaving the campus, I asked one of the history professors to recommend a text to give me the essential coverage needed for the required half-point. His recommendation—a veritable tome—I purchased in Brunswick, read and reread during the summer. There would be no slipping up.

I spent most of the summer in Maine at our Wayne camp on a pleasant mix of activities, with a few days now and then at Belgrade helping my grandparents. Early in the summer I searched for nesting birds around our camp. I found one, a spotted sandpiper, tame enough for me to get close for shots of the bird on its nest. The results, with my Kodak, were not worth saving, but at least I had photographed my first bird. Date: June 16, 1927. A ritual was baked-bean suppers at the Androscroggin Yacht Club every Saturday night. When Eleanor was with me, we went dancing at one of the local night spots. The most local, in Wayne, bore the romantic name Moon Glow.

As summer drew to an end, I considered myself an authority on Roman history. On September 19, I took the Cadillac to Brunswick for the required examination. I was confident about passing it, though without official indication of having succeeded until two days later when, in my bug, I arrived at Bowdoin and was told that I could enroll as a sophomore. I was now a fully fledged Bowdoin student! Again I roomed in the same dormitory, across the hall from my room of the year before and with a new roommate.

IN MY SOPHOMORE YEAR at Bowdoin, starting in 1927, I fulfilled all course requirements with none of the nagging worries of my freshman year. I remained the ardent movie fan, missing few good local shows. My parents often came to our home football games and customarily invited me afterwards to dine with them at Brunswick's Eagle Hotel where they stayed overnight. Eleanor and I exchanged letters weekly, each keeping in touch with the other on our problems, frequently scholastic, or on our social doings. My vacations were invariably in Middleton, as were many weekends except for a few at Belgrade. I continued taking home movies of people, relatives as well as friends at Bowdoin and elsewhere. No arm-twisting did I need to show my films. Indeed, I would gladly set up my projector and screen at a mere hint from anyone wanting to see such-and-such a film.

Following Dr. Gross's earlier advice, I registered in Introductory Zoology, taught by Dr. Manton Copeland. At last I had entered a field of study profoundly exciting me. Dr. Copeland himself, of moderate height, round-shouldered, wearing rimless glasses, kindly in demeanor, precise in his lectures and instructions, took a personal interest in me as he did in all his students. From the beginning I felt at home in his biology laboratory, willingly spending more time than required on experiments and reports.

If I thought there were too many distractions during my freshman year, they were minimal compared to those in the first semester of my sophomore year. Besides taking three other courses in addition to zoology, I was immediately in the midst of rushing at the Psi U house: hosting freshmen and urging them to pledge Psi U by impressing upon them the genuine fellowship among Psi U's everywhere. Altogether thirteen freshmen pledged—poor souls toward whom in the next week or so our attitudes would turn hostile and become increasingly so as Hell Week approached.

My feelings during Hell Week surprised me. Now a sophomore, I had expected my attitude would be hostile. Instead, I found myself compassionate. Although I had a paddle, I wielded it lightly and only then on pledges who had been commanded to make the round in the dining room for wallops from *all* the brothers. Preceding the initiation ceremonies, I was asked to blindfold and escort one of the pledges from his solitary confinement to the chapter hall. I wondered what was running through his mind as I led him along. Perhaps he was thinking about food more than anything else, as I had the year before.

Now that I was an associate editor of the *Orient,* my work was cut out for me as never before. Although I continued writing up various interviews and reviewing lectures by college guests, I delegated freshmen cub reporters to cover numerous events while I took the responsibility of editing, sometimes even rewriting, their efforts. And I constantly fretted about getting sufficient copy from them to help fill an issue, but I usually managed somehow.

It seemed that scarcely a day passed when I was not pounding my typewriter at some point between classes, after midnight, or on weekends away, and always using only two fingers as I did for the rest of my life. What prompted me, I sometimes wondered, to give so much time to the *Orient?* I had no thoughts of becoming a journalist or a professional writer of any sort. I simply liked to write and to see the results in print. The fact that I was competing for a higher post on the *Orient* staff was incidental.

My 1927 Thanksgiving recess in Middleton was particularly memorable thanks to the visit of my grandparents, away from Belgrade and for the first time in a home with electricity. Grandmother, despite her partial deafness, could hear well over the radio and listened to it at every opportunity. Of course, I showed them my movies—the first movies they had ever seen—including shots of themselves. Both gasped, then laughed, at the way they appeared on the screen.

Back in Brunswick, I learned that there would be three plays written by students for presentation at Christmas house party time. I couldn't resist trying out for a part and to my astonishment won a leading role in one—*Late-229*, based on a story by John Galsworthy. The lead, a physician, released from prison, arrives home unexpectedly, to the dismay of his family. The principal scene—the doctor's arrival, the family's mixed reaction to him, and the doctor's dignified departure clearly intimating his obvious disappointment—was poignant, drawing on my talent as no other play ever had.

Rehearsals for the play soon began, further complicating my life, as if I didn't have enough classes and work for the *Orient*. However, I would not let my concern about performing in the play mar my pleasure during the forthcoming house party. Eleanor arrived in time for the dinner and dance at the Psi U house. Although she and I parted long after midnight, I picked her up in the early morning to attend a class with me and later have lunch. After lunch, I soon left her with friends while I hurried to the Cumberland Theater to dress for my role. Eleanor and friends arrived by curtain time. The formal dance in the gym that night, with praises from Eleanor and others ringing in my ears for my afternoon performance at the Cumberland, coupled with my relief at having the show over with, was one I always remember with pure pleasure.

During my Christmas vacation at home, Uncle Bill played Santa Claus at the sanatorium, visiting the patients. With just the right physical shape, all he had to do was dress in the traditional regalia and let his natural jocularity come forth. He was perfect.

Toward the end of my freshman year, I had become acquainted with Charles C. Dunbar, a sophomore in another fraternity. Although not caring about birds, Charlie liked camping and mountain-climbing as I did, and he induced me to join the Bowdoin Outing Club. Now, at its scheduled meeting in January, 1928, came the decision to climb Mount Washington after the midyear examinations. We realized the risks as the great mountain, at 6,288 feet, was noted for its sudden, tempestuous storms resultig in loss of human life. Hence, we gave careful attention to acquiring suitable apparel and emergency equipment. The excursion, ten of us in the party including Ed Dana, Clark Sears, and Charlie Dunbar, entrained on February 2 for Gorham, New Hampshire, from there hiking the thirteen miles (I carrying my movie camera) to our headquarters, the Appalachian Mountain Club huts in Pinkham Notch.

Early the next morning, in absolutely clear weather, we began the six-hour assent on the Carriage Road to the summit, arriving at midafternoon. I wore snowshoes as far as the Halfway House and then clamp-on "creepers." Not unexpectedly, the temperature at the summit was subzero. The sky was nearly cloudless; there was scarcely any wind. How lucky could we have been! (As I viewed the snow-clad scene, my memory jumped back to that summer day in 1924 when, with Eleanor, Miss Wadleigh, Lawrence Kinney, and Harry Berry, I looked down from this very spot on a raging thunderstorm.) We made the descent in three hours, except for the few members on skis who made it in two.

The day following, our last, we hiked to Glen Ellis Falls and the Crystal Cascades to see how these summer attractions looked in the dead of winter. In the afternoon, Charlie and I walked up to Hermit Lake, hoping to view the head wall of Tuckerman's Ravine, but in a matter of minutes we were enveloped in a blinding snowstorm, and consequently lost no time in following our disappearing tracks back to the huts.

Dr. Gross had already returned from South America, by way of Costa Rica, on January 20. Twice he had written to me, the first time with a report for publication in the *Orient*. Soon after his arrival, I hurried to greet him. Although he was voluble in telling me of his successes, he declined to let me write about them for the *Orient*: "That would be advertising," he said.

At the start of the second semester, there were five students besides myself registered in Ornithology, the course consisting of lectures, laboratory work, and, in spring, field trips. Dr. Gross usually based lectures on his own studies such on the herring gull and the tropicbirds in Bermuda. Illustrating them with lantern slides, his objective was twofold: to show what he had learned from his own research, and always to point out the need for still more studies. For laboratory work, the primary purpose was identification of local bird species from preserved specimens—"bird skins"—in Bowdoin's collection. He showed us how "to key them out" to species with the use of Frank M. Chapman's *Handbook of Birds of Eastern North America.*

To give us an appreciation of a bird skin, how it is "put up" (preserved for study) and why careful handling of it is necessary, he gave us a demonstration and then required each of us to prepare a skin. For the demonstration and for individual practice, he had a good supply of ruffed grouse— fortunately large birds, easy to handle. I went further by mounting my specimen, inserting glass eyes and perching the bird as naturally as possible on a branch. For years I kept it as a souvenir, the only bird I ever mounted among the many hundreds I would put up as skins.

An exceptional event for the Psi Upsilon Fraternity, as a national organization, was scheduled in Montreal on March 17 when it would install a new chapter, Epsilon Phi, at McGill University. All Psi U's were invited to the ceremony. Since Montreal could be reached directly by train from Portland, why should not we from the Kappa chapter attend? A notable temptation: there was no such thing as Prohibition in Canada!

I must admit that I had never drunk an alcoholic beverage of any sort. This may have been due to Father's stern warnings about the "evils" of hard liquor after his experiences in superintending employees. Perhaps not; I have no answer. At the Psi U house there was occasional drinking when one or two of the brothers managed to get a bottle of bootleg gin or whiskey. But there was no drinking, conspicuously at least, before house-party dinners or during the dances thereafter.

About a dozen of us from our Kappa chapter attended the installation, including Ed Dana and Clark Sears. Having registered at the Hotel Mount Royal, the first thing we did after getting our rooms was to make a beeline to the nearest dispensary for bottles of liquor. I chose a fancy one, of apricot brandy—not that I knew brandy from any other drink. I simply liked the look of the bottle. The installation ceremonies, most impressive, were in the afternoon, followed by a fine banquet. Afterwards, Ed, Clark, and I took in a hockey game between Montreal and Ottawa. When I returned, I found my roommate and our other Kappa brothers, without regard for moderation in drinking, rip-roaring drunk; they would soon become dreadfully sick.

Nevertheless, every one of us made the train to Portland early in the morning. For those with a bottle of liquor came the question: how to smuggle it into the United States past the Customs inspectors when we reach the border? Each had his own idea. Mine was to go to the men's room and there, in the wastebasket, wrap up my precious cargo in the soiled towels. After we crossed the border, it was still there! I cherished my fancy bottle for years to come.

Soon after returning from Montreal, I learned that Ed Dana had been elected editor-in-chief of the *Orient* and I one of the two managing editors, who would take turns making up an issue. My first would be for April 25. This was a wholly new and more responsible task: selecting feature stories, writing headlines, arranging articles on the several pages, obtaining cuts, locating fillers for gaps, and, withal, editing material when necessary. Getting out an issue meant, practically, my living in the Brunswick Record Office, where the *Orient* was printed. All along I was thankful for Ed Dana, who had solutions for the problems forever cropping up.

As the spring vacation approached, I reminded Dr. Gross of his offer to take me at that time with Thornton Burgess to see and photograph the heath hen on Martha's Vineyard. True to his word, he would make arrangements. When I announced my intention at the Psi U house of spending some of my vacation with the heath hen, there came astonished queries and comments such as, "Who in hell is the heath hen? She must be *some* gal!" I was prepared with explanations, though I'm sure that some never believed I would spend vacation time with a bird.

On the morning of April 5, my parents delivered me at the South Station. Already aboard the train were Dr. Gross and Thornton Burgess, whom I now met for the first time, although I had heard him lecture at Bowdoin the year before. We arrived in New Bedford in midafternoon and there boarded the steamer bound for the Vineyard. At the dock we were greeted by the warden of the Heath Hen Reservation and driven by him, first to his home, where we would stay while on the Vineyard, then to the reservation for a tour of it. Primarily of scrub oaks, the reservation included a large open field, the traditional display ground of the remaining three heath hens, all males. In the middle of the field had been permanently erected a large wooden blind, head-high, suitable for accommodating two people, and with peepholes on all sides. Food, mainly corn, had been liberally scattered around the blind to attract the heath hens close.

Well before dawn the next day, Thornton Burgess and I, both of us carrying still and motion-picture cameras, crept into the blind. Seated on campstools, our eyes at peepholes, we waited expectantly. We began hearing vesper sparrows singing in the distance. And then a partridge-like bird suddenly flew in a hundred feet away, crouched, and for about twenty minutes stayed motionless except for head movements. Any doubts about its identity were dispelled when the bird at last stood up and performed as a male prairie chicken should: stamping the ground with his feet, lifting his long, pointed neck feathers upward and forward while inflating beneath them orange-red air sacs that produced a hollow-sounding *whooooooo-doooooooh* as they deflated.

After repeating the display twice, the heath hen jumped up, fluttered and whirled, came down in the opposite direction, and cackled several times. There being no bird to perform before or to respond, that was the end of the show. He calmly walked toward us and circled the blind several times without showing the slightest alarm, foraging on corn as our cameras clicked and whirred. After what seemed a short time, he took off for the scrub oaks. Late in the afternoon we entered the blind again. Before sunset all three males showed up. They behaved in much the same way as the lone bird had in the morning—flying in, crouching, displaying briefly, foraging, then flying off as the dusk gathered.

Besides my opportunity to see and photograph the last three heath hens, I had been fortunate to have three days just to be with Dr. Gross and Thornton Burgess on the Vineyard. They had become close friends, and were forever teasing each other. I could hardly believe my eyes when, one day, I watched them rolling around and wrestling on a road bank, both laughing, behaving like teenagers.

With spring at hand in Brunswick, laboratory work in Ornithology turned to field trips, at first in cars to nearby coastal bays to observe chiefly waterfowl. In early May, starting about the tenth, we began early morning bird walks in the neighborhood, first arriving at daybreak in the Gross kitchen for coffee and doughnuts. The doughnuts were sugar-coated, including one made of rubber. Woe unto the sleepy fellow, arriving late, who chose it! His momentary embarrassment broke any existing formality and started off the morning in merriment. In the short walk following, we usually saw well over fifty species, some of which we had seen earlier only as bird skins in the laboratory.

For the Ivy Review, *The Show-Off*, scheduled by the Masque and Gown for May 24, I tried out for a short part and won it. I came to regret having done so as rehearsals took so much time, just sitting around and waiting for my brief appearance. In mid-May I tried out for the DeAlva S. Alexander Prize Speaking Contest and was informed that I had been selected as one of the nine participants. The date of the contest would be June 18 and I could give the declamation of my choice. Naturally it would be my old reliable, Poe's "The Raven." Rehearsals would begin after the final examinations.

Remarkably, busy as I was in May, I found the time to participate in two socials events. One was Eleanor's Junior Prom at Wheaton on June 4, and the other consisted of the Ivy activities at Bowdoin, starting June 23. Eleanor was unable to make Brunswick for the party the first night. Consequently, I spent it alone at work in the biology laboratory, preparing for an illustrated talk on the heath hen to the bird class the following morning. By late afternoon, Eleanor and my parents arrived in time for dinner at the Eagle Hotel. Before long I had to break away from the table and head for the Cumberland Theater for my little stint in *The Show-Off*. Eleanor and my parents were there by curtain time, and afterwards, my parents departed for Wayne, leaving us without a car. But no problem; a fraternity brother kindly loaned us his for a day's outing at Poland Spring, returning in time for the formal dinner at the house, followed by the Gym Dance, "the best yet," Eleanor and I declared. In the morning we visited with the Grosses.

My second semester had not been long under way when Dr. Gross announced in his class that he would be teaching ornithology in the coming summer at the University of Michigan Biological Station. (The man who usually taught the course would be on leave of absence.) The station was in northern Lower Michigan, not at the University in Ann Arbor. I remember Dr. Gross looking pointedly at me while making the announcement and, after class, my inquiring about the possibility of attending. But there the matter rested until long after the trip to Martha's Vineyard and we were well along in his ornithology course.

By that time Dr. Gross had come to realize my intense enthusiasm for birds and made it clear to me that a summer at the Michigan station would be ideal for me. I could take the advanced course in ornithology, allowing me ample time for studying birds at their nests. The American woodcock would be an especially fine species to study as so little was known about that important game bird. On May 19, I agreed to go, provided my father approved, as he did, generously supplying the funds.

But I had little time at this point to think about going to Michigan. Once the Ivy Activities were over, I had the responsibility of getting out the last issue of the *Orient* for the academic year. And there were my final examinations to prepare for and take. Meanwhile, I learned that I had been elected a member of the Masque and Gown. On June 10, Dr. and Mrs. Gross and their three children were already packing to leave for Michigan; I bade them good-bye, saying it would not be long before I would be seeing them all in a new environment.

My parents, Aunt Millie and Uncle Bill, and Oscar Adler arrived in Brunswick on June 12, the day I took my last examination, and drove me to Wayne. I went twice to Brunswick to rehearse for the Alexander contest. Finally on the day of the contest, off we all went to Brunswick, I formally dressed. I justified my confidence in "The Raven" by winning second prize among the nine contestants. What pleased me most was winning before Mr. Adler, the first person in my life to cultivate my desire to perform before an audience.

The next day we all headed for Middleton. For me the

rush was on in the next couple of days to get ready for Michigan by obtaining and packing the clothing necessary for field work. However, I squeezed in time for visits with Eleanor, to show her and Mr. Adler my movies of the heath hen. On June 22, I was delivered by a sanatorium employee to the South Station in Boston, bound for my first venture west of the Hudson—"way out west," so it seemed to me.

In the early morning I got off the train in Cheboygan, Michigan, after an interminably bumpy overnight ride from Detroit. In a biological station truck with driver awaiting me, we set out through downtown Cheboygan, a declining lumbering center that still boasted the biggest and tallest sawdust pile in the country; rattled over some thirteen miles of dusty farm roads; turned into scrubby woods on a long winding road—more like a trail—in which the truck labored up to its hubs in sand; and finally reached the station, in more sand, on the shore of Douglas Lake.

The setting was utterly bleak. Back from the lake stood huge pine stumps blackened by fire and, between them, stretches of bare sand sprinkled with carbon. Here and there a few aspens, some low shrubs, and brackens straggled for life. Why such desolation?

I soon learned that this part of northern Lower Michigan, about twenty-five miles south of the present-day bridge across the Straits of Mackinac, had supported magnificent forests until decimated by lumbering operations in the 1870s. By the turn of the century, repeated fires had caused further devastation, creating a virtual wasteland. In 1908, the University of Michigan acquired a large tract of this wasteland by gift and purchase. Here a year later, the university established the biological station, which began its first session on July 5.

When I arrived, the station was beginning its nineteenth consecutive session. Housing facilities comprised an asphalt-roofed kitchen and dining hall, nine wood-framed laboratories, thirty-four wood-framed houses for faculty and students, and tents with canopies of mosquito netting for the rest of the students, including myself. A network of boardwalks kept everyone from wallowing in sand from one building to another. There was neither plumbing nor electricity. Kerosene lanterns and lamps provided the little illumination needed in summer so far north. The rule was lights out at 10:00 P.M.

This primitiveness suited me; it was so much like camping out. My tent, which I shared with another student, was for sleeping only. My desk in the laboratory I rarely used. The outdoors was my laboratory, so it was for nearly all students.

Field trips in Ornithology and other courses were on foot or by boat, seldom far from the station. Vehicles for transporting classes overland were unavailable. Thus, for the entire eight weeks, students and faculty, numbering about a hundred, were more or less confined. We depended on the immediate environment for our studies, and on ourselves for our recreation and for entertainment on Saturday nights.

Welcoming me wholeheartedly and brimming with his perpetual enthusiasm, Dr. Gross had me searching for birds before I had unpacked. No American woodcock could I find, as I had hoped, but hermit thrushes were numerous and I chose them for my study.

Research in ornithology at the station was devoted primarily to life histories of particular species. Dr. Gross, whose own research centered on life histories, soon had all his students using burlap-covered, or tent-covered, blinds for close-up observations of birds at their nests. Although blinds for such purposes were not new to the station, what was new— much to the astonishment of station personnel—were blinds on towers, which Dr. Gross had his students construct for watching birds high in trees. One little boy, walking by one of the towers with his father, was heard to ask, "Why did they put that outhouse way up there?"

My study of the hermit thrush at the biological station introduced me to research, its challenges, its satisfactions, and its limitless opportunities anywhere in the world. I now considered myself a would-be ornithologist. How and where I would educate myself further and eventually support myself were yet to be resolved.

Once my Michigan summer was well over half gone, I began giving thought, in letters to my parents and Eleanor, as to when I should conclude it. I could see no point, nor could Dr. Gross, in staying for the last two weeks of the session with the nesting season over. Therefore, I wrote Father suggesting that, in early August, he and Mother pick up Eleanor and drive to Buffalo, to meet me there on my arrival by boat from Detroit (I would reach Detroit by train from Cheboygan). Father agreed and so we met in Buffalo, August 8, the next day touring the Niagara Falls area on both the American and Canadian sides before heading for home.

CHAPTER 8 / *Bowdoin Junior*

BACK AT HOME FROM Michigan in the summer of 1928, I had no car. My bug had reached the point of no further repairs the previous winter. Father had turned it in and negotiated for a new car—a Model A Ford Roadster, complete with all the extras including rumble seat. The summer ended all too soon, or so it seemed. Eleanor had begun her senior year at Wheaton. I had driven her there proudly in my roadster on September 20. Three days later, having stuffed the car with personal belongings, I headed for Bowdoin to start my junior year of 1928–29.

This time, on arriving in Brunswick, I drove directly to the Psi U house where I would live. Ed Dana, now a senior, had invited me to room with him along with Theron Spring, also a senior, a quiet, soft-spoken chap. Our room was the Nursery, a commodious wing on the third floor with large windows on both the north and south sides. A bedroom for the three of us extended from the east side.

Already the house was bustling with hospitality as rushing was in progress. I entertained two prospects from Kents Hill and did my best, in spite of interruption by problems in getting out the *Orient,* to corral more pledges. We succeeded in obtaining fourteen, the largest delegation ever. Hell Week at the house got under way on November 1; initiation was November 9. Throughout, all the procedures from most of the stunts to the final, serious ceremony and banquet, conformed to those of the two previous years.

Among the courses for which I registered were Comparative Anatomy of the Vertebrates, taught by Dr. Gross, and Special Field Investigations, during which, under Dr. Gross's direction, I would summarize my studies of the hermit thrush in Michigan, review the literature on the species in the Bowdoin library, and then prepare an article that would incorporate all results I deemed significant. By early December, I had been through all the relevant literature available and was ready to start writing up my study of the species in the coming weeks.

Bowdoin, as mentioned, enjoyed the benefits of the Mayhew Fund, established to provide lectures on birds. Now, in 1928, came the John Warren Achorn Lectureship, another fund for lectures on birds and birdlife. Chosen as the first Achorn lecturer was Dr. Robert Cushman Murphy of the American Museum of Natural History. His presentation, "The Birds of Peru," was scheduled for January 3, 1929, at the Cumberland Theater. Illustrated with motion pictures and hand-colored lantern slides, and narrated in Dr. Murphy's inimitable style of precise diction with flashes of humor, it impressed me as much as had William L. Finley's performance. In this case, the man himself made even more impact on me than his pictures.

Reviewing the literature on the hermit thrush taught me a good lesson: detailed as I thought my notes were on what I had observed in Michigan, they were too sparse. I would nevertheless have to go ahead with what I had. Dr. Gross went over my first manuscript with a critical eye, pointing out its weaknesses, suggesting points I should incorporate. I reworked the manuscript accordingly, making a new copy. On this Dr. Gross indicated more improvements. Again I reworked it and typed a third copy. This time Dr. Gross felt that I had an article suitable for publication. Thus encouraged, I submitted it to *Nature Magazine*, but it was immediately rejected without comment. Probably it was too factual, not light enough to sustain the interest of the general reader. Dr. Gross considered the article more suited to an ornithological journal, in which case I would have to rework it to meet the style of the particular journal chosen. The mere thought of reworking it yet again was more than I could bear. Realizing this, Dr. Gross advised me to set the work aside for the time being and write instead about the demise of the heath hen. I had seen the last remaining heath hens; I had photographed them. Furthermore, I now had at hand for reference his monograph, *The Heath Hen*, just published (1928) by the Boston Society of

Natural History. Right away I set to work, during spare time in the remaining six weeks of the semester, on an article about the heath hen.

At the beginning of the second semester, in February, I added another course to my curriculum, registering in Botany, taught by Dr. Copeland. The course was required since I was majoring in biology. By no means required but nonetheless tempting was a role in this year's Commencement Play, Shakespeare's *King Lear*. I appeared at the designated time for tryouts on March 14, and read several parts. Three days later I learned that I would be the Duke of Albany and was given a list of rehearsal dates. So I had done it again; crowding even more my extracurricular activities.

Without Christmas house parties the previous December, because of a smallpox epidemic, the campus was now beginning to show excitement over the Winter Hop, Thursday and Friday, March 21–22. On Thursday evening Eleanor arrived in my car with a friend as a date for Ed Dana. They were late, yet in time for the house dance that night. The next morning in the science building, Dr. Gross was kind enough to give a few of us his lecture on tropical birds. After lunch there was time for a little bridge before going to the Cumberland Theater for the Masque and Gown production. Then followed the formal dinner at the house and the Gym Dance, as always with a big band that made dancing irresistible.

Every year, before spring vacation, it was traditional for the outgoing editors of *The Bowdoin Orient* to produce *The Bowdoin Occident*, mock edition with ample opportunity to make fun of situations, often involving faculty, which may or may not have taken place. Generally, most names were humorously misspelled though recognizable.

For reasons I fail to remember, the production of the year's *Occident* was largely turned over to me. (And this despite my learning a few days earlier that my competitor for editor-in-chief had won and that all my responsibilities for the *Orient* would cease after spring vacation.) Although already blessed with an abundance of good copy, I was nevertheless not deterred from writing the long, lead article and printing it under a six-column banner headline GROUS-MAGEE MURDER CASE STIRS COUNTRYSIDE, with the three-column

subtitle "SHAMROCK," BELOVED PUSS OF BRUNSWICK
TRACK MAN, MURDERED BY CRAZED SCIENTIST OF
BOWDOIN. The story was pure fabrication. Dr. Gross and
Jack (John J.) Magee were next door neighbors and friends. I
showed the proof to Dr. Gross, who thought it uproarious,
but I missed showing it to Jack Magee because he was out
of town.

With the issue of the *Occident* now ready for distribution,
my headline story, and some of articles I had selected and
titled, so greatly shocked a couple of *Orient* editors, who happened to see the issue before distribution, that they called an
emergency meeting of the entire *Orient* staff in the Brunswick
Record Office. Should this issue be published? It was chock-
full of insults. Some of the articles were too close to the bald
truth. Thus ran the objections. Even so, here was the issue,
printed and dated March 27, ready to go. And so it was
distributed.

With the *Occident* at large the next day, telephones in the
president's and dean's offices buzzed. My brothers in the Psi
U house could hardly believe what they were reading, especially since I had edited it. I could be fired from college, they
warned.

Fortunately, whatever fury there was ended with vacation
beginning the next day. No punishment was forthcoming.
After vacation, on April 10, President Sills called a meeting in
his office of the entire staff of the *Orient*, past and present,
expressing his grave concern about the bad taste exhibited in
the last *Occident*. He read several letters of complaint from
alumni. But not once did he raise his voice in condemnation.
His was "a heart to heart talk," I wrote in my diary.

A final note: When Jack Magee, whose fiery disposition as
track coach was legendary, eventually saw the *Occident* involving him in the so-called murder case, he was enraged.
Learning that I was the author, although he did not know me,
he was heard to say that I was a skunk with an odor I couldn't
get away from. In due course, after vacation, I introduced
myself to Jack Magee and received the outburst of anger I expected. Only mildly did I succeed in pacifying him.

After the hubbub about the *Occident*, I welcomed spring
vacation as never before. Leaving Brunswick with me in my

car at the end of March was Dr. Gross, bound for Martha's Vineyard. He would stay with us in Middleton that night and we would deliver him early in the morning at the South Station in Boston. I would shortly join him on the Vineyard and we would see and photograph, toward evening, the one lone heath hen. This accomplished, the next morning early Dr. Gross and I left the Vineyard, he for Brunswick, I for Middleton.

While I was still on vacation in Middleton, a family friend showed me an American wood cock on its ground nest in some woods near Danvers. The bird sat absolutely motionless, its plumage mimicking its immediate surroundings. After letting us approach to within about five feet, it abruptly flushed straight up, wings whistling, and was away over the treetops. In the nest were four spotted eggs, symmetrically arranged. Three days later, Eleanor with me, I returned to find the woodcock still nesting. Later I remarked to Eleanor that I had developed more interest in the woodcock than I had in any other bird species. It was a bird I wanted very much to study.

Back in Brunswick, my vacation over, an important event pending on Saturday, April 20, was the Senior Prom at Wheaton. Eleanor was looking forward to my coming and, besides, she was anxious to have me bring a date for a classmate. I had no trouble inducing Moon (David P.) Mullin, a sophomore in my house, to come along with me as the much-needed date. Moon and I set off to Middleton on the Thursday, passing the night there, and headed for Norton the next day, forgetting all about this being April 19, Patriot's Day, and some of the roads being blocked off for the Boston Marathon. How I managed I fail to remember, but we arrived in time for the dinner and were later comfortably lodged. The next day, a rainy one, Eleanor's class of 1929 spared no effort to keep us entertained until the main event—the Prom in the evening. It was just as I expected, decorations were superb and the music lively. Actually, I thought it surpassed all the parties I had attended during Eleanor's four years at Wheaton. After taking the two girls out for lunch the day following, Moon and I returned them to the college and set out for Brunswick.

Toward mid-April, Dr. Gross and his class had discovered

a pair of bald eagles nesting high in a tree close to, and over-looking, an inlet of the Kennebec River south of Bath. About one hundred feet back and farther up on a slope was a very tall tree. Near the top of this, Dr. Gross suggested, would be an ideal location for a blind from which to watch and photo-graph activities at the nest. Consequently, during the next few days, Dr. Gross, some of his class, and I proceeded with his suggestion, first nailing slim boards across the tree trunk for a ladder, then tugging up boards and two-by-four-inch beams for the blind platform, and finally upright supports for the covering. By early May 4 we could watch the eagles from the blind, provided we entered it before daybreak and re-mained as motionless as possible. Should the birds become in any way aware of us, they would leave the nest and stay away from it. I kept Eleanor posted on what Dr. Gross had us doing about the eagle nest and suggested that, when she came for the Ivy Activities, she bring clothing suitable for tree-climbing. I knew she would be excited to see the eagles.

After three days in mid-May attending the ninety-sixth convention of the Psi Upsilon Fraternity in Washington, I was behind in my courses; hence there was much catching-up on my hands. At the same time, I was determined to continue working on my heath hen article. Looming were three days of Ivy Activities starting on May 22. Meanwhile, on May 20, there was a Mayhew Lecture, "The Filming of the Golden Eagle," by Captain C. W. R. Knight in the Pastime Theater. Capt. Knight, a Britisher, delighted all of us with his subtle humor and his obvious affection for his subject perched on the stage with him. In his film he showed the eagle flying in slow motion—an accomplishment in bird photography which, up to this time, was new to me.

Eleanor arrived in her own car, late but in time for the for-mal dinner at the house and the dances to follow at our house and others. It was sometime after 1:00 A.M. when Eleanor and I stopped dancing at the house, she to go upstairs to put on her knickers and long boots and I to don some old clothes at the dormitory. When we appeared thus garbed at the house before leaving, several couples stared at us in disbelief and someone asked where in the world we were heading at this time of night. We explained about going to watch nesting eagles. Leaving the others mystified, we drove off into the night toward Bath.

Dawn was breaking by the time we reached the base of the tree supporting the blind and started climbing the ladder. Eleanor put her hands on the ladder in the same places from which I withdrew my feet—and she made it. Once we were huddled together, we looked down on the nest through a big peephole. Alas, when it was bright enough for us to see the nest, there was no eagle on it. Apparently we had disturbed the bird in our climbing and it had left. (We did catch a glimpse of an eagle soaring in the distance.) We lingered for a short while, hoping that one of the eagles might return, then descended from the blind and returned to Brunswick. After breakfast, we drove to Belgrade for a day's visit with my grandparents, though we spent more time catching up on sleep than we did in conversation.

I have since marveled at how much in these days I took Eleanor for granted. That she liked birds, I knew, and that she enjoyed camping and mountain-climbing, but assuming that she would willingly leave a dance, change into rough clothes, and do what we did that night of May 22, was taking her more for granted than I ever stopped to realize.

The weather we had for Ivy Day, May 24, was perfect. I was delighted to have my parents on hand for the traditional exercises, from the opening prayer to the class poem and the oration, followed by the presentation of gifts to the planting of the ivy. The great day culminated as always for Eleanor and me with the Gym Dance, the women resplendent in colorful gowns, everyone responding to the popular music of the time played by one of the better known bands.

In the evening of May 29, at the last meeting of our Psi U chapter for the academic year, I was elected the next year's president. I was more than complimented; I was deeply moved by the trust expressed in me to maintain the standards of the fraternity in 1929.

Now that classes were over, there were examinations coming up. I needed time to prepare for them. And there were rehearsals for *King Lear* to attend. How I found the time, I will never know. On June 12, I finished reworking and sent off my article, "The Passing of the Heath Hen," with photographs to *Forest and Stream*, a widely circulated magazine. Now the wait for the response would begin. Then I drove to Middleton to collect Mother for Eleanor's graduation from Wheaton, June 18. The ceremonies over, Eleanor returned with us to Middleton, where we left Mother while we went on to Bowdoin to dance at the Senior Hop that night.

King Lear was staged the next evening outdoors in front of the Walker Art Building on its paved terrace. Serving as background was the building's classical Romanesque facade enhanced by bronze sculptures. The weather could not have been finer. Seated with Eleanor in the audience, extending from below the terrace, were my parents and grandparents, Auntie Brown, Uncle Bill, and Aunt Millie, all of whom had gathered for the occasion. Many times thereafter they remarked about the fine production and how much they had enjoyed it under the stars.

King Lear marked the terminus of my junior year at Bowdoin, but long before the year drew to a close I had become increasingly concerned about having no trips for birds in the offing for the early summer. Dr. Gross was going to Wisconsin to undertake a field investigation of prairie chickens for that state and would be provided with an assistant. What should I do? Dr. Gross was ready with advice: "Undertake your own investigation. Go to Great Duck Island off Maine's northeast coast and study the herring gulls nesting there in abundance; band and photograph them too."

CHAPTER 9 / *Sea Island Adventure*

A MAP SHOWED Great Duck Island, about two miles long and a half-mile wide, lying ten miles off Mount Desert Island in the open sea. The lighthouse on its southern tip, I soon learned, was manned by three keepers. They and their families were the island's sole occupants. Monthly visits by the government lighthouse tender, lobster fishermen who came to pull their traps near shore, and an underwater telephone cable were the only contacts with the mainland.

The more I considered the problems of reaching the island and living there on my own, the more I was convinced about needing a man Friday. Whom did I know well enough to take along? And who liked me well enough to endure the isolation—and birds to boot?

I thought at once of Charlie Dunbar, a good friend and fellow member of the Bowdoin Outing Club. Although he cared not one iota for birds, or science for that matter, he enjoyed camping, among other outdoor activities. A sea island adventure might appeal to him. Luckily it did. He agreed to accompany me.

Back in Middleton, on June 21, 1929, I set to work acquiring equipment for the Great Duck Island undertaking. Earlier in the year I had purchased a tent—a huge A-shaped edifice. Made of canvas and waterproof, the tent had a portico held up by metal poles; inside was room enough for two cots and a center table. A heavy tarpaulin floor was sewn to the walls and there was a screened back window with a curtain that could be rolled down. The entrance was protected by canvas flaps and a curtain of mosquito netting that could be tied closed. The two main tent poles were metal and telescoped. Everything was dark green except the mosquito netting. I named my temporary home Green Mansion. It weighed seventy-five pounds.

In the next two weeks, Charlie in Portland and I in Middleton planned the adventure with only the vaguest concept of what was in store. We would drive in my car to Northeast Harbor and hire a lobsterman to deliver us to the island in his boat. Since we were going to camp out, we would make ourselves entirely independent of the lighthouse keepers and take our own food. Charlie appointed himself in charge of provisions and purchased three cartonsful of tins. He also appointed himself cook—chief can-opener. I borrowed the Bowdoin publicity department's Graflex and bought a supply of film; obtained a supply of bird bands, gull size, from the Bureau of Biological Survey in Washington. Then we assembled folding cots, blankets, cooking utensils, ax, kerosene lantern, flashlights. We would meet in Portland on July 5 and proceed to Northeast Harbor.

During the two weeks in Middleton I became more impatient with each passing day and was glad the last was the Fourth of July, when Uncle Bill, Eleanor, and I set off the fireworks at the sanatorium.

When I picked up Charlie in Portland the next day, he had more paraphernalia including a revolver—for "target practice," he said. We arrived as planned at Northeast Harbor, found our lobsterman, piled our duffel into the stern of his boat, stored our car, and got under way courtesy of a converted Packard motor, a dinghy in tow. Dense fog lay "outside" as it had, we were told, for the fifteen preceding days. Soon we were in it.

Somewhere in the nothingness ahead was Great Duck Island. We kept on for two hours. Our skipper had not hesitated to take us out and seemed not in the least bit concerned. He was relying on the sluggish southeast wind for direction and measuring distance by estimating his boat's running time. Suddenly he stopped the motor, listening, he explained, for the Great Duck foghorn. We strained our ears in the silence. He started the motor again. I realized at once what a friendly sound the motor made and squelched the thought of its not restarting. After a few minutes, he stopped the motor again. Again no foghorn. The silence was dreadful.

I have forgotten how many times we stopped and started. But I will not forget the sound of the foghorn when at last we heard it, above the motor's chugging, a loud bellow repeated rapidly three times. The skipper stopped the motor to make certain of its direction. We heard a thunderous roar of surf, and I had the scary feeling of nearing the base of a cataract. Then the foghorn sounded again. Without the motor to muffle it, the blast was deafening and nerve-shattering. Moments later I caught a glimpse of mountainous surf only fifty feet away.

There would be no landing here, our skipper informed us, because this was the southern tip of the island, exposed to the open sea and rimmed by high ledges. We must go to the island's less exposed western side, where the slope to the sea was gradual, although there would still be surf, he hastened to add.

Soon we were heading in toward the skipper's chosen landfall. We could begin to see a dark, rocky shore and much breaking surf. When the motor was cut off I could hear the roar. The skipper threw out the anchor.

We pulled the dinghy to the side of the boat, but it would not stay without being held. Charlie volunteered to do the holding while I jumped in and took the duffel, which the skipper passed me piece by piece. I worried about Charlie, his hand on the dinghy and his feet in the boat. When the dinghy lurched away from the boat, he was stretched like a bridge between the two. He could, I thought, be stretched beyond endurance.

If making a landfall was risky business, the skipper showed no indication of it. Seated and rowing, he headed for the shore, choosing a space between two high rocks wide enough to admit the dinghy. He waited for a lull between rollers. When it came he rushed in, rowing furiously and reaching the space between the rocks in the nick of time. Charlie, who had been waiting with painter in hand, jumped for one of the rocks, green with slippery seaweed. He landed, one foot sliding off before the other arrived. Result: Charlie was sprawled over the rock on his stomach, while the uncontrolled dinghy crunched against the rock. Charlie scrambled to his feet; the dinghy was now being pulled seaward by the undertow of an incoming roller. Charlie pulled frantically to get it back and lost his footing. Result: Charlie was sprawled on his back with his feet in the air. The roller wedged the dinghy high and dry between the rocks where it stayed. A perfect landing!

The skipper, in a hurry to unload and be off to Northeast Harbor before dark, passed us our duffel and we heaped it on a rock well above tide line. We shoved him off with a hasty farewell.

We had scarcely noticed that the afternoon light was fading, because we had been more than ordinarily occupied; but now, quite alone in the fog, we realized we had little time to lose if we expected to set up Green Mansion before nightfall. We left our duffel where we had piled it and struck out in the direction of the foghorn. It had to be near the lighthouse and its keepers. We felt obliged to make ourselves known to them, declare our intentions, and find out where we could camp.

As soon as we left the shore we were walking around enormous boulders and thick clumps of spruce, then into a grassy area where we disturbed a flock of sheep. A little further on we faced an imposing, dense stand of spruce impossible to circumvent. Somehow we had to get though, for the foghorn was sounding off on the other side, so we fought our way into it. Each tree we touched showered us; sticky spider webs glued themselves to our faces, tickling our noses; dead branch stubs jabbed us. Fairly breathless and increasingly frustrated in this jungle of tortures, we suddenly emerged into an open area where, before we had time to straighten up and catch our breath, pandemonium broke loose.

Dozens of gulls took to the air, screaming and jabbering, obviously alarmed. In the dimness ahead we could make out many others rising as the alarm spread. We had, of course, entered the gull colony, my first introduction to a sea bird colony of any kind. As gulls circled above us, one after another swooped down menacingly to within two or three feet of our heads, veered off, circled up, and then came down to renew the attack. One particularly angry bird dove at Charlie. Just as it reached a point a few inches above his head, it lowered its feet and kicked off his hat. Surprised, Charlie grabbed for his hat, exclaiming above the tumult, "I didn't know I was supposed to take off my hat in this ——— place."

The foghorn was still ahead, so we had no alternative but to pass through the colony. With each step in the uncertain light, more gulls swooped low over us. I remember stepping over numerous nests I wanted to inspect, but this was no time to be an ornithologist.

A quarter-mile after we cleared the colony, we confronted a row of three white houses with lights coming from their lower windows. Beyond the roof of one I noticed the lighthouse, a massive white cylinder disappearing skyward. Above it, as though disconnected, was a hazy gleam of the light itself. The foghorn was somewhere near the base, but it didn't seem as deafening as when we had first heard it from the boat. This was natural enough, though I didn't stop to think about it, because it was blasting seaward.

Before we could decide which house to approach, we discerned a tall figure moving toward one of them from the lighthouse. We hailed the man and introduced ourselves. The figure belonged to the head keeper, who was not a little surprised by human sounds coming out of the fog. In a somewhat gruff voice he invited us into his house, where we could appraise each other by lamplight. He turned out to be a rawboned, middle-aged man with a rather surly expression. Charlie and I felt decidedly uncomfortable and no less so a few moments later when we met his wife, a short, heavily set woman close to his age, with wide, bespectacled face, sharp voice, and prominent teeth. She greeted us in a perfunctory manner over the blaring of a radio that she did not turn down. If she was surprised by us, she didn't show it. In the room was a lad of eleven or twelve—their only child—who displayed an exuberance his parents lacked. To him our appearance and the reasons we gave for being there seemed to foretell excitement in an otherwise dull existence.

Shouting above the radio we explained where our duffel was and how we intended to camp out. The keeper said he had no objection since the island was not government-owned and therefore not under his jurisdiction. As for a place to set up camp, he recommended a high spot above the east cliffs where we would not be bothered by sheep and would be clear of the gull colony. The "boys" would help us get our duffel over there. Upon this remark, the youngster left the house in haste.

The couple seemed to warm up slightly to our intentions. They yelled out directions as to how we could get fresh water from the catch basin—a cistern that collected rain from the roofs of the buildings; the wife would be glad to cook some food for us; we could come and listen to the radio. This was a lonely place, they assured us, and the only other persons here were the first and second assistant keepers and their families. By this time the boy was back with two others a little older who belonged to the second assistant keeper. They were ready, they said, with two wheelbarrows and lanterns.

The boys seemed to know where our duffel was piled. We trudged along after them in the dim light of the lanterns. The boys were in high spirits; for them this was a real lark, and it took them little time to locate our gear. Most of it we heaped on the wheelbarrows; the rest Charlie and I carried. Finally we arrived at our destination. We observed faintly that we were in a little open area. Not twenty feet away the ground fell away and from below we heard heavy surf.

Now to set up Green Mansion, in a light rain that had begun to fall. I shook its great mass from the sack and unfolded yards of it. Eventually the tent began to take shape and before long all five of us were inside. I think the boys wanted to stay with us, for they had much to say about how snug Green Mansion was and what fun it would be to spend the night. Some persuasion was necessary to convince them that the capacity was limited to two before they made their reluctant way home. This was the last time we would see the second assistant keeper's two sons because on the following day they left the island with their parents for an annual vacation.

Wearily, after lighting our lantern, Charlie and I made the inside of Green Mansion livable by putting up the cots and shoving all accessories under them. Charlie thereupon assumed his first duties as cook. When we were finally ready to try out our beds, Charlie brought forth his revolver, carefully placed it under his cot, and gave me a silly grin. "It's just in case," he said. In case of what, I wondered. A sheep attack?

Charlie, settled in his cot, was asleep in a twinkling, but I was at the mercy of the island's night and its incessant sounds: the periodic bellowing of the foghorn, the roaring, crashing, and banging of the surf against the cliffs below us. I began imagining shifts in the tempo and mood of the sounds. Sometimes the foghorn seemed to be slowing and more doleful—raising my hopes that it might not sound again—only to regain renewed vigor for the next outburst.

During a momentary lull, I heard several odd little sounds and held my breath to identify them. Again I heard them, more of them, this time above the night's din. Now they were occurring frequently: stammering, purring, chuckling sounds—the repertoire was indescribable. And the sounds were getting closer and coming from all directions. I groped for my flashlight and snapped it on, rolled out of my cot, parted the tent flaps, and stepped under the portico. To my astonishment the sounds were coming not only from the air and ground, they were coming from *under* the ground. But not a thing could I see, since the beam of my flashlight failed to penetrate the fog.

Had I not known that Leach's storm-petrels—sea birds of swallow size—frequented Great Duck Island in the summer, that they nested in burrows and remained there out of sight in the daytime, and that they were notable for a remarkably varied vocabulary, I would never have guessed that I was hearing birds.

Back in my cot, sleep was still impossible as I contemplated the storm-petrels I had yet to see. Why all the different calls? Probably they were greetings between birds returning from the sea and their mates, which had spent the day in their burrows. Then I began noticing that the calls of one storm-petrel had a muffled quality and I soon realized why. The unfortunate bird was *under* Green Mansion. We had set the tent over a burrow, blocking the entrance and imprisoning the poor creature. The thought that we would have to take down and move Green Mansion on the morrow made me very tired indeed. I fell asleep.

Sometime later in the night I awoke with a start—the foghorn had ceased its remonstrations. Moreover, the rain had stopped and the surf had lost its punch. Fair weather was in the offing. Again I fell asleep, but not before dreamily considering the happy prospect of really seeing Great Duck Island for the first time.

We awoke early. Brilliant rays of light streamed in between the tent flaps, and I could see clear sky under the window cover. We burst out of our cots to look around and found ourselves on a grassy and mossy crest, backed by tall spruces, overlooking the Atlantic from a granite escarpment that dropped to boulders glistening in the breaking surf.

Breakfast was a nuisance. I gathered the driest dead branches I could find and encouraged them to burn, whereupon Charlie prepared his first culinary offerings: fried eggs, bacon, and boiled coffee. While we ate we made plans for the day. There was the island with its gull colony to explore, then a blind to build for photography. And Green Mansion had to be moved. When I told Charlie that we were living among petrels and that the tent was covering a burrow, he was incredulous.

"How do you know?" he asked.

"Because I heard them last night," I replied somewhat peevishly, remembering how well he had slept through the night's hubbub.

"Well, last night isn't this morning," he quipped. "I don't see any petrels."

"They're underground." As I said this I noticed near his feet a hole about the circumference of a man's arm. "You're standing on one now."

I pushed my hand and forearm into the hole. The earth was soft and damp. I found that the burrow angled abruptly. Using my forearm as a lever, I widened the burrow and pushed around the bend, my upper arm disappearing.

"What makes you think you're going to find a bird down there?" Charlie asked. I was beginning to ask the same question of myself.

When there was scarcely an inch of my arm left, my hand entered a warm, dry chamber, and my fingers felt a feathery body and a gently pecking bill. Underneath the bird was one egg. I said nothing but smiled triumphantly, eliciting an expression of disbelief from Charlie.

"Now don't tell me you've got a petrel," he exclaimed.

In general appearance the petrel suggested a large swallow—of martin size. Its tail was moderately long and slightly forked; its wings were long and narrow. But any similarity to a swallow ceased on closer inspection. Its feet were webbed, its bill hooked, and its nostrils prominently tubed and extended forward on the top of the bill. It was dark gray except for a white patch on the rump. It did not make a sound. Apparently, protestations were not part of its varied vocabulary.

I passed the bird to Charlie. No sooner had he taken it than it regurgitated a greenish fluid with a pungent odor.

"The darn thing is sick, it's vomiting," Charlie observed. He promptly handed the bird back to me.

"No, it's all right. Just a habit whenever it's disturbed. Probably defensive. Anyway, it's quite effective; see how quickly you gave it up."

"Then what is the stuff?" Charlie wanted to know.

"It comes from the stomach. It's always somewhat oily because the bird's food is quite oily in content."

"Then maybe it should be called petrol," Charlie countered.

I told Charlie that the name petrel is derived from "little Peter" from the bird's way of "walking" on the water as Saint Peter did in the Scriptures. Charlie wondered why the petrels weren't flying around us. I explained that they spend the daytime far out at sea. Only during the nesting season, and at night, do they come to land. But Charlie was bound to have the last word: "I see, they stay in all day so that they can be out all night."

When I put the petrel down at the burrow's entrance, it quickly hurried in and out of sight. Although in the vicinity of Green Mansion we found more than a dozen burrows, there was an area nearby without them where we would move the tent before evening.

Spruces dominated the interior of the island. But on its western side, beyond the spruces, the island was open, sloping to a shore of ledges and loose rocks with light surf. Back from the shore were sheep in a pasture of short grasses and lichen-encrusted boulders; spruces, mostly standing alone, some pinnacled, others flat-topped, and a few dead, bleached, and gaunt; and some five thousand herring gulls.

Of the many so-called "sea gulls," the herring gull was in 1929 and has been ever since among the most common on the Maine coast. One indisputable explanation for its success is that it is a scavenger, content to take whatever food—dead or alive, fresh or putrified—it may find on the water, on the shore, or inland. It has learned to follow boats from fishing vessels to ferries, to wait for the departure of picnickers from beaches, and to make periodic visits to community dumps.

Although far from the herring gull's food sources, Great Duck Island compensated by providing isolation from mainland disturbances and mammalian predators. It also offered enough space for the gulls to form a nesting colony protected from intrusion. On the morning of July 6, after fighting through the spruces of the island's interior and emerging at the edge of the herring gull colony, we stopped, fascinated. Never in my life had I seen so many gulls. They were everywhere: on the ground, standing on boulders, and perching on trees. Those nearest saw us immediately and stood as rigid as wax figures, suspicious and tense. What next?

We took a few steps. Suddenly the alarm was sounded. Up rose a gray-and-white cloud of beating wings, punctuated by discordant screams and calls. Soon the cloud turned into a swirling multitude of vociferous forms, many of which were circling over us and looking down threateningly. We proceeded boldly into the colony to find nests. When unusually aggressive gulls dove at us, Charlie pulled his hat down tight on his head. He was taking no chances.

Finding nests was no problem. All were on the ground a few feet apart and openly exposed, often at the bases of rocks or beside clumps of grass. They were largely of grass and seaweed packed down and cupped. The majority held eggs, usually three, the colors of which were predominantly drab green and spotted dark brown; a few already contained newly hatched chicks covered with grayish down and spotted like the eggs. Opportunities for study and photography were endless.

Charlie, who had already had enough of nests, patiently seated himself on an old stump with gulls storming above him. Eventually, near the shore on the ledge itself, I found an exceptionally large nest in which crouched two baby chicks with eyes closed. The ledge and surroundings were ruggedly picturesque. When I picked up one of the chicks, it kept its eyes closed and held itself stiffly. In my hand for a few minutes, however, it stood up somewhat shakily on its oversized, webbed feet, opened its eyes, yawned, then settled down in my palm. Pure innocence and charm. I had found my nest.

It was noon by the time we had explored the island and returned to Green Mansion. The head keeper, his wife, and their son appeared soon after lunch, showing unexpected interest in how we were getting along and asking us to supper. In the afternoon Charlie helped me build my blind, at best a crude affair, supported by spruce poles and covered with burlap I had brought along for the purpose. We set it about six feet away from the chosen gull nest, then left so that the adult birds would have ample time to get used to it before the next day. We removed the contents of Green Mansion, took it down, set it up again where there were no petrel burrows, and moved in. We had time to band a dozen gull chicks before washing up for supper.

The head keeper's house was spotless; there were no rugs or other embellishments, and the furniture was plain and unupholstered. Supper was ready when we arrived. We ate in the kitchen.

Food was plentiful and delicious, but there is nothing else I remember pleasantly about the supper and evening that followed. The radio blared from the adjoining living room. Our host was loud-mouthed and profane and our hostess hardly less so. The keeper would talk only about the problems of running the lighthouse and foghorn. He had to do all the work himself, he complained, because his assistants were lazy and uncooperative.

It was after dark when we started back to Green Mansion. Under the clear, star-studded sky, I felt a keen sense of relief, and so did Charlie. The evening had been an ordeal. "They're strange folks," I remember remarking.

Right after breakfast on our second morning I gathered the Bowdoin Graflex, a tripod, some film, food for lunch, and started for the gull blind. I prevailed upon Charlie to accompany me. He could help by walking away from the blind after

I had entered, thus directing the gulls' attention to him and causing them to forget that there had been two of us. "Besides," I teased him, "the gulls pay more attention to you than they do me."

Charlie waited outside the blind while I crawled inside, set up my Graflex on the tripod, and cut a hole in the burlap through which to see and photograph the nest when the birds returned to it. I also cut peepholes on the other sides of the blind for watching events around me. Then Charlie was on his way out of the colony, the gulls circling above him and following.

The colony settled down. In a few minutes, the ledge chicks, recovering from crouching and "freezing" at our intrusion, were toddling about the nest and peeping plaintively. Shortly thereafter their mother dropped down and, still a little apprehensive, took hesitating steps to the side of the nest. At last, all suspicions allayed, she stepped on the nest and settled over the brood. The camera made a sharp sound when I took my first picture. Instantly the mother jumped into the air, her chicks froze, and all the gulls within hearing distance took flight. As I took more pictures, the birds paid less and less attention to the noise, and finally none at all. I obtained all the pictures I wanted.

The hours that followed were the first I had spent watching activities in a sea bird colony. At the start, my attention centered on the ledge family: how the female cared for her chicks and how the chicks reacted to her mate when he arrived to feed them, pecking at his bill until he regurgitated the food he had brought. The ledge nest, it so happened, was one of several in the immediate vicinity of the blind. All had chicks nearly the same age. Watching these nests I became aware of how neighboring families interacted, squabbling over their territories, and so on. Never a dull moment did I have and at times I was fairly dizzy, looking out first one peephole, then another, trying to keep track of the goings-on.

Charlie, at Green Mansion when I returned in the late afternoon, couldn't believe that I had been in a blind all of ten hours. When I assured him that I had had an intensely rewarding session and that the hours had passed all too quickly, he seemed dumbfounded, concluding that he never expected to understand the makings of an ornithologist or any person who could bear watching birds for more than five minutes.

But Charlie had had an enjoyable day too. He had explored the eastern shore at high and low tides; had put Green Mansion's interior in order and, outside, had used rock slabs to construct an open fireplace and a table; and had met and hobnobbed with the first assistant keeper. As a matter of fact, Charlie told me triumphantly, the assistant keeper and his wife had asked us to supper that very evening.

"What's the assistant keeper like?" I wanted to know.

"Oh, he's a quiet person, almost gentle," Charlie told me, "and he doesn't smile. Seems rather queer."

The assistant keeper and his wife were perhaps in their late forties. He was of slight build and stooped at the shoulders. Occasionally he showed a glimmer of pleasantry, but he never smiled, as Charlie had noted. His wife was short and quite stout, with a round, rather sad face.

Their general appearance belied a warmth of character, for when we arrived for supper we were welcomed in the friendliest manner. They were immediately interested in our work. Their home was neat, clean, and comfortably furnished; numerous knickknacks here and there gave it a homey look. In no time we felt very much at ease.

With the start of supper, conversation flowed easily. But it was not long before we were discussing the social relationships of the three families on the island. The man was soon speaking emphatically and bitterly about the head keeper, while his wife interjected comments at every opportunity. They were making serious accusations. Then came a hair-raising statement from her: "Yesterday the keeper threatened to kill my husband."

Eating was forgotten. I was so astonished that I must have sat in my chair as if stunned. This couple, at first so quiet and gentle, suddenly revealed a deep-rooted anger! Were they telling the truth or were they exaggerating? Whatever the answer, there was real reason for their solemness. Furthermore, our presence was giving them a chance to pour out feelings long pent up.

Charlie and I became gravely concerned. Here was a

situation which, if entirely true, might mean serious trouble. We probed the couple with questions, and their answers came easily.

In their opinion the head keeper had an unsavory reputation and had obtained government employment as a refuge. I don't remember whether I finished my supper or not. I was much too occupied contemplating the situation which had the makings of a grim melodrama: people isolated on an island where a madman is in control and where the only means of calling for help—the telephone—is in the madman's house. What was there to do about it?

After supper we conversed for about an hour on the same topic. Just as we were about to depart, the assistant keeper cautioned us to be careful because "that man probably suspects you of spying on him and making ready to tell on him when you get to the mainland." I felt hairs standing on the back of my neck.

Our walk back to Green Mansion was through a night as clear as the one before, but we were too fraught with worries to take much notice.

"Sewall," Charlie said, "this is not a healthy place. It's time to think about getting off."

I refused to agree with him outwardly. "After all, we've just started our work," I stated firmly, "and haven't anything to show for our expense and efforts." I persuaded Charlie to stick it out.

On each of the next eight days I devoted six or more hours to the gull colony, usually in the morning, from my blind by the gulls' nest on the ledge. The ledge family made me realize for the first time just how rapidly young sea birds grow and how intricate bird behavior and social relationships are. On each succeeding morning when I arrived at the blind, the chicks had changed so greatly in appearance that I could hardly recognize them. Every day I watched the activities of the gull family—its strife with neighbors and the changing attitudes of the chicks and their parents. At first I took notes in great detail, but soon events got ahead of me and I gave up note-taking. I had not anticipated such complexities: in Michigan, the summer before, I had found it comparatively simple to record activities of a single family of hermit thrushes.

In any case, the entire experience gave me a new respect for the problems of ornithological research, as well as a fondness for colonial sea birds which greatly influenced my choice for adventures in many far-flung places in the ensuing years.

Every afternoon Charlie helped me band young gulls. The weather continued to be favorable, with bright skies and cottony clouds borne from the mainland by westerly winds. Fog usually set in at night, bringing on the foghorn, but its doleful bellowings no longer disturbed me. I had become as accustomed to their regularity as to the ticking of a clock. During these eight days we had followed our resolve to keep away from the lighthouse. We had not seen the keepers, although several times the head keeper's wife had sent us her boy with biscuits for our supper.

In the evening of July 16 at Green Mansion, we enjoyed supper in the twilight and sat and talked under the portico until fog and dampness drove us inside. I was soon in my cot and nearly asleep when I heard the assistant keeper's voice outside. He wanted to see Charlie.

A conversation took place in low undertones, although I could hear enough to know that the assistant keeper was agitated. In a few moments Charlie burst into the tent, grabbed his revolver and some bullets from under his cot, and went out. I heard a few more words, then Charlie returned empty-handed.

Fairly beside myself, I demanded, "What in the devil is going on?"

"Oh, he thinks he should have the revolver for self-protection. The head keeper is on a rampage and is threatening him." Charlie spoke casually—much too casually for my peace of mind.

"Don't tell me you gave him your revolver," I said, knowing full well that he had. "Are you losing your mind?"

Charlie said nothing. After a few moments I continued, "If he uses that revolver to murder, you'll be an accessory or something. You should have refused to let him have it."

I soon resigned myself to the situation. The man had the weapon. I tried to steel myself for whatever might happen. Gone was the hopeful ornithologist in me. Tomorrow we would arrange to get off the island. I tried to sleep.

Right after breakfast I set out for the head keeper's house, determined to contact the lobsterman in Northeast Harbor and have him get us as soon as possible.

The boy was playing in the yard. Once on the porch I heard the radio. Things must be normal. When I knocked at the door, a harsh voice told me to come in. The keeper and his wife were seated at the table just finishing breakfast, their expressions impassive. With their permission, I made my call and found that the lobsterman would be out to take us off in the morning.

"So you're leaving in the morning?" the keeper asked, having heard my part of the phone conversation. "I thought you were going to stay a while longer."

"Well," I hesitated, thinking quickly, "we've accomplished everything sooner than I expected we would. Also, I've run out of film." Then I thanked his wife and him for letting me use their phone and giving us some food now and then.

"Come back again sometime. Maybe we'll see you off in the morning."

Maybe! Why did he use that word? How could we get off in the morning without his seeing us? The word stuck in my mind for the rest of the day while we banded our last gulls, while we packed our duffel in the evening, while I was going to sleep, while we folded up our cots and collapsed Green Mansion and wadded it into its sack in the morning.

The lobsterman arrived as arranged on July 18. There was no "maybe" about it; the head keeper saw us off. But no assistant keeper was in sight.

From Northeast Harbor we were to drive directly to Portland where I would leave Charlie at his home; then I would head for Wayne to open and live at the camp, taking meals with Aunt Mame and Uncle Luther, while I awaited the arrival of my parents on July 20.

When we were ashore at Northeast Harbor, Charlie produced the revolver from his duffel bag.

"Where did that come from?" I exploded. "I thought you had given the thing away."

"So did I," Charlie replied, "but early in the morning when I went for some water the assistant keeper saw me and returned it, thanked me profusely, and said it was no good to him."

"No good to him; what did he mean?"

"He tried it; couldn't hit a thing."

"What did he try?"

"A gull!"

CHAPTER 10 / *Bowdoin Senior*

HAPPY AS I WAS to see Father and Mother, and eager to tell them about my sojourn on Great Duck Island, I was stopped short when Father handed me two letters that had come for me at Middleton from *Forest and Stream,* one accepting my heath hen article for "an early issue" of the magazine and the other containing a check in payment for the manuscript. I must have jumped for joy. Then Mother gave me important news: Eleanor had gotten a job, starting next September, to teach in Edgartown High School on Martha's Vineyard. Of all the coincidences, Martha's Vineyard!

From July on, my 1929 summer in Wayne lived up to its predecessors for enjoyment. Eleanor, Auntie Brown, Uncle Bill, and Aunt Millie joined us for long visits. (Aunt Millie expressed repeatedly her pleasure about having my heath hen article accepted, serving toward fulfilling her wish in my becoming a writer.) Never did I or my parents fail to spend some time with my grandparents in Belgrade. Eleanor and I got in our mountain-climbing, this time twin-peaked Mount Bigelow.

My parents departed for Middleton on August 26, Eleanor and I a few days later. Eleanor may have been more excited about her first job than the rest of us, but nobody would have known it from the way we reacted. No question about it, Father decided, all of us would take her to Edgartown in our new Buick. And so we did. Driving to Woods Hole, we put the car on the steamer to Oak Bluffs and from there drove to the house in Edgartown where Eleanor would board. The rest of us spent the night at the Kelly House in town. Before leaving the next day we toured the island, Eleanor with us, not failing to include its colorful southwest promontory, Gay

Head. After my earlier trip to Martha's Vineyard for heath hens, I discovered that there was more to Martha's Vineyard than scrub oaks.

On September 20, I arrived back at Bowdoin in my roadster for my senior year, 1929–30. I again occupied the Nursery. My previous year's roommates, Theron Spring and Edward Dana, had graduated. My new roommates were Pete Ridlon, classmate and companion about whom I have written, and John Creighton, Jr., a sophomore—handsome, deep-voiced and brilliant, with a ready sense of humor.

Rushing of freshmen was at once under way. Now that I was president of the house, I felt more keenly than ever many responsibilities, in this case acquiring the best freshmen delegation possible in number and quality. Ultimately we acquired fifteen, one more than the year before.

Amid the hubbub of rushing I had to give attention to courses since, obviously, my education came first. Majoring in biology, I signed up for all the remaining courses Bowdoin offered in that field.

Classes had begun when I received from the publisher of *Forest and Stream* a copy of the October, 1929, issue containing my article, "The Passing of the Heath Hen." It was the lead article. Excited, of course, I rushed the copy to Dr. Gross who lost no time in passing it on to President Sills. From several brothers in my house, who were taking "Casey's Lit" (the familiar campus name for the president's popular course, Literature), I heard how the president had spoken glowingly of the article and about his pleasure that it had come from a Bowdoin undergraduate.

Initiation was scheduled for November 1. Beforehand there was much expected of me: chairing the Friday night meetings of the brothers in the chapter hall, largely on business matters but also on other problems needing attention; making certain that each freshman pledge was assigned one or more guardians to oversee his class work, offer him encouragement when necessary, and follow up on his progress in whatever extracurricular project or projects he had chosen; and, above all, to assure that the traditions of Hell Week were maintained without injuries or damage to property.

Thinking ahead to my role as president in the initiation

ceremony itself, I decided to memorize and recite rather than read the ritual from the dais. Then I would step down from the dais, stand before each delegate in turn and, while looking directly at him and addressing him by full name, ask him to pledge his everlasting loyalty to the Psi Upsilon Fraternity. Upon his compliance, I would then congratulate him and extend the fraternity's grip. The fact that I looked into many heavily moist eyes bore proof enough that my presentation was as effective as I had intended.

With the Psi U initiation over, it seemed that the rest of my senior year proceeded at a more rapid pace than in my earlier three years at Bowdoin. Thanksgiving recess in Middleton, with my parents, Aunt Millie and Uncle Bill, Eleanor (vacationing from Martha's Vineyard), and Auntie Brown, was over in no time.

At the Bowdoin Christmas house party, December 19–20, Mother was one of the chaperons, coming to Brunswick alone on a train; Eleanor arrived on another. My roommates and I turned over the Nursery to them. Father and Auntie Brown met all three of us at the train home on the twenty-first. The party lived up to the high expectations for Bowdoin house parties, so long established. Especially did Eleanor and I like the music of Perley Breed at the Gym Dance.

Like the Thanksgiving weekend, the Christmas recess in Middleton seemed to be over in no time too. Christmas Day was festive, as the presence of Uncle Bill and Aunt Millie always made it so, and on New Year's Day, Father, along with Eleanor and Auntie Brown, drove me to the train bound for Brunswick. Eleanor would soon be returning to Martha's Vineyard.

During January in Brunswick and the recess in Middleton after the midyear exams, I used odd moments and late evenings to write a popular article about my experiences with herring gulls on Great Duck Island. In mid-February, I put the finishing touches on the article while spending a snug weekend with my grandparents in Belgrade. More important to me than the article were the precious moments at the farm; I realized that this would probably be my last winter visit there. Time was obviously catching up with my grandparents. Henceforth, they would be spending winters with my parents in Middleton, unable to maintain the farm themselves at that time of year.

On April 8, when I considered my article on the herring gulls at Great Duck Island in as good shape as it would ever be, I submitted it to *Nature Magazine*. Lo and behold, nine days later came a letter accepting it, with the offer of a substantial honorarium. Suddenly I felt rich, rich enough— considering also the fee I had received from the heath hen article—to purchase a real professional still camera. I eventually chose a Graflex equipped with a Protar VIIa lens and a double extension bellows, and bought a Crown A tripod for support when necessary.

Sometime early in the second semester, Dr. Gross told me that he would be in Wisconsin again that summer conducting the state's prairie chicken investigation, which would leave me after graduation to undertake a bird project on my own. I was anxious to work on the coast with sea birds. But where? Luckily I became acquainted with a junior, Paul A. Walker, who was interested in Maine's coastal birds. Learning of Paul's and my interest, Stanley W. Hyde of Yarmouth, Maine, an older man sitting in on Dr. Gross's ornithology course to increase his knowledge of birds, advised us to go to the Sugar Loaf Islands at the mouth of the Kennebec River near Popham Beach. Terns nested there in abundance, he said, and we were welcome to stay in his cottage at Popham Beach and use his rowboat to reach the islands. He would not be using the cottage early in the summer while the terns were nesting. Paul and I gratefully accepted his offer. We would meet at Popham Beach and work with the terns right after my commencement.

Why, I will never know, but despite all the activities scheduled ahead, I succumbed to trying out for a role in the Commencement Play, *Romeo and Juliet*. Expecting a minor role, if any at all, I was instead selected as Friar Lawrence, a major one. From April on, I consequently became committed to long rehearsals, many at the most inconvenient times.

There is no question that my desire to become an ornithologist by profession was inspired by Dr. Gross. I liked his way of life, which combined teaching with the opportunity to study and photograph birds anywhere. But it was not until I returned from my 1928 summer with him in Michigan that I actually decided on ornithology. Back at Bowdoin that fall I let Dr. Gross know how, after graduating, I wanted to work toward and earn a Ph.D. in ornithology. This would require a minimum of three years.

During my years in college the almost certain route in the United States to becoming a professional ornithologist was to enter the graduate school at Cornell University in Ithaca, New York, and obtain a doctorate under Arthur A. Allen. Cornell was the only institution at the time to offer a program leading to a doctorate in ornithology as such. Dr. Gross, thoroughly supportive of my decision, wrote to Dr. Allen recommending me for graduate work and received a highly favorable reply from Dr. Allen accepting me. Thus, the stage was set for me to apply for entrance. I would go to Cornell in September, 1930.

All along my parents were aware of my mounting enthusiasm for professional ornithology and had not once objected. Father loved the practice of medicine, the profession of his own choice. If he ever harbored any hope that I too might go into medicine, he never as much intimated it. What pleased him, as well as Mother, was that I had found a profession that excited me. "How lucky I am to have such a son," I once heard Father say. "My good friend Dr. ———— has a son Sewall's age with no desire to do anything other than to hang around and pick up odd jobs."

On the weekend of April 25–28, 1930, I journeyed all the way by rail from Brunswick to Ithaca, to spend a mere three hours with Dr. Allen in his office at Cornell University. Never mind the complications of changing trains to reach Ithaca in upstate New York, I was determined to meet Dr. Allen and clarify questions about academic requirements and procedures as well as living conditions. He could not have been more helpful in so short a time. A handsome man of moderate stature with a pleasant face, accentuated by dark eyebrows and a trim, black mustache, he immediately made me feel at ease. I never regretted making the trip, complicated and brief as it was, for there was much that I learned.

Dr. Allen would be chairman of my three-man doctoral committee. Upon his recommendation, the two other members would be Dr. Albert Hazen Wright, vertebrate zoologist, and Dr. James G. Needham, entomologist and famed as the

"Father of Limnology." During my first year I would be expected to attend Dr. Allen's classes and to take courses given by Dr. Wright and courses in Dr. Needham's department. I would not be working for grades or credit. Before the end of my first year, I would have to prove my ability to read at least two foreign languages. As for a place to live, Dr. Allen felt sure that he could find a room for me in one of the faculty houses. After my first year, I would be relatively free of courses, enabling me to pursue research undistracted. As for the subject of my research and doctoral thesis, I expressed a keen desire to center it on the American woodcock. This pleased Dr. Allen as it was, he said, an important game bird, yet comparatively little was known about its breeding habits.

During the course of the interview, Dr. Allen told me that the "Laboratory of Ornithology" was merely a name that he used on his letterhead. The laboratory bore no official status in the university complex. The name was used to justify the teaching and promotion of ornithology in the Department of Entomology which Dr. Needham chaired.

Soon after I returned to Bowdoin from Cornell, I and all the other seniors began preparing for the major examinations during the upcoming week of May 12. With confidence I looked forward to mine in biology, certain that I would make a good showing. Happily I did, justifying my confidence and at the same time increasing the high regard in which both Drs. Gross and Copeland held me.

Eleanor was with me for the Ivy Activities in late May following the major exams. After the Ivy exercises of the junior class in the afternoon of May 23, we seniors attended our last chapel, a ceremony for which we donned caps and gowns for the first time. We occupied, as all seniors do, the aisle-facing benches closest to the dais. Eleanor joined the audience in one of the other aisle-facing benches. After the brief address from the pulpit, solemnly and slowly we marched down the center aisle, led by the class marshall, past our audience, and out of the chapel.

As always, Ivy Activities terminated with a gala dance in the gym, sparked this time by the exotic music of the Ipana Troubadours. Then came two weeks of final examinations. Ever so gradually the campus population of underclassmen dwindled as they finished their exams until we were practically a campus of seniors only. On Sunday afternoon, June 15, at 5:00, properly in cap and gown, we attended the Baccalaureate service in the Church on the Hill, just outside the campus, where we would graduate four days later. President Sills addressed us on the subject of loyalties.

Two days later, June 17, was Class Day. Well in advance of this occasion my class met, not only to elect officers and marshal for this year and years to come, but to select participants in the day's exercises. I was elected to give the opening address, others to give a poem, the oration, the class history, the closing address, and to write an ode. Our exercises took place by tradition under the Thorndike Oak at 3:00 P.M. Included was smoking the pipe of peace, singing the ode, and finally walking over the campus, stopping before the principal buildings to give a cheer.

For this occasion and the events of the next two days, my parents, Aunt Millie and Uncle Bill, Aunt Mame and Uncle Luther, Auntie Brown, and Eleanor had taken up residence either in the Eagle Hotel or in lodgings elsewhere. After the Class Day exercises, Eleanor and I were invited by friends for dinner in Bath, returning later to Brunswick for the Class of 1930 Dance in the gym.

Alumni Day followed on June 18, the campus thronging with representatives of earlier classes. Unfortunately the weather was bad, raining intermittently. This meant that the Commencement Play, *Romeo and Juliet,* would have to be staged that night in the Cumberland Theater instead of outdoors on the spacious terrace of the art building—a bitter disappointment to all of us taking part in the production.

Father insisted, before going to the show, that I, Eleanor, Auntie Brown, and my admiring relatives be his guests for a shore dinner at the New Meadows Inn just outside of town. The dinner was no pleasure for me because I was on pins and needles, as I always was before going on the stage, but this time more than ever as I had a major role to play. I had to break away early anyway for the Cumberland Theater, there to get made up and into costume. The play went off smoothly, despite the stage's cramped conditions. As for my role, Friar Lawrence, I gave a couple of lines that were not as Shakespeare had written them, but only the prompter knew. How blessed was my relief when the show was over.

June 19, 1930, was the day of days when I graduated from Bowdoin College. The commencement procession to the Church on the Hill had formed on the campus by 10:00 A.M. All participants, except the band, were in academic regalia. The procession was led by the honorary marshall, then came the band, followed in pairs by the college officers, distinguished guests, recipients-to-be of honorary degrees, the faculty, and, drawing up the rear, we seniors. Once in the church, the officers, distinguished guests, and those to receive honorary degrees occupied the dais, seniors the front pews below the dais.

The ceremony, presided over by President Sills, opened with prayer, followed by addresses from four seniors who had the highest scholastic ranking in the class. Then came the conferring of degrees—first, the honorary ones upon citizens who had made worthy contributions to society, and second, either Bachelor of Arts or Bachelor of Science degrees upon us. Each of us, called to the dais by name, on receiving a diploma with a congratulatory handshake from President Sills, made certain immediately thereafter to switch the tassel on our mortarboards to the left side, indicating graduated status.

Following the benediction and the ceremony over, as quickly as I could, I sought my family, Eleanor, and Auntie Brown to receive their congratulations and embraces. Together we made our way to the Moulton Union for a reception by President and Mrs. Sills and then to the gym for the Commencement Dinner, the final event of the 125th Commencement.

Farewells from classmates to classmates ensued, all aware that never again would all of us be together at one time. Aunt Millie and Uncle Bill, Aunt Mame and Uncle Luther left for their homes in their respective cars. Auntie Brown returned to Middleton with Father and Mother in their car. Eleanor stayed with me while I loaded my car with my last personal effects at the Psi U house and we were soon off to Middleton.

Two days later, June 21, Paul Walker and I arrived in our cars at Popham Beach, as planned months earlier, to photograph the terns on the Sugar Loaf Islands. Aboard my car were my precious new camera and materials for the blind in which I would use it. We set up housekeeping in Mr. Hyde's cottage, thanks to his offer of it, and found his rowboat in excellent shape and ready for use.

In view of Mr. Hyde's cottage were the Sugar Loaf Islands—two ledges rising from the tidal churn where the Kennebec River flows into the Gulf of Maine. Upper Sugar Loaf, the larger of the two, was our obvious choice for we could easily discern its thriving tern colony as well as better opportunities for landing on it.

As we were to learn, Upper Sugar Loaf had a surface area at high tide of approximately an acre and a half, consisting of irregular ledge shelves rising step-like thirty feet above the high tide line to a more or less level summit. We estimated that the nesting bird population consisted of 350 pairs of common terns, six pairs of roseate terns, and three pairs of Arctic terns. Most nests were in grassy crevices, sometimes sheltered by overhanging ledge shelves.

Paul and I set foot on Upper Sugar Loaf on June 22. Losing no time we set up my blind—it was large enough to accommodate the two of us—on a high point where I could be close enough to several attractive nests. Some of the eggs were hatching. Making sure that the blind was well tied down by guys, we left at once so as not to disturb the birds further and give them time to get used to the blind by the time of our return the next day.

I kept no journal of our activities in the ensuing eight days. It was just as well because it would have been a hodgepodge. We were forever frustrated by all sorts of problems. Sometimes it was the weather, prohibiting good photography. More often it was waiting for the right tide to allow us to row out to the island or back without being forced off course, either up the river or out to sea. While on the island I was always pressed for time to obtain the particular tern shots I wanted before I would have to leave the island because of the tide. Paul had little time himself to spend in the blind. Much of the time he spent rowing me out to the island or back, or waiting for the opportunity. His patience I will never forget.

Nor will I forget his companionship during the long hours, sometimes half-days, we had to kill just waiting on the mainland or on the island.

We called it quits on June 30, dismantling the blind and bringing it back to the mainland, then packing our cars. The next day we departed our separate ways, I heading directly to Middleton, anxious to get into my darkroom in the cellar of my home, there to develop my film. The results with my new Graflex were more successful than I ever dared hope. In the near future, the prints I made from the negatives would serve me well.

CHAPTER 11 / *Cornell Graduate Student, First Year*

AFTER THE SOJOURN with the Sugar Loaf island terns, my 1930 summer followed with no further ornithological activities but my attending Cornell University for graduate work was more than ever on my mind. The realization that no firm arrangements for living in Ithaca had been made also concerned me. In April, Dr. Allen had told me that he knew of a room in a faculty home he felt sure he could obtain for me. He would inquire and let me know.

By late August, I was so concerned about not hearing from Dr. Allen that I wrote to him. No response. Eleanor departed for Martha's Vineyard, returning to her job. Finally, in a letter dated September 16, Dr. Allen replied that the room he had hoped to reserve for me would not be available, and advised me to get in touch with him upon my arrival in case I had trouble finding one. In the same letter Dr. Allen added: "George Sutton, the bird artist, is coming here for work this fall and he has written also regarding a room."

George Sutton, the bird artist? I concluded that he must be George *Miksch* Sutton, whose series of frontispieces of woodpeckers in full color had been appearing recently in *Bird-Lore.* Imagine having such a talented man as a fellow student! I assumed correctly that he would be a graduate student. I looked forward to knowing him.

Since registration for Cornell students would be September 22–23 and instruction would begin on the twenty-fifth, I was soon off in my new roadster on the twenty-second for a day's drive, reaching Ithaca before sundown and concerned about finding a room. Luck was with me for, as I drove up the hill from downtown Ithaca toward the Cornell campus, I crossed Lake Street on which I spotted a sign pointing to a three-storied house bearing the notice about rooms for rent. No time did I lose. I was greeted at the door by three spinsters who escorted me to their last remaining untaken room, on the third floor. With a comfortable-looking bed, a bureau, two chairs, and a desk, I took it gladly. My hostesses would serve me breakfast; for other meals I would be on my own, at restaurants or cafeterias uphill on the campus or in College-town, reached from the campus by a bridge south over Casca-dilla Gorge.

In the spring when I visited Ithaca, Dr. Allen had met me at the train and driven me directly to McGraw Hall for our conference in his office; afterwards he drove me directly back to the station. I had been so intent on my conversation with Dr. Allen as to pay little attention to the Cornell campus, let alone McGraw Hall.

One of the oldest buildings of the university, founded in 1865, McGraw truly showed its age. Much of the central interior had once been a three-storied museum of natural history, but in the passing of time and growth of the university it had been encroached upon for space to suit other purposes. Its exhibit cases on the main floor and balconies had been shoved close together to make room for offices, classrooms, and laboratories, reached by a maze of narrow passageways.

Following breakfast the first morning I promptly drove up to the campus, a steep ascent, seeking McGraw Hall on the west side of the campus quadrangle and therein, after getting confused a few times, finding Dr. Allen in his office on the second floor. Welcoming me warmly and introducing me to his assistant, Peter Paul Kellogg, Dr. Allen gave me a tour of the old building. First he led me up one flight of stairs on the north side of the building to Dr. Wright's vertebrate laboratory, then down half a flight into ornithology's "Grad Lab"—a huge room accommodating several big desks. He assigned me to my desk by a large window providing a magnificent view of the city below. Then we went downstairs to the ornithology classroom with a big table running its length, the walls flanked by steel cases containing bird skins, and finally to the basement with its darkrooms for photographic purposes and its corridors walled by all sorts of refrigerators for storage of vertebrate specimens, bird or otherwise, of varying sizes. The south side of McGraw was devoted to geology.

Now that I had my desk and had gotten my bearings on the campus, I proceeded at once to register and pay fees, standing in line it seemed for hours to take care of all routine entrance matters. I remember my next ten days as a veritable whirl. There were classes to meet, those in entomology given on the so-called "Ag Campus," adjoining the main campus a mile or so away from McGraw Hall. There were arrangements to make for preparing myself to show reading ability in two foreign languages, in my case French and German.

I met and held conferences with Drs. Wright and Needham, who seemed pleased to serve on my doctoral committee. They could not have shown greater interest in my objectives as a graduate student and my professional intentions later. I was immediately at ease with them, as with Dr. Allen.

In the Grad Lab I soon became acquainted with the other students and their projects: George B. Saunders, studying the distribution and behavior of the two North American species of meadowlarks; Wilfred A. Welter, focusing his attention on the (long-billed) marsh wren; Elizabeth Kingsbury, investigating the life history of the bobolink; James Crouch, working on the cedar waxwing. The enthusiasm of all for their projects was infectious. Moreover, the attitude of everyone toward the work of fellow students was cooperative, each willingly sharing experiences as well as giving assistance and advice.

Then on October 2 arrived a new member of the Grad Lab: George Sutton, following his return from Southampton Island in the Arctic. With his presence an increased enthusiasm permeated the atmosphere. In an unbelievably short period he had talked with every student, offering help or useful ideas as well as encouragement. Finding that I was to study the American woodcock, he was delighted. Right off he asked whether he could do the frontispiece when my work was published. He could indeed, was my response.

In the next several days George and I took long walks and dined together. We were drawn to each other through so many mutual interests that in no time we became close friends. Although nine years my senior, to me George seemed my age. About my height, he was slightly heavier with a fair complexion and wearing a thin mustache. He bore a naturally serious expression, bordering on a scowl. But with people, greeting and talking with them, any such expression disappeared. Basically, he was an extrovert.

Since George was older than I, it was only natural that I was curious as to what he had been doing and why graduate work now. I soon learned that his professional career had begun in 1919 in association with the Carnegie Museum in Pittsburgh, Pennsylvania. Among his many friends in the Pittsburgh area was John Bonner Semple, a munitions inventor-manufacturer and a born sportsman whom George persuaded to sponsor and participate in ornithological expeditions for the benefit of the Carnegie Museum. In 1925 came a turn of events for George when the Board of Game Commissioners of Pennsylvania urged him to head their Bureau of Research and Information. To make their offer sufficiently attractive, he would be called "state ornithologist." George accepted but was soon in politics, which he detested. "What I wanted to be," he said, "was an ornithologist knowledgeable enough to draw birds well, write good books, and teach younger people."

Thus, in the summer of 1929, George broke away from the Game Commission and registered as a graduate student at Cornell University for a Ph.D. under Dr. Allen. His thesis would be a report on his year-long exploration of Southampton Island in the North American Far North, and he set out at once.

Now here we were at Cornell. George, already having done his research, would be a graduate student for only two more years during which he would write his thesis and fulfill course and language requirements. Of course, Dr. Allen chaired his committee. The other two members of it were Dr. Wright and Walter King Stone of the Fine Arts Department.

George was rooming in the top-floor apartment in the home of the late Louis Agassiz Fuertes, north of the campus across Fall Creek Gorge on Wyckoff Avenue. Having studied under Fuertes years before at the Fuertes summer home on Cayuga Lake, George knew the family well and took me during one of our walks to meet Fuertes's widow, who continued to occupy the family home. A little person, most cordial in manner and ever ready with a humorous remark, Mrs. Fuertes was a delight. I would drop in with George to visit with her several times in the academic year getting under way.

George and I had barely known each other before I made it clear to him that I could never hope to draw birds, as I had neither the inclination nor talent. My forte was photographing birds and, to prove it, I showed him my collection of tern pictures taken the previous summer. Not only was he greatly impressed, but he insisted right then and there that I select some of them immediately for publication in a paper, explaining the behavior shown in each photograph and analyzing the use of feathers during the behavior. I went ahead with the text in spare moments during the ensuing weeks—now and then receiving George's help on technical expressions—and finally submitted the paper for publication in *The Wilson Bulletin*. It was accepted and appeared in the September issue for 1931.

As our acquaintance grew closer, George revealed a tantalizing prospect for late next spring. He told me that by chance—not by prior planning—he had returned from Southampton Island late the summer before by ship to Churchill, Manitoba, which lies back from the mouth of the great Churchill River on the west side of Hudson Bay, and from there he had taken the train back to the United States. While killing a few days waiting for the train, he found not far south of Churchill numerous Harris' sparrows on what probably had been their breeding grounds earlier in the year. As George explained, Harris' sparrows breed in north-central Canada west of Hudson Bay and were the only remaining North American bird species for which eggs had never been found. Always they nested so early in the spring that their eggs had hatched before people arrived. But now the Canadian government had built a railroad that could bring people to Churchill ahead of the breeding season. Here was an opportunity to beat the Harris' sparrows north, be there when they nested and laid their eggs—and be the first to find the eggs. George said he would propose to J. B. Semple, when in Pittsburgh over Thanksgiving, that Semple organize and finance an expedition, on behalf of the Carnegie Museum, to find the eggs. No doubt J. B. (as George always called him) would join the expedition. Then George asked me outright, "Would you like to go as photographer?" I jumped at the prospect and silently thanked my tern pictures for inspiring the question in the first place.

Already a traditional program of the Laboratory of Ornithology was a seminar every Monday evening which we as graduate students were expected to attend, while anyone else interested in birds, whether on the campus (student or teacher) or in town, was welcome. Whatever the program— usually announced in advance—it began with a reading of the local bird list on which were checked off the species seen in the past week by persons present in the room. If anyone reported a species out of season or range, he or she was immediately given the third degree and forced to defend the identification by describing the bird in minute detail. Failure meant no entry of the species on the week's list.

The first semester had been under way about a month when there was an exodus of all of us from the Grad Lab to attend the meeting of the American Ornithologists' Union, October 20–23, at the Peabody Museum in Salem, Massachusetts. The A.O.U., the leading organization of professional ornithologists in the United States and Canada, met once a year in one part or another of either country. That it should meet this year so close to my home in Middleton seemed too good to be true.

Dr. Allen had already left for the meeting, taking George Sutton with him in order for both to attend the business meeting on Monday, October 20. Before they departed, I invited George to stay overnight after the sessions with my parents and me at our home a few miles away. He accepted gladly. The first day of the A.O.U. meeting was devoted to business sessions of the Council, Fellows, and Members. Associates, which included all of us in the Grad Lab except George, were excluded. George had earlier been elected a Member in recognition of his accomplishments in Pennsylvania.

I was on hand promptly for all the public sessions on Tuesday through Thursday. Just about the first person I ran into was Dr. Gross, all smiles and for good reason: on Monday he had been elected a Fellow in recognition of his work on the heath hen and other birds. Gradually, among the 180 or so people attending the three days of public sessions, I began to see and even meet some of the people who to me, heretofore, had simply been distinguished names in ornithology.

Close to sixty papers were given during the three days. On the second and third days, "General Sessions" and "Technical Sessions" ran concurrently in different rooms. This was regular practice at A.O.U. meetings, I was to learn, and frequently resulted in persons leaving one room while a paper was being given and rushing to the other room to hear the paper there, and *vice versa*. There was constant traffic, back and forth, in and out; those giving papers paid no heed, seemingly expecting walk-outs and walk-ins. On studying my eight-page program, I was in a dilemma; there were so many good papers to choose from, some of them conflicting. But there were at least two papers I would hear regardless of conflicts with others: Dr. Allen's success story of raising ruffed grouse in captivity, and George Sutton's account of his year with the birds on Southampton Island. I noted no walk-outs from either paper.

By Friday, when George left with me for Ithaca after staying at my home for three nights, he had won two more staunch admirers—my parents. In letters to me thereafter, Mother almost always asked to be remembered to George.

Back from the A.O.U. meeting, it was time for me to "think woodcock" and get on with my research on the species. First of all, I needed specimens. To obtain them, Dr. Allen broadcast over the radio urging local sportsmen to give their long-billed quarry to the Laboratory of Ornithology for scientific purposes. In no time I had all the woodcock needed for external and internal anatomical studies, for analysis of stomach contents, and for study skins. For expert instruction in the technique of preparing study skins, I was grateful to George Sutton.

I also began an extensive search of the literature for information about woodcock. Here I had a great advantage—access to the Cornell Library with one of the most extensive collections of ornithological books and journals in any library in the country. Weeks of searching lay ahead, which included making out reference cards to articles about woodcock for later consultation.

Ornithological literature at the time (1930–31) consisted largely of regional lists of birds, reports on taxonomic studies, and treatises on life histories, migration, and food habits. The result of my labors was an enormous file of data on the distribution and relative abundance of woodcock in the various states and Canadian provinces within its range, but very little on the life history of the species. There were half a dozen detailed descriptions of flight-singing, a few miscellaneous observations on incubating birds and injury-feigning, and some reports of birds carrying their young. Obviously, I had much field work cut out for myself, come spring.

My turn for performing at a Monday-night seminar was scheduled soon after the next Christmas holidays. I decided to give a talk on the terns and gulls of the Maine coast and illustrate it with lantern slides, forty altogether, from the best of my photographs. The slides would be glass and would have to be hand-colored. Early in December, allowing myself plenty of time, I set to work on them with water colors and brushes.

Hand-coloring glass slides! No artist myself, I had to learn. Fortunately, I had George Sutton to teach me at least the fundamentals of putting on water colors. I had seen so many ghastly colored slides projected at seminars—solid blue for sky and solid green for foliage, frequently overlapping; the color patterns of birds so smudged as to be barely recognizable—that I was determined to have mine as faithful to the subjects as my crude talents would allow. After struggling at odd hours for days or nights, sometimes so mismanaging the colors as to require washing the slides and starting over, I was ready for the seminar on January 12, 1931. In a way it was a significant date in my career as it marked the first illustrated talk or lecture I ever gave.

Between early December, when I began coloring lantern slides and my showing them on January 12, there were other developments. George had just returned from Thanksgiving in Pittsburgh where, true to his word, he had proposed to J. B. that I go with them in the spring to Churchill as photographer. J. B. was entirely agreeable. All of my expenses would be paid; my negatives would become the property of the Carnegie Museum, although I was assured use of prints from them for my own purposes. Besides my being photographer on the expedition, George and J. B. thought that I should assist them in collecting birds and preparing their skins for the Carnegie Museum when bad weather prohibited photography. In the munitions business himself, J. B. offered to acquire for me at cost a Winchester 12-gauge, double-barreled shotgun, equipped with an auxiliary .410 barrel that could be inserted in one of the regular barrels for small birds. I gladly accepted his offer with the provision that I would have the gun for practice long before leaving Ithaca. (I had never shot a bird in my life.) The weapon, properly disassembled in its sturdy carrying case, arrived early enough as promised.

Ever since summer, Eleanor and I had kept up a steady exchange of correspondence about our ups and downs, mostly ups. In December Eleanor was elated to be offered a teaching job, starting in January, in Pembroke just a few miles southeast of Boston. Much as she liked Martha's Vineyard, the lovely island itself as well as her friends there, she was happy to come to the mainland for teaching and thus be able to spend her weekends with Auntie Brown in Middleton.

As during my Bowdoin days, Christmas at home was full of pleasures with my family, this time including my grandparents. Eleanor and I were on the go, taking in movies, having parties with friends. All too soon it was time to go our separate ways, Eleanor to Pembroke and I to Ithaca. This time I left my roadster, deciding to reach Ithaca by train and bus, not needing my car until I could pick it up when I returned for the Easter recess.

Back at the Grad Lab, I was deflated by George Sutton's change in attitude toward me. Barely did he speak aside from greeting me and answering my questions curtly. Had I offended him? He assured me that I hadn't. Was our trip next spring to Hudson Bay called off? It wasn't, he replied emphatically. For the next several days he continued solemn. Upon his arrival at the Grad Lab he greeted me in a matter-of-fact manner, then went directly to his desk where he settled down to work. He asked none of us to have lunch with him. I was totally mystified by his behavior. Then came the day when George was himself again—outgoing, making comical observations on one or another of us, or on some current event. Following my lecture at the Monday-night seminar, he couldn't have complimented me more highly.

It was not long after my seminar when Mrs. Fuertes asked George if he knew of a young man "congenial to him" who would like to occupy next fall the vacant room next to his in her top-floor apartment. George thought of me at once, said he would sound me out, and he did. I accepted the opportunity without a moment's hesitation.

For us at the Grad Lab, life in winter was not all work. On returning from supper we often played a couple of vigorous rounds of slapjack, using two packs of cards always available for the purpose on the center table. Lucky was the player whose hand escaped without a bruise, a scratch, or gouge if it was the first one to come down on the suddenly upturned jack. We were content to settle down to work after the rounds, nursing whatever wounds we might have acquired.

If ice and snow conditions were favorable, suitably garbed we gathered in the evening on Beebe Lake, northeast of the main campus, to skate or to take rides on the toboggan chute that ended up on the lake. On sparkling days we skied on the local golf course, even tried some steep slopes, though taking all sorts of sprawls and rarely reaching bottom.

Never were we lacking for opportunities to attend concerts and lectures sponsored by the university. Frequently we enjoyed the hospitality of Glenside, the Allen home on woodsy Kline Road which declined circuitously from Cayuga Heights to near Cayuga Lake level. Mrs. Allen, a pleasant, scholarly lady, delighted as much as her husband in entertaining us at receptions following programs by visiting ornithologists or on other occasions warranting social gatherings.

In late March, I was home in Middleton for the Easter recess, almost as glad to have my roadster again as I was to be with my parents and with Eleanor who was home on her vacation. Besides my usual activities on vacations, I gave much attention to equipment and necessities for the upcoming Hudson Bay expedition. I had to shop and buy two heavy blankets and some heavy clothing. Then I had a blind to make for photography: first, to construct its folding frame; second, to fit and sew a concealing cover for slipping over the frame when unfolded and standing. All this paraphernalia had to be packed, including film for my camera, and shipped off directly to the Carnegie Museum from whence it would be transshipped with the expedition's other equipment to Churchill.

I drove back to Ithaca on April 8, going first to the Grad Lab where I found George Sutton in another slump, greeting me but saying little more. Why? He had been to Pittsburgh, as he had been at Christmas, and returned in the same mood. Confident that in a few days he would be himself again—and that there would come a day soon when I would know the reason for the "post-Pittsburgh" slumps—I paid little attention to him. In any case, his slumps never again occurred.

In the weeks to follow I devoted afternoons and evenings, when not involved with classes, to field work on woodcock. I chose for the site of my study the Connecticut Hill Game Preserve belonging to the New York State Department of Conservation. The Preserve, southwest of Ithaca and about twenty-eight miles round-trip from the Cornell campus, embraced abandoned farmland consisting of fallow fields fringed by high shrubs and secondary woods.

Woodcock, early arrivals in the state, were probably nesting. My procedure was to locate the singing fields where the males gathered, one to a field, after sundown. Each male, once on the field, began uttering his peculiar *peent* sounds. Finally, when it was dark enough, he undertook a flight-song, spiraling upward for about two hundred feet, his wings whistling, then after circling and still whistling, he began a zigzag descent, chippering vocally until he neared the place where he had started, then ceased. In a few moments the bird, again on the ground, began peenting. Soon he ascended for another flight-song. The number of flight-songs performed depended on how long twilight prevailed. With total darkness, flight-singing stopped.

My studies during the early evenings at the preserve required recording all kinds of observations. For example: the relations of flight-singing to weather; measuring the amount of light required for flight-singing periods; the duration of flight-singing in relation to season; the area covered during flight-singing.

My original notion was that male woodcock performed near their nests. All I had to do, so I thought, was to search the vicinity of the singing fields thoroughly and I would run onto the nests. How wrong I was! Despite the hours of searching, not a nest did I find. Evidently the female woodcock flies to the singing field to mate with the male, then leaves. The male apparently hasn't any knowledge of where the nest is or where the female goes.

I ceased studying woodcock at Connecticut Hill in early May, sooner than I would have ordinarily, but mid-May, the time to leave for Hudson Bay, was fast approaching. I had already fulfilled the requirement to read French and German, yet there were still courses to finish in advance.

My first year at Cornell had been a gratifying experience, not only academically but personally. In particular did I come to admire the qualities of Dr. Allen. In his calm, unassuming yet persuasive way, he generated enthusiasm and encouragement. He was an unswerving optimist. His personal warmth made him easily approachable. He was never too busy or too tired to give me his undivided attention.

Inseparable from his prevailing optimism was his great sense of humor, his boundless capacity for the light touch. Whenever speaking at a seminar, in class, or in practically any situation, he could not pass up an opportunity to arouse a smile or laugh. Puns he found irresistible, and the more outrageous the better. He liked to tell stories involving amusing experiences at his own expense and he thoroughly enjoyed writing limericks. Invariably his humor was gentle, without rancor, and never intended to embarrass anyone.

Dr. Albert Hazen Wright—we called him Uncle Bert—was an entertaining instructor. His subject was vertebrate zoology (exclusive of birds), although his main interest was in reptiles and amphibians. In both laboratory and field he frequently interrupted his lectures with a story on himself or someone else that had nothing to do with the subject. He kept all of us up to date on the Boston Red Sox, baseball fan that he was. He knew the batting average of every player. One of his peculiarities in lecturing was to use the word "now" indiscriminately. This "now" frog; this "now" book. In no way did this habit fail to enhance his lectures; we simply accepted it as typically Uncle Bert.

One of the Last Three Heath Hens. Martha's Vineyard, April 6, 1928.

ᴀɪʀ ᴏꜰ Wɪʟʟᴏᴡ Pᴛᴀʀᴍɪɢᴀɴ. Churchill, Manitoba, 1931.

SEMIPALMATED PLOVER IN DISTRACTION DISPLAY. Churchill, Manitoba, 1931.

ναparte's Gull Chicks in Nest. Churchill, Manitoba, 1931.

BONAPARTE'S GULL. Churchill, Manitoba, 1931.

AMERICAN WOODCOCK ON NEST. Connecticut Hill near Ithaca, New York, May 15, 1932.

ᴛʟᴀɴᴛɪᴄ Pᴜꜰꜰɪɴ Cᴀʀʀʏɪɴɢ Hᴇʀʀɪɴɢ Fʀʏ ᴛᴏ Iᴛs Cʜɪᴄᴋ. Machias Seal Island, 1932.

BOREAL CHICKADEE. Grand Manan, New Brunswick, late June, 1935.

ᴘɪɴɢ Plover. Jones Beach State Bird Sanctuary on Long Island, June 13, 1935.

CHAPTER 12 / *To Hudson Bay*

THE ITINERARY FOR our Hudson Bay expedition was now set. Accordingly, I left Ithaca on May 16, 1931, bound for Middleton. That same day George Sutton headed for the Carnegie Museum to meet with J. B. Semple and together line up equipment for camping, collecting birds, and preparing skins. Happy was this day for me when I moved out of my third-floor room on State Street, harboring the pleasant prospect of living in the Fuertes home, come fall.

Middleton on May 17 was a slow day for me. Eleanor was still away teaching in Pembroke and my parents were attending out-of-town meetings. After putting my car away and packing, I had time to spare in the afternoon and decided to look for birds in the local lowland woods. The next morning I awoke with my face and hands broken out in big red blotches, my lips parched, my eyelids burning. Paying too much attention to birds the previous afternoon, I had gotten into some poison ivy. Father, appalled, swabbed my face and hands with a dressing of some sort, though it failed to relieve the misery or improve my looks. In the late afternoon, in accordance with my schedule, Father drove me into Boston's South Station. Tugging a big suitcase plus a Graflex camera and a Winchester 12-gauge shotgun, each in its own carrying case, I made it from Father's car to the train about to head west.

Later, hungry and entering the dining car, I was escorted to a two-seated table, assigned one of the two empty seats, and handed a menu. A few moments later a man was assigned the seat opposite me, given a menu, but instead of looking at the menu he looked at me, rigid and stared, obviously repulsed at what he saw. To allay his fears that I might have some horrible disease, I pointed to my face and quietly said, "Poison ivy," whereupon he turned to his menu, never again giving me as much as a glance.

My immediate destination was Chicago where I would visit, for two nights and a day between, with Bowdoin friends who had been Psi U undergraduates when I was a senior. I had told them about my forthcoming adventure and they had insisted that I stop off and let them show me the town. Indeed they did, shocked as they were at my appearance and embarrassed when introducing me to anyone. We toured the Field Museum, the Aquarium, the Lincoln Park Zoo, and even the grounds for the World's Fair in 1933. By the time they put me aboard the train bound north on the second morning, I had begun to look fairly respectable. On the third morning my problem was barely noticeable.

I slept soundly that night in my Pullman sleeper, awaking in Superior, Wisconsin, for breakfast in the dining car. Afterwards, the view from the train began with the forest and lake country of northern Minnesota, then the prairie country of southern Manitoba, and ending in the big, modern city of Winnipeg in the evening of May 21. George and Mr. Semple were waiting for me at the station.

At last here was the great J. B., about whose character and traits George had discoursed often, especially his enthusiasm for field projects. At times George had spoken of J. B.'s tendencies to be unbearably imperious, to pontificate, and to play practical jokes. I hardly knew what I would be expecting of this man before me: short, of heavy build, his hair closely cropped, his manner congenial. George had forewarned me to address him always as "Mr. Semple," as only George and very few other people had the privilege of calling him "J. B." in his presence.

After our night's stay at the Fort Garry Hotel and a little hasty shopping, all three of us were aboard the Hudson Bay Railroad on its weekly, thousand-mile trip to Churchill. Now began a new experience, a journey from spring back to winter. All day the vernal green gradually disappeared as we traversed country consistently flat and monotonous. For us, passing the time included mainly eating, sleeping, and playing three-handed contract bridge. Few birds did we ever see. The next morning we reached the halfway stop, The Pas, the

only community of any consequence, where the arrival of the
weekly train north was its big event. Vast numbers of people,
including many Indians, were awaiting on the platform. Since
we had over an hour to get out and stretch our legs, we left
the train and headed directly to the brushy outskirts of the
town to look for birds. Among them were a few Harris' sparrows, the first I had ever seen.

Here was the bird whose undiscovered eggs we were
after. I was impressed as much by the large size of the Harris'
sparrow as I was by its distinctive appearance: a pink bill in
contrast to a black crown, face, and throat, and white underparts. The sexes were alike.

Our long train ride to Churchill finally ended the next evening, May 24. All that day we saw harbingers of what to expect:
snow. From the train we stepped into it, two feet deep, and
we in our spring attire. A gust of bitter wind whisked off
George's straw hat. Waiting to greet us was Bert (Albert C.)
Lloyd whom J. B. had engaged as the fourth member of our
party. A good ornithologist, Bert already knew the Churchill
region from previous experience.

There was no standing around in this frigid weather for
any of us. Heaping our luggage into a tractor-truck, we made
for the headquarters of the construction camp to meet the
boss (I never knew his name) of the Department of Railways
and Canals. He was unaware of our coming.

We had some explaining to do. We were here to look for
birds and would disturb nobody; we had the necessary docu-
ments from the government granting us permission to come
and stay, to carry on with our project. We wanted to establish
our camp on the outskirts of town near the mouth of the
Churchill River. Meanwhile, we were in desperate need of ac-
commodations until we had the camp.

Although obviously taken by surprise by our unan-
nounced appearance, the boss was nonetheless agreeable to
meeting our needs. He assigned us some rooms and gave us
permission to take meals in the mess hall with the workmen,
all sixteen hundred of them, who were building the grain elevator. He would have his men set up our camp, actually a
tent, ready for occupancy by the following afternoon.

At six o'clock the next morning we all piled into the mess

hall with the whole working crew. There were no greetings, no conversations. Food was plentiful and excellent. We were there to consume it, to stoke our furnaces in the shortest possible time, and be off.

Churchill in 1931 was an enterprise, not a town. Here by the Churchill River a huge grain elevator of cemented gravel was under construction for storage of grain from the western provinces before transportation by ship to foreign ports. On higher ground along the river between the elevator and Hudson Bay were rows of bunkhouses, a hospital, banks, and headquarters of the Royal Canadian Mounted Police.

A short walk south and east of Churchill brought us into Arctic tundra—bare, mossy, and cushion-like with occasional shallow lakes, some large enough to bear such names as Landing and Rosabelle. Dwarf willows, crowberry, and juniper fronds comprised the few shrubs. The sole interruptions in this otherwise open plain were outcroppings of bare granite.

We were at the southern limits of the Arctic tundra, for barely six miles south of Churchill was the timberline, the northernmost limit of the spruce forest, its trees here stunted, gnarled, and twisted, intermixed with tundra growth. We called this area "the bush" and it was important to us because this was the nesting habitat of the Harris' sparrow. Fortunately, in the bush nearest Churchill, the Department of Railways and Canals had a gravel pit to which, once the snow had disappeared, the company sent its cars frequently for the necessary building material. We were welcome to ride on the cars. Indeed, the engineers and firemen stopped to give us a ride whenever we waved to them.

Churchill was still in the grip of winter. Hudson Bay was covered with massive ice chunks and Churchill River was icebound several miles back from the bay. There was considerable snow cover in and around Churchill with some snowdrifts as high as ten feet. How were we going to live in a tent? I went to sleep the first night in my snug room after much wondering about it.

Our camp, as we had hoped, was on the south side of Churchill near the mouth of the river. Already it had a floor with a frame for a tent, used in the previous year. Now, as authorized by the company's boss, some workmen in the morning shoveled snow off the floor, put up the company's ready-made tent over the frame, carried in and set up a stove, lugged in armfuls of wood for the little heat we could expect, brought in chairs, and helped us set up a worktable. Beds? None. We had our own sleeping bags to spread out on the floor. J. B., very much a private person, had his silk tent mounted on a platform a few feet away from ours. In it he put his personal effects including his sleeping bag. No stove did he want.

By afternoon we were already preparing bird skins in our camp, establishing a routine followed in the days ahead. Our specimens we collected on the nearby tundra, or further south in the bush, in the morning and prepared them as skins in the afternoon. J. B. did very little collecting himself and never prepared skins, but greatly enjoyed watching *us* prepare specimens, praising our work and the fine collection growing daily. I became fairly proficient and speedy when it came to skinning the birds, but there was no way I could keep up with George in "putting up" the skins afterwards. With a small bird in good condition to begin with, George could skin it out, insert the materials to recreate the shape of the bird, and sew it up in fifteen to twenty minutes. Becoming impatient with my slowness in putting up specimens, George suggested that I just skin the birds and let him put them up. This procedure I gladly accepted, shortening our time spent on specimens.

My photography in the beginning amounted to shooting scenic effects, people, and company activities. Photographing birds would have to wait until they nested and I could get close to them. The snow was fast disappearing as the days grew warmer. Bird migration was at its height. Willow ptarmigan, permanent residents, were numerous about our camp. I took pleasure in photographing a particular pair, both seemingly fearless. The cock stood on a ledge, his rich chestnut-colored neck feathers contrasting sharply with his otherwise white winter plumage.

On May 27, Bert Lloyd had great news for us. He had returned from the bush where he had seen a Harris' sparrow. (Our quarry we had beaten north by three days!) From now on at least one of us explored the bush daily, watching for the arrival of more Harris' sparrows.

The sparrow was very much on our minds as we prepared skins or lay in our sleeping bags. Questions. Speculations. In the first place, where did it nest? On the ground, in a shrub or tree? Nobody knew. And how would we find the nests? George's advice: look everywhere—on the ground, under bushes, in trees, in holes in the ground. And watch the birds constantly. The easiest way to find some nests is to watch a bird that has a piece of grass, or a feather, or a twig in its bill. Keep your eye on the bird and follow it as it may be taking whatever it has to the nest.

Before we realized it, nearly a week had passed which had included long treks to the bush (often missing a noon meal), skins to prepare, and field notes to write up on our return. Spring was progressing rapidly. The mosquitoes had arrived in force, frustrating our observations through the bobbinets we wore over our heads. I had already succeeded in photographing a tree sparrow nesting and found later a few nests of other species; I photographed the adults occupying them.

We had yet to find a Harris' sparrow nest but were confident that we would. When we did, the eggs were to be collected immediately, to avoid our losing them should a predator discover them first. Much as we wanted photographs of the eggs in a nest, and the nest in its original position, the eggs safely preserved would be more important. Furthermore, the parent birds should be collected along with the eggs as proof that the eggs were those of the Harris' sparrow.

All this time it seemed certain that it would be one of the four of us who would find the first set of eggs. Then suddenly any such confidence was shattered. Four Canadians had come to find the eggs. We had rivals! George called them "our enemy."

The four of us were asleep early on the night of June 7 when we were awakened by male voices outside the tent. After they announced who they were and where they were from (Alberta), we invited them in while we stayed in our bags. We were civil but hardly hospitable as we responded to their queries about the birds we had been seeing—knowing full well what they were leading up to. Yes, the Harris' sparrows were here in abundance but we had found no nests. Telling us that they had arrived by train (the same one we had come on a week before) and were camping in a freight car, they departed, expressing their hope that we would soon become better acquainted. After this visitation was over, we could hear J. B. in his tent muttering about those intrusive Canadians.

Now we were wide awake with no more restful sleep in prospect. Furthest from the thought of anyone of us in our party was becoming famous as the discoverer of the Harris' sparrow eggs. Our major concern: find the eggs before the Canadians do!

In the following days at least two of us searched the bush daily, ever alert for any signs of a Harris' sparrow with nesting inclinations. Whenever the weather was pleasant with a sky conducive to photography, I worked with my camera on nesting birds, wherever they might be.

On June 15, a dull day for photography, I stayed in the bush to watch for Harris' sparrows. Despite all the hours I spent, I experienced only a few moments of excitement when I saw a Harris' sparrow with grass in its beak dropping to the ground some distance away. It did not repeat the act. Later I inspected the area where the bird had disappeared with the grass, but all I could find was a bunch of grass, with a hole in it, under a shrub. A mouse nest, probably.

The next day, June 16, George Sutton found the first nest of the Harris' sparrow with four eggs. Here, in his own words, he tells about his discovery.

At a little before nine o'clock, while marching across an all but impassable bog, I frightened from a sphagnum island underfoot a slim, dark-backed bird. It made no outcry, but from an explosive flutter of its wings I knew it had left a nest. I searched a moment, parting with my hand the tough, slender twigs of flowering Labrador tea. And there was the nest—with four eggs that in the cool shadow had a dark appearance. The mother bird, by this time, was chirping in alarm. I looked at her briefly with my glass. A Harris' sparrow! I raised the gun, took careful aim, and fired. Marking the nest, I ran to pick her up. Upon my return, the male appeared. I shot him also, for I knew the record would not be complete unless I shot both parent birds. To say that I was happy is to describe my feelings all too tamely. I was beside myself. Shooting those important specimens had taken control. I had been so excited I had hardly been able to hold the gun properly. As I knelt to examine the nest a thrill the like of which I have never felt before passed through me. And I talked aloud! "Here!" I said, "Here in this beautiful place!" At my fingertips lay treasures that were beyond price. Mine was Man's first glimpse of the eggs of the Harris' sparrow, in the lovely bird's wilderness home.

Then I began to wonder how many other nests had been found that morning. The enemy! My comrades! Had they, too, been favored by Heaven with a sign? I had a wild desire to gather everybody about me—friend and foe alike—so that we might work together, compare notes, make plans, take photographs. I looked at my watch. Perhaps some Canadian had found a nest at eight o'clock! Perhaps several nests had been found before nine o'clock that morning! I fired my shotgun loudly as I could (have you ever tried this?) three times, and was a little surprised, as the echoes died, that no familiar form of friend nor unfamiliar form of foe materialized. I fired again. There was no answer.

So, happy in a way that was quite new to me, but dubious as to the priority of my achievement, I hippity-hopped across the bogs. I wasn't much of an ornithologist those next few hours. . . . At a little before noon I chanced to see Bert Lloyd ahead of me. I started to call him—then decided not to. A wild fear seized me. Perhaps all this happiness of the last three hours was unwarranted. Perhaps all this had been some weird hallucination. I knelt on the moss, opened my collecting creel, got out those two specimens I had shot at the nest, and looked at them closely. Yes, they were Harris' sparrows, there could not be the slightest doubt of that. They were not white-crowned sparrows, nor fox sparrows, nor tree sparrows. No, there was nothing wrong with me this time.

"Bert!" I shouted, trying to keep my voice normal. And Bert turned and came. "What luck?" I asked. And Bert gave me the usual report—plenty of birds, mated pairs too, but no nest. Queer that he couldn't see how boiling over I was with excitement.

So I told him. And Bert's response was the response of a good friend, a good sport, a good ornithologist. His words were cordial and the exultant delight that shone from his face was genuine. I showed him the specimens. And from that time until the reunion of our party that evening, the two of us wondered how many other nests had been found that day.

To be perfectly honest, I was hoping that nobody else had found a nest. In a vague sort of way I wanted my good friend J. B. to have the thrill of it all—but he had been successful in so many ways that I felt this purely ornithological triumph might quite justly be mine. And Sewall—well, if Sewall had found a nest before nine o'clock that morning he was just too lucky for tolerance. But the Canadians!

Bert and I got back about six o'clock. We were a little late at the mess hall. The workmen frowned as we came in, for they knew the cook would be angry, and we were wet and dirty. But we didn't care. Let them frown. Let them despise us. We were above being despised. J. B. and Sewall were busy stoking—almost too busy to notice us. We sat down. When there was a clatter of departing workmen I leaned toward J. B. and said, "Did you find the nest today?" J. B. said he hadn't. "I found one—with four eggs in it," I rejoined. And the stoking stopped.

I have never, neither before nor since, seen J. B. look as he looked at precisely that moment. He may have been wishing that he had found the nest. He may have been as jealous as a successful, vigorous, fair-minded, generous sportsman can at times be. He may quite possibly have hated me for my insolence. But I think he was happy. *

It was not until June 20 that the next Harris' sparrow nest, also with four eggs, was found—and I found it. I had missed my claim to fame by four days. Thereafter, nests were found by all of us including the Canadians.

On June 21, J. B. announced that he, George, and I would be leaving Churchill, terminating the expedition, on July 6. (Bert Lloyd would continue staying at Churchill.) This would give us two more weeks for collecting and, best of all for me, for photography. The nesting season was under way in full force. I found nests nearly every day as did members of my party who called them to my attention. In no time at all I had pictures of such common species as the Hoyt's horned lark, the hoary redpoll, and both the Lapland and Smith's longspurs.

Several species of shorebirds were common. When with their nests or young, they were ideal subjects for the camera because they were approachable. Once, on finding a least sandpiper nest containing eggs and wanting to photograph the bird on it, I set up my blind very close to the nest and crawled in with my camera. Before I was ready to take shots, the bird had already returned to the nest. After I took the pic-

*George Miksch Sutton, *Birds in the Wilderness* (New York: Macmillan), 1936.

tures and stepped out of the blind, the sandpiper continued to sit on the nest. My blind would have been unnecessary.

When I neared shorebirds with their broods of chicks, the parents frequently put on distraction displays—broken-wing acts—excellent for photography. I took shots of a semipalmated plover's efforts—waving its wings, crouching with spread, white-tipped tail, and then running away rodentlike, as if enticing me to follow. A stilt sandpiper performed before me with equal fervor, though it lacked the striking color patterns of the semipalmated plover's to accentuate the performance.

But the departure date was approaching too rapidly for me because many pairs of Bonaparte's gulls were now nesting in some of the isolated spruce trees bordering the lakes on the tundra and in the bush. Besides being attracted to these little black-headed gulls, I was fascinated with the idea of gulls of any size nesting in trees. Furthermore, little was known about the Bonaparte's breeding habits. Mustering my courage, I asked J. B. if he would sponsor my staying another week so as to investigate and photograph the gulls. Bert Lloyd would be staying. All the Canadians had left except one, Arthur C. Twomey, with whom Bert and I had struck up a close acquaintance. Arthur had become as fascinated as I by the gulls. J. B. was agreeable and wished us well as we accompanied him and George to the train in the evening of July 6. At the time we thought of the weather that had greeted us the evening of May 24!

The usual nest of the Bonaparte's gull, a compact construction of twigs, lichens, and mosses, fits deeply into the thickly foliaged branch of a spruce. On July 11, Bert and I found one such nest eight feet up in a spruce, its position given away by an adult flying from it, protesting our presence. In the nest were two newly hatched chicks and one pipped egg. So that I could photograph the contents, Bert climbed the tree, carefully loosened the nest from the branch, and passed both nest and contents down to me on the ground and in sunlight. I lost no time in taking pictures and passing the nest up to Bert who placed it firmly in its original position. I learned later that my photographs of the newly hatched chicks were the first ever taken.

Not surprisingly, much of my last day, July 13, was devoted to packing, but I found the time for one last visit to the bush. I was back for supper to stoke in the mess hall with Bert Lloyd and Arthur Twomey. After they had helped me with my luggage to the railroad station, we had an hour or more to reminisce before the train began to pull out at ten o'clock. I saw from my window the aborning grain elevator silhouetted against the sunset and watched it disappear from view as the train picked up speed.

What an expedition it had been! We had not only achieved our goal—becoming the first to find the eggs of the Harris' sparrow—but we had also made a fine collection of bird specimens representing eighty-eight species, and I had exposed over five hundred negatives which should provide ample coverage of twenty bird species and miscellaneous shots of many others.

CHAPTER 13/*Cornell Graduate Student, Second Year*

BY JULY 20, 1931, I was with my parents in Wayne where they had preceded me. I had been met at the South Station, Boston, by one of the sanatorium staff and driven to Middleton, where I picked up my car and rushed to see Eleanor and Auntie Brown. Immediately Eleanor and I made plans for being together in Wayne from August 1 to 12.

Never was Wayne lovelier nor Lake Androscoggin more enticing than in that period— especially Lake Androscoggin in the evening of August 2. There was no breeze; the stars sparkled. I asked Eleanor, "How about going out on the lake in the rowboat, first putting a blanket and some pillows on the floor to lie on, and then just let the boat drift?" "Wonderful idea," was her quick reply. Little did she know I had something special in mind. Once out on the lake I revealed it: "Eleanor, will you marry me?" Her sweet, softly spoken response: "I'd love to." How long we drifted on the lake thereafter seemed timeless. We talked on and on about how we wanted our future together, how many children we should have, where we would live. I remember only one decision: Eleanor would announce the engagement formally during the Christmas period. As if the engagement would be a surprise! Many of our relatives and friends would wonder why we had taken so long. After all, we had been going together, beginning in high school, for about ten years.

Our sojourn in Wayne over, Eleanor and I returned to Middleton where I set to work developing and printing the Churchill photographs. I found the time to play tennis with Eleanor until she had to be back teaching in Pembroke, to have an occasional round of golf with Father, and to play croquet in the evening with Father and the sanatorium doctors.

George Sutton was delighted with the photographs, prints of which I rushed to him in batches as soon as they were ready.

In late September, I returned to Ithaca for my second year of graduate work, this time under living circumstances so much more pleasant than the previous year's as to defy comparison. In the Fuertes home on Wyckoff Avenue, Mrs. Fuertes was at home to greet me, as was George Sutton. According to previous arrangements, George and I were to have three rooms on the top floor to ourselves. In one room would be our beds. In the second, we would keep our clothes and have ample room for storage of personal paraphernalia and field equipment. And in the third, a large room running the length of the north side of the house, which had been Louis Fuertes's studio, we would be free to work whenever we wanted to get away from the hubbub of the Grad Lab.

Mrs. Fuertes insisted that we have breakfast every morning with her. Endowed with both charm and wit, never losing an opportunity for a quip, she started out our days on a happy note. She adored movies. When there was a good one in town, George, or I, or the both of us escorted her.

The Grad Lab had come to life. Among the new arrivals was John T. Emlen whom we liked at once. He looked hardly old enough to be out of high school. And back from his observations on the birds of Madagascar was Austin Rand, who would be writing his thesis on the birdlife of that remote island.

Already there was excitement in the air about attending the forty-ninth meeting of the American Ornithologists' Union at the Book-Cadillac Hotel in Detroit, and the Museum of Zoology at the University of Michigan, Ann Arbor. Scheduled for October 20–23, invitations were already out to send in artwork for exhibits and to apply for spaces on the program during which to give papers.

Upon George Sutton's insistence, I lost no time in having several of my favorite photographs of Churchill birds blown up in large prints, framed, and sent promptly. I was informed by mail that my request to show photographs of Churchill birds had not only been granted, but that I was invited to show my lantern slides during the last afternoon as one of the three special attractions at the Cranbrook Institute of Science in Bloomfield Hills. Right then and there I could see that my work was cut out for me as I had chosen thirty-five photographs for lantern slides to hand-color, with George's promise to help with his artistry.

I drove to the meeting, Bill Welter and John Emlen accompanying me. There were fifty-four papers on the program. During the first evening, George told of his explorations of Southampton Island about which he was writing his thesis. I was pleased to see Dr. Gross again and hear him report on his bird studies the previous summer along the Canadian Labrador. Then came my turn on the program at Cranbrook. After giving my introduction I asked to have the lights out. To my horror the slides barely showed up on the screen! The best I could do was to describe what the slides showed. This I did, having them projected as briefly as possible. Then I sat down in utter dismay as the house lights came on. Suddenly from far back in the auditorium came a loud voice, "There was something wrong with the projector; be patient, we have another projector." The replacement projector set up, I asked for lights out as before. This time the slides showed up on the screen in their full brilliance as I ran them with the accompanying remarks I had intended to make in the first place. When the lights came on, the entire audience was standing, giving me a prolonged ovation that made up for my initial dismay.

By the time I had returned to Ithaca, I needed to give special attention to the woodcock migration, following up on information I had gleaned from the literature. I must go, I decided, to the Cape May Peninsula in New Jersey, in particular to Cape May Point at its southern tip where many woodcock, after breeding in northeastern North America, congregate temporarily before continuing south across or around Delaware Bay. Since the southward flights are heaviest during the first two weeks of November, I set out in my car and stayed for four days, November 8–11, in the village of Cape May Point, rooming in the back of a store, thanks to the kindness of the storekeeper who lived with his family above it.

Two local lads, who were familiar with woodcock and hunted them, guided me to a hedgerow on the outskirts of town where woodcock gathered. This was shortly before sunset on November 8. We concealed ourselves along the western side of the hedgerow, which ran north and south, and thus we faced the sunset. As the sky darkened and twilight conditions approached those during which male woodcock begin flight-singing in the spring, a woodcock suddenly flushed from its hide at our backs and dashed across the sky in front of us. Then another flushed not far away, flew over our heads, and alighted in the field. Soon there were birds rising from different places, usually from hedgerows, and hurrying in various directions close to the ground. After a lapse of about twenty minutes, all this activity was over as quickly as it had begun. Presumably the woodcock had either come down in the open cultivated fields to secure food lacking in their daytime hides, or had continued their journey southward.

Before daybreak the following morning I started for the same hedgerow. Once quietly seated beside it, I waited for the lighting conditions to match those when activity had ceased the previous evening. As I had hoped, woodcock began to fly about again. A majority rose from the fields and alighted beside the hedgerows. By sunrise I saw no more woodcock. Actually I had seen fewer birds during the morning activity than the evening before. Some of the birds had either had their fill of food and were already in their daytime habitat or had migrated southward and not been replaced by birds from the north. In the following evenings I saw steadily fewer birds. I returned to Ithaca aware that I should come back to Cape May a year hence to determine whether or not my observations were typical.

There would be no more field work until the beginning of the woodcock's breeding season in the spring. But I was not without work. I was taking five courses, some of which needed making up, and I had a part of my thesis to write, bringing together all the data I had gathered on the distribution of the species throughout its range.

George Sutton was occupied almost daily writing his thesis, "The Exploration of Southampton Island, Hudson Bay." I enjoyed rooming with him. Upon retiring or before falling asleep, we sometimes quizzed each other on the scientific names of birds, or discussed personalities we knew, pointing up their favorable or unfavorable traits. We expressed our opinions on movies we had just seen, or New York shows which had recently come to Ithaca, and university concerts to which we had regular tickets.

Sometimes we held conversations concerning our own outlooks on life. One evening, soon after we had started rooming together, I talked about Eleanor and how we intended to marry soon. He remarked how much he had liked her on meeting her with my family at the time of the Salem A.O.U. meeting. Then he told me how he had become engaged to a lovely girl in Pittsburgh and that they planned to marry as soon as he returned from his year on Southampton. He was deeply in love with her and, while he was on Southampton, they agreed to talk with each other by radio every Friday night. Mysteriously, about halfway through the year, she no longer contacted him and he could not reach her. When George returned from his year of absence, he learned that his dearly beloved had married.

Whatever heartbreak George must have suffered, he had at least overcome it by the time he reached Ithaca in early October. But the heartbreak was revived later while he was in Pittsburgh at Christmas and again the following Easter. The circumstances that had twice aroused his peculiarly solemn behavior, or slumps, I had no way of knowing. Thereafter, George must have steeled himself against any such display of emotion because I never saw it again. I have always suspected that the loss of the girl he loved so deeply, and was to have married, stopped him from ever again falling in love. He remained a bachelor all his life.

George was popular among members of the art department and prominent business people in town. An entertaining conversationalist and story-teller, able to sing and to play the piano with gusto, he was in much demand at their parties. Not liking to arrive at parties alone, he often induced me to accompany him, provided he was sure in the first place that this arrangement was agreeable to the hosts and hostesses. Invariably the parties were strenuous affairs, involving all sorts of games, and lasting frequently until after midnight.

My recesses or vacations with my family, Eleanor, and Auntie Brown were subdued affairs by contrast. But I always looked forward to them and never more so than in my 1931 Christmas recess coming up in Middleton. Eleanor would have her engagement announced on December 19. The next day the local newspaper reported on the occasion: "On Saturday afternoon Mrs. Benjamin Brown of Maple Street gave a bridge tea in honor of her niece, Miss Eleanor Rice, daughter of Mr. Walter B. Rice formerly of Middleton. Mrs. Brown announced Miss Rice's engagement to Sewall Pettingill, son of Dr. and Mrs. Olin S. Pettingill of the Essex Sanatorium. Mr. Pettingill is at present a student at Cornell. The young people at the party were high school friends and classmates at Wheaton where Miss Rice graduated . . . ."

Parties ensued in the days from the announcement of our engagement until after New Year's. Then it was Pembroke for Eleanor, Ithaca and back to work for me. I had my research on woodcock anatomy to complete and George had his thesis to put in final form. To keep ourselves fit in these winter months, we often went skiing or took long hikes. Through the winter, very much on my mind was the coming spring for two reasons: Eleanor had promised to spend a week of her spring vacation with me in Ithaca; and I would have to spend as much time as I could investigating the nesting habits of woodcock— the real core of my thesis.

Eleanor courageously departed alone in her car from her school as soon as it closed Friday afternoon, April 15, tackled the 360 miles to Ithaca and arrived on Saturday afternoon. I met her at Willard Strait Hall, the student union, where I had reserved a room for her. In the week that followed she scarcely had time to spend in her room other than to sleep and dress. George threw a big dinner party for her, Mrs. Fuertes a luncheon, and the Allens had a special tea party in her honor. Besides my giving her a tour of the local state parks, including Taughannock with its spectacular gorge headed by the 215-foot falls, I took her to Connecticut Hill for two early evening sessions of listening to flight-singing of woodcock. If the week had been strenuous for her, there was no sign of it when we parted company for her drive back to Pembroke. I was relieved to get a wire from her, as soon as she had arrived, and delighted with her letter afterwards, praising everyone she met as well as all the parties and the trips we took.

While Eleanor was in Ithaca, Father wrote that Oscar Adler had died on April 21. His health had been steadily worsening ever since I had last seen him when he attended my participation in the Alexander Prize Speaking Contest at Bowdoin in June of 1928. I was saddened as I recalled my younger days at Greenwood Mountain observing his skill in painting landscapes and his knack for coaching plays.

On May 10, 1932, George Sutton became *Dr.* George Sutton, having submitted his thesis and passed his doctoral examination. Losing no time, he took off forthwith on an expedition to Saskatchewan for the Carnegie Museum and I would not see him again until fall.

May was already here and woodcock were nesting. Needing nests for observations, I let it be known to all my friends that I wanted to know about any nests found and where I could see them. I advertised a reward in the local newspaper to anyone who could show me a nest. Since woodcock have coloration imitating the dead leaves of the forest floor on which they nest, sit motionless on their nests, and will not leave their nests until practically stepped on, finding their nests required inspecting vast areas—and some luck besides.

I chose Connecticut Hill for my searching. I knew that woodcock were in the area, having observed them flight-singing there earlier in the season. Although I have no idea how many acres of ground I covered in my searching, I succeeded in finding two nests, one on May 13, the other on May 15. The nests were not far from each other and I was happy to discover that incubation of the eggs had only begun.

The situation was ideal. I could live not far from the nests. I set up Green Mansion (of Great Duck Island days), acquired cooking utensils and food supplies. There would be no driving back to Ithaca for eating and sleeping. Mine would be a hermit's life.

During the next four days I spent the daylight hours either searching for more nests or just napping. From sundown until sunup, I watched one nest or the other from a blind, sometimes using a flashlight to spot any action. The question I wanted most to settle: do the males ever come to their nests? I never heard them flight-singing near the nests, nor did I ever see one male near either nest. I concluded, as I had the year before, that the males probably did not even know the whereabouts of nests.

At the end of the fourth day I began to feel ill. Was it my food, my cooking? The next morning, I felt so sick that I closed up Green Mansion and headed for my room in the Fuertes home. Mrs. Fuertes was away but upon looking at myself in the mirror, I saw my chest covered with red spots and realized I had the measles.

I drove immediately to the university infirmary where I was put to bed with a temperature of 104 degrees. I had my parents wired and notified my good friend George Saunders, fellow graduate student, of my predicament. Knowing where Green Mansion was, he took it down at once and, with all its accompanying furnishings, put it in the Grad Lab. I never dreamed that my parents would come all the way to Ithaca to see me, simply because I had the measles, but they arrived within a couple of days and stayed overnight at Willard Strait. Satisfied that my case of measles would run its normal course, with no danger of complications, they left for Middleton the next day.

Not until the first week of June did I feel normal again. By then my Connecticut Hill nests were empty. I assumed they had produced chicks because there were empty shells in them, but I could find neither woodcock family in the area. How unlucky could I be, afflicted with measles at such an important time? But then came a stroke of luck.

On June 17, Adjer Smyth (a fellow graduate student) showed me a woodcock nest with three eggs he had found on a little island in North Spencer Pond not far south of Ithaca. About three hundred yards in circumference, the island was near enough to shore for me to wade out to it, but the water was too deep for woodcock to wade ashore. From island to mainland they would have to fly. The next day the eggs hatched. What I had, in a sense, was a captive brood I could find every day and the progress of which I could follow. Adjer's find had actually saved my thesis.

Daily, hidden from view, I watched the activities and behavior of the parent woodcock and her brood. Each day I captured at least one chick to weigh and measure it for growth as well as to photograph it. By the fourteenth day the last of the chicks was able to fly from the island and I never saw it again. Considering its rapid development, I estimated that the young woodcock must have been fully grown on its twenty-fifth day.

Thanks to the successful conclusion of my study of the island woodcock, I considered my research over for the season. I packed up at the Fuertes home and, on July 2, drove home to Middleton.

CHAPTER 14 / *Sojourn with Puffins*

IN MY CORRESPONDENCE and visits with Edward Dana, following our years at Bowdoin, I often expressed my wish to land on Machias Seal Island just to see and photograph Atlantic puffins. While recovering from measles at Cornell in late May and downright discouraged because my woodcock study had seemed hopelessly interrupted, I began wondering what I would do with birds, come summer. I wrote and suggested to Ed that we go to Machias Seal Island. He was graduating from Harvard Law School, and would want a vacation as well as an undisturbed place to study for his bar examinations in late summer. His response was prompt and enthusiastic. The trip was on! By the time he replied I had had the good fortune of the island woodcock to save my study in June, but we nevertheless proceeded with our plan.

Machias Seal Island, ten miles off Maine's northeastern coast at the mouth of the Bay of Fundy, consists largely of ledge and is treeless with about ten acres of grass-covered interior. The island supported a lighthouse, a fog-signal station, and homes for the keeper, the assistant keeper, and their families. The lighthouse and other facilities were Canadian-owned and operated, the personnel also being Canadian, from nearby Grand Manan, New Brunswick. Landing on the island was impossible when the sea was rough as it had neither harbor nor dock.

On July 5, 1932, I set out from Middleton, staying that night with Ed in Portland. The next day we visited with my grandparents in Belgrade where they still kept their farm in operation. On July 8 we arrived in the fishing village of Cutler, Maine. There Gene Farris, a fisherman, was expecting us as we had previously arranged with him to take us out to the island in his boat. At the time, Cutler and its outlying sea were shrouded with fog; but to find the island in the fog was no problem for Gene, and the sea itself was calm. Ed and I were soon aboard with all our necessities for camping and were on our way in early afternoon.

In a short while we knew that the island lay ahead as we could hear its foghorn. As the sound grew louder I could make out the dark shoreline of the island. And then over our boat flew several puffins—my first view of those extraordinary birds!

On the lee side of the island, Gene eased his boat up on a slanting ledge where he always landed. Waiting for us on shore were Edgar Russell, the head keeper of the lighthouse; Alma, his wife; twelve-year-old son Ronny; and Harvey Benson, the assistant keeper who was a relative of the Russells. They were expecting us as they had been notified in advance by radio when we would come and of our intent to stay on the island, camping out for a week to photograph birds. Quickly, Edgar and Harvey helped us unload so that Gene could back off the landing ledge. He waved us farewell and shouted the promise that he would be back for us in a week.

Now we had time to introduce ourselves. Alma said she would be glad to serve us meals in her house. Edgar and Harvey helped carry our gear to our campsite on the lee side of an old lighthouse they called "The Castle." There we put up my Green Mansion, and spread blankets on its canvas floor for sleeping. We were at home. All the time we had been fog-bound and the foghorn, not far from where we had set up the tent, never ceased to sound off with clock-like regularity—two loud quick blasts followed by a minute of silence, then two more quick blasts, and so on. How could we ever sleep?

Alma was a marvelous cook as our supper of fish chowder proved. This meal, like the others to follow, was not begun without Edgar first saying grace. At no time were the Russells wanting for food. Besides bounties from the sea surrounding them, they kept three cows and numerous chickens, and Alma made her own butter.

After supper and weary of the day, Ed and I retired to Green Mansion. Before long we adjusted to the foghorn and fell asleep, only to awaken hours later with a start. Why? The foghorn had stopped. Peering outside our tent we could see the adjacent mainland.

Following breakfast we inspected the island, finding much of the grassy interior away from the buildings alive with nesting terns—a few roseate and common terns but mostly Arctic. Their abundance tended to distract our attention from a few pairs of spotted sandpipers and savannah sparrows, as well as tree and barn swallows in the air. In the soil below the terns were numerous burrows of Leach's storm-petrels.

The puffins—those pigeon-sized sea birds with the parrot-like beaks which had lured us to the island in the first place—occupied the higher southwestern shore, full in the face of the strong southwesterly winds. On one of the flattish-topped boulders, high enough to overlook the island interior as well as the sea, stood several puffins until they took off into the wind when we drew too close. Climbing up on the boulder where the puffins had been, and looking down on the seaward side, we noted a wall of loose rocks with deep crevices where the puffins nested. I later estimated that there must have been as many as four hundred pairs of puffins in the colony, along with a few razorbills.

I decided that the place for my blind—steel-framed with burlap covering—was on the highest of the boulders. There I erected it and anchored it down well with ropes. I did not go into the blind but stood off some distance and, with binoculars, watched the reaction of the puffins to this sudden change in their surroundings. Gradually they began to accept the blind, paying little attention to it, even dropping down beside it.

Convinced that I had chosen the right location for the blind, I returned to Green Mansion for my camera. Imagine my surprise when, on returning, I saw two puffins standing on the blind's hammocky top! My blind had created a new, desirable height and the puffins would soon be vying with one another for its extremely limited surface.

The two puffins flew off the top, as did the others from the boulder, when I entered the blind. Before long, however, puffins began circling the area, coming in steadily closer, finally landing around the blind. From peepholes I looked out upon a most sedate group of birds. The sexes were alike. They stood perfectly still on their bright red feet, only moving their heads from side to side, focusing first one eye on the blind and then the other. I noticed their flawless attire—immaculately white underparts in sharp contrast to jet-black backs, wings, and tails. And those astonishing faces and beaks! I wanted to catch a puffin and give it the once-over.

The next day I entered the blind with my "puffin gloves," the heaviest winter gloves I owned, brought especially for handling puffins, which are noted for their vicious bites. As I had expected, a puffin soon alighted on the top of my blind, its feet sinking into the loose burlap. Putting on my gloves and making certain of the location of the bird's feet, with one hand I pinched its feet and held it while with the other I reached out through a peephole and brought it below. Although the bird struggled mightily, not a sound did it utter.

Wishing to see my captive in better light, I took it out of the blind to the level interior of the island. There I studied its remarkable avian face. The forward half of the high, narrow beak was red, the basal half deep blue and distinctly framed by a yellow fillet. The mouth was lined with yellow, its corners bright orange, while the rest of the face was grayish-white. This strange color combination gave me the weird feeling of looking at a mask hiding the features of an ordinary bird—a mask actually seeming to be tied by a white string around the back of its head. Each eye, triangular in shape with a dark, lash-like line extending back from it, suggested a chink carelessly cut in the mask. Of course, the eye proper was perfectly oval with bare, vermilion lids. The illusion of three-sidedness was due to two bluish scales, one above and the other, a long one, below, and the illusion of lashes was due to a peculiar fold in the skin back from the eye. I was about through meticulously examining the puffin when I realized that I had not seen its nostrils. I had not looked at the bird's head from below. This I did and saw two slit-like openings almost paralleling the cutting edge of the upper mandible. Why their unique, obscure position was a mystery to me.

Through with giving my captive the once-over, I released it on the ground but it could not take off because the surface was flat and sheltered from the wind. Immediately it made a beeline toward the ledge on which my blind stood, keeping its wings outspread as an aid in maintaining balance. Once at the foot of the ledge, it started pattering to the top and jumped off into the slight oncoming wind. Gravity pulled it down, though it managed sufficient momentum in its descent to sustain flight and was soon over the sea.

During the week on the island, I spent many hours in the blind from day to day, sometimes taking photographs but more often just having fun watching puffins gathered in the vicinity of the blind. Their number seemed to be governed by wind. The more wind, the more puffins; and the more puffins, the more activity.

Never had I observed a colony of sea birds that was less vocal. No screaming, no loud gabbling as in gull colonies. The few sounds puffins uttered, mouths barely open if at all, matched perfectly the birds' solemn appearance. The sounds had a sepulchral tone, reminding me of the lowing of cattle in a hay-filled barn.

Abundant though the puffins were about my blind and on neighboring ledges during the day, they all disappeared at night. Either they spent the night on the sea or passed it among the rocks below. Their departure was gradual. Invariably, a few lingered on the higher ledges longer than the others, their white "waistcoats" barely discernible in the twilight.

I was highly entertained one afternoon by a puffin running in and out among the rocks with a mouth full of feathers and grasses. Obviously, it desired to build a nest but could find no place in which to start it. All suitable places were evidently occupied. Every so often with renewed courage, it disappeared into another crevice, only to reappear with its mouth still full of nesting material, discouraged.

Without doubt the most amusing behavior was "bill-clicking." Two puffins approached each other and, without uttering a sound, proceeded to slap the sides of their bills together. A clicking sound resulted. The performance often continued for several minutes and quite frequently attracted other loitering puffins. Sometimes they looked on, seemingly interested, or entered the performance, thus increasing the number of participants and amount of clicking. Occasionally, bill-clicking became a regional free-for-all. Bill-clicking must have been a form of social play. The nesting season was well under way, so it was not a means of pairing, nor was it a case of fighting as the birds appeared altogether too mildly disposed.

I became aware that there were chicks in the crevices below when the adult birds began returning from the sea with fish dangling from the sides of their bills. Rarely did a puffin arrive with just one fish—more often with a half-dozen or more. The fish were generally of the same size, usually herring fry.

I wondered how a puffin could catch such fish in quantities. How could it catch first one fish and, holding that, open its bill to catch another without losing the first fish? Probably the answer lies in the fact that the roof of the puffin's mouth has numerous hard ridges between which the fish are wedged as they are caught, and consequently held. In any case, the fish-catching technique of the puffin is a remarkable energy-conserver. One trip to the sea is good for more than one fish.

Several times I turned my blind over to Ed Dana, as I knew he would enjoy watching puffins as much as I did. Like me, however, he became anxious to inspect the rocky wall in which the birds nested and, furthermore, to see some of the nests and chicks. Fortunately, for a helper we had Ronny Russell, a youngster still slim and able to slither into some of the crevices where the nests were beyond our reach.

Puffins have only one egg and the sexes are equally attentive in keeping it at uniform temperature—in other words, they take turns incubating it. As we watched outside we would see one puffin fly to the passageway leading to its nest and enter; then in a few moments its mate would appear from the same passageway, straighten up and scan the surroundings, stretch and yawn, and soon fly out to sea.

The result of a puffin egg's hatching is a disappointment, as Ronny revealed when coming out of a crevice with a baby puffin. One would expect a downy creature with at least some of the appeal of its parents. Instead, the result is a plump, slow-moving chick with loose, dusky down, thick black bill, dull blurry eyes, and dark feet. Placed on a rock exposed to the sun, the homely youngster strove to find its accustomed darkness by inching in the direction of the nearest shadowy spot, meanwhile complaining feebly.

During our seven days on Machias Seal Island we had exceptionally good weather. Every day, Ed Dana faithfully studied for his bar exams but always allowed plenty of time to investigate different parts of the island. As the second evening approached, Edgar Russell led Ed up inside the lighthouse to show him how one lighted the great light with its enormous, powerful lenses. The light itself revolved on mercury and was turned by what looked like a grandfather clock weight that hung the full height of the lighthouse—one reason that lighthouses are built so high. With the coming of the last evening, Ed lit the light himself under Edgar Russell's watchful eye.

All along we greatly enjoyed eating with the Russells. During one of the last meals they told us they would be moving back to their home on Grand Manan and issued us a standing invitation to visit them. Gene Farris arrived on July 15 as promised. Soon Ed and I with all our gear were aboard his boat, but not until we had thanked our hosts for their thoughtfulness, with special words of praise for Alma's cooking.

On our return to Cutler, Gene suggested that the following day we should visit Old Man Island, not far from Cutler, where double-crested cormorants and a few greater black-backed gulls nested. He knew a fisherman in Cutler who would take us out—the sea tomorrow had every promise of being calm—and stay offshore while I photographed some of the nesting cormorants and Ed watched from a distance.

Old Man Island, about ten acres in size, was locally called "The Old Man" because of its odd shape. It had steep, rocky sides rising some forty feet above the tides. On the upper slopes and on top were stunted spruce and fir, most of them dead. The aspect of The Old Man was bizarre and more so in the summer with the blackish cormorants nesting in the dead trees.

We accepted Gene's suggestion. Once ashore in the morning, Ed and I scrambled up The Old Man, I with my blind and camera. I set up the blind near one of the dead trees which supported a cormorant nest containing three half-grown young. The nesting adults soon came to the nest, then disappeared seaward. Eventually, one of them returned to the nest, gave a croak, and opened its mouth. At once the young started cheeping loudly, each in turn tickling the parent's gullet with its bill. Finally, one at a time, each youngster plunged in, pushing and wriggling down the parent's throat until it reached food.

Ed had, from a distance, watched what I had been photographing. On our way back to Cutler, Ed remarked that the feeding performance was "positively lewd" and that cormorants themselves, except for their emerald eyes, were "truly revolting birds."

Once we had landed in Cutler and shifted our gear to my car, I drove Ed to his home in Portland, first stopping in Wayne on the way to pick up Eleanor, then returning with Eleanor late that night to Wayne. She had arrived there the day before with my parents. Knowing all too well that I would want to get into my darkroom in Middleton as soon as possible to develop the pictures I had taken on Machias Seal Island, she was ready to go back to Middleton with me in a couple of days. My hopes for good puffin pictures lived up to my highest expectations. I would have some pictures to show at the A.O.U. meeting in October.

The remainder of my summer passed quickly as well as pleasantly, partly in Wayne, partly in Middleton. Eleanor was happier than ever because in September she would be teaching at the Hadley School in Swampscott, near enough to Middleton so that she could drive to school daily and live at Auntie Brown's home.

At some point in the summer, Eleanor chose December 31 as the date for our wedding and soon we began discussing whom we should include in the wedding party. We would be married in the white Congregational Church downhill from Auntie's house and across the main road. The minister was the Reverend Wilbert Wolf, but I had a suggestion: to invite the Reverend Henry E. Dunnack of Augusta, Maine, who had married my father and mother, to join the Reverend Wolf in marrying us. Eleanor liked the idea at once, and said that Father, not I, should invite him. The Reverend Mr. Dunnack was happy to accept.

CHAPTER 15 / *Doctorate from Cornell*

SUMMER OF 1932 over, I began my last year of graduate work at Cornell. I was warmly welcomed back to Ithaca by Mrs. Fuertes on October 1 and again offered her third floor. George Sutton, my roommate, was yet to arrive; he was still at his home in Bethany, West Virginia, after his summer of ornithological work in Saskatchewan. He would come any day to take up his appointment as Curator of the Louis Agassiz Fuertes Memorial Collection of Birds.

I returned to Cornell for my third year with a nagging concern because I had to face my qualifying examination for the doctorate, said to be more exacting than the final. Much as I dreaded meeting with my doctoral committee, scheduled for soon after I arrived, I need not have. Each committee member in turn reported favorably from the instructors in the courses I had taken and my general attitude in coping with them. Nothing further said by each committee member, they voted to waive my qualifying examination. I never heard sweeter music!

I set to work writing a short paper on a particular aspect of my woodcock study and also coloring a series of my best puffin slides, both efforts for the A.O.U. meeting, October 17–20. George arrived barely in time to help me finish some of the better slides.

The A.O.U. meeting was in Quebec City. Headquarters were in the castle-like Hotel Frontenac and sessions in La Salle des Promotions, Laval University. The whole affair was superbly managed. I was moved especially by the friendliness of Aldo Leopold and several other distinguished A.O.U. members who went out of their way to compliment me on my contributions to the program and how well I presented them.

From November 2 to 10, I revisited Cape May Point, New Jersey, to compare the woodcock migration with what I had observed of it the year before. No remarkable numbers did I observe at any time as on the evening of November 8, 1931. My conclusion, borne out by the observations of others in earlier years, was that only severe weather from the west forced the birds eastward from their normally direct southern course.

After the Cape May Point trip, I picked up work on my thesis, trying hard to concentrate on the job, but the wedding on December 31, even though still a month and a half away, was proving increasingly distracting. We had planned a big wedding. There were invitations to have printed and many friends to whom they should be sent. George would be my best man, and I invited five Psi U brothers of my Bowdoin years to be ushers. Eleanor's matron of honor would be her Wheaton roommate, Marita Kneeland, and she invited two Wheaton classmates as attendants.

During my Thanksgiving recess in Middleton, Eleanor and I planned events prior to the wedding, the wedding itself, and what we should do afterwards. The formal dinner on the night of the thirtieth would be second in importance only to the wedding the next day.

Soon after I returned to Ithaca I acquired the necessary formal attire including cutaway coat and striped pants. In the meantime I received a disturbing letter from Eleanor that her father was gravely ill in the Worcester State Hospital. His condition had worsened by the time I reached home on December 18 and he died on December 23. All of the family, shocked and saddened, attended Mr. Rice's funeral in Salem during the afternoon of December 25.

Despite her grief, Eleanor was determined that we should go ahead with wedding plans, except to cancel the formal dinner the night before.

Members of the wedding party arrived on December 30. George and the ushers stayed at my house, Mr. Dunnack in a guest room at the sanatorium. After a dinner together at my house—a stag dinner of sorts—we went in various cars to the church where we were joined by Eleanor and her party to rehearse for the wedding on the morrow. The church was decorated in Christmas green with tinsel.

At 4:00 P.M. on December 31, the ceremony began. Never was Eleanor more beautiful, coming up the aisle on the arm of her uncle, Harry Boyd. She wore her mother's wedding gown of silk muslin with trimming of rose point lace and satin ribbon, and she carried a bouquet of roses.

Following the ceremony, we all walked up the hill across from the church to Auntie Brown's house for a reception, leisurely and prolonged, nobody in a hurry to leave. Eleanor quietly disappeared upstairs, changed clothes, came down to join me. Saying our farewells, before long we were in our car and headed for the Andover Inn where we would stay over New Year's Day.

No honeymoon ensued—it would come in June, once Eleanor was through teaching and I, we hoped, had obtained my doctorate. On January 2, Eleanor and I appeared at my home in Middleton where my parents had designated their front guest room as "our room" when we were home together. By January 3, she was teaching; by January 4, I was in Ithaca.

At one point during the preceding November, Dr. Allen had told me that the Ithaca Night School, which was held in the local high school, planned to offer a winter course in ornithology early in the new year. Would I be interested in teaching it? I would indeed, but I failed to ask just what would be expected of me—my mind was on the wedding. January, 1933 seemed years away.

On January 4 at 7:00 P.M., I met my class which consisted of fifteen students ranging in age, I judged, from twenty to sixty-five; only two of them were in middle age. Their taking the night course was for credit. This meeting on the fourth was brief, simply enabling me to give instructions on materials each class member should bring and to outline the objectives of the course. We would meet from 7:00 to 9:00 P.M. every Monday and Thursday in January, February, and March.

If ever my ingenuity was taxed—giving a *night* course in ornithology in *winter!* No field trips; no opportunity to see, hear, and consequently identify live birds. From his laboratory, Dr. Allen let me borrow bird skins, lantern-slide projector for showing his or my slides, or anything else that might be useful.

Morning and afternoon on practically every Monday and Thursday I devoted to preparations for the evening class. At first, I worked up rough notes to follow in lecturing on the anatomy, physiology, and behavior of birds. Then for each class, I started gathering up bird skins representing the different groups of birds (for example, woodpeckers), carried them in my car to the school and displayed them on tables in my classroom. My objective was to show the means by which each species can be identified. Now and then I gave a talk with lantern slides on my various trips. I also gave quizzes on identification, the results of which always encouraged me for they showed that I was accomplishing more than I ever expected in a night course. I met my class for the last time on March 23 and watched it graduate four days later. I have long wondered how much ornithology I actually taught during those three winter months. Would any of the students ever recognize the birds in the wild that they had seen only as skins or on slides?

My other five days of the week during those three months were devoted to work on my thesis. I was soon far along in describing the woodcock's plumages, feather tracts, skeleton, and life history (including migration), and setting down my principal findings from field research. But my information on the breeding distribution of the species was too sparse, the library not yielding the data I needed. Hence, in late January I mailed out over three hundred questionnaires to ornithologists in all of the states and Canadian provinces where woodcock bred, or were reputed to breed, for estimates of abundance, for dates of arrival and departure, and for precise breeding dates.

How happy I was when Eleanor boarded the train in Boston on February 17 to spend her week's vacation with me in Ithaca. Mrs. Fuertes arranged in advance for us to occupy her son's vacant apartment in Collegetown. After arriving, Eleanor quickly sensed the work I had to do on woodcock distribution. As the questionnaires came in, she proceeded to help organize the information. But our week was not all work. Mrs. Fuertes, George Sutton, and the Allens arranged all sorts of social occasions for introducing my bride. At numerous times during the week when we were alone, Eleanor and I were trying to decide where to go on our belated honeymoon. We were still trying to decide when I put her aboard the train for Boston, her vacation over.

During the entire winter period when I was teaching and writing my thesis, the country was in the depths of the Great Depression. Salaries were being cut at Eleanor's school and at the Essex Sanatorium. Banks were closed on March 4. (Father sent me money in registered letters to help me pay my bills.) The situation that concerned me: what would I do for a job after I had my Ph.D.? I registered at the Cornell Bureau of Education Service for a possible teaching job the following year. I applied to every teacher's agency the bureau could recommend. Both Drs. Allen and Gross wrote generously about me in letters to accompany my applications.

In early April, George Sutton left for field work in the Big Bend country of southwestern Texas.

In mid-April, I was alarmed to learn that the date for my doctoral examination had been moved ahead, to May 30, owing to one member of my doctoral committee wanting to leave Ithaca by June 1. What unnerved me particularly was the need to have my thesis ready by then. Much of the writing was still incomplete and needed polishing. Then it would have to be professionally typed and bound. All this seemed impossible. "Do the best you can," was Dr. Allen's comforting remark to my expressed worry.

At the time I received this alarming news, Eleanor was already on the train, Ithaca bound, for a week's vacation. We stayed at Willard Strait. This time, thesis or no thesis, I wanted Eleanor to visit Washington, D.C. and, besides, I needed to look up some woodcock records in the U.S. National Museum. So to Washington we drove one day, spending the next day there, and then returning.

Quite by chance at the museum we met a young man who had just returned from Cobb Island, one of the sand barrier islands off the coast of Cape Charles, Virginia, where he had found coastal birds breeding in abundance. Sensing our immediate interest in the island, then learning the reason for it, the young man responded, "Cobb Island is just the place for you!" He advised us to drive down the cape to the little seaside town of Oyster, there leave the car and negotiate with a fisherman to take us out to the island, eight miles across a shallow sound, locally called the Broadwater. The owner and sole occupant of the island was Captain George W. Cobb, who welcomed people liking birds. He might let us camp.

Eleanor and I had already made up our minds by the time we were back in Ithaca, her vacation over, and I had put her aboard the train: it would be Cobb Island for our honeymoon next June. I now had five weeks left before the day of my doctoral examination. At that time I must present three bound copies of my thesis: the ribbon copy for the Cornell library, the first carbon copy for Dr. Allen as chairman of my doctoral committee, and the second carbon copy that would be mine. As fast as I could type the pages and correct them (my typing was sloppy), I turned them over to a professional typist. I also had to make three photocopies of each of my drawings and three prints of each photograph I chose to use. All this involved darkroom work that only I could do.

All my time was not devoted to the thesis, however. I needed to check on my woodcock plots at Connecticut Hill. There were social occasions I could not avoid, and I could not resist passing up a good movie, often taking Mrs. Fuertes with me. Yet, it seemed that I spent most of my time in McGraw, especially nights, getting in bed sometimes just before dawn.

By May 29, my thesis was professionally typed only in part, hence still unbound and not ready for presentation at the examination the next day. I reported this distressful situation to Dr. Allen who calmly responded, "Never mind, I will explain the situation to the committee and they will understand."

Following Dr. Allen's instructions, I appeared at the office on May 30 at 9:00 A.M. The two other members of my committee had arrived. Dr. Allen seated me in his office facing a circle of a few people who included, besides my committee, members of the biological faculty invited to attend. My examination proceeded.

At the start I was naturally apprehensive, if not a little nervous. Nevertheless, I felt a marked degree of confidence. This was due largely to my experience in teaching at the night school and to my reviewing some of the important texts in past courses I had taken since coming to Cornell.

The questions leveled at me were not intended to trip me up or to make me feel ill at ease. Generally, they were worded to test the depth of my knowledge of field procedures in biology. In a shorter time than I ever anticipated, Dr. Allen asked if there were any more questions. There being none, he asked me to leave his office, close its door, and wait outside. In a matter of only a few minutes, he stepped out of his office smiling broadly, approached me with his right hand extended and shook mine, saying "Congratulations, Dr. Pettingill!" Taking me by the arm he escorted me back to his office where each person present came forward to shake my hand.

With my examination passed, my committee granted me no more than fourteen days to submit my thesis, completed and bound. With these steps taken, I would fulfill requirements for my Ph.D. from Cornell.

Soon all 557 pages of my thesis had been typed and the thirty-five accompanying plates mounted. The work remaining consisted of collating the pages and plates to make up the three volumes, and getting the three volumes bound. Since the local bindery was crowded with orders, I worried lest it could not meet my deadline of June 12. But, glory be, it succeeded.

On schedule, I lugged all three bound volumes into Dr. Allen's office and placed them before him on his desk. There they rested, each three-and-a-half inches thick and bearing the simple title:

THE AMERICAN WOODCOCK
Philohela minor (Gmelin)

Although Dr. Allen was already familiar with the contents, having reviewed and advised me on all parts of the text before it was professionally typed, on seeing these books his face produced a pleased expression that said everything without words. Passing me my copy, he remarked in a meaningful tone how proud he was to have had me as a graduate student. When I said good-bye and shook his hand, I thanked him wholeheartedly, as I was deeply indebted to him for the meticulous attention he had always given me and for his unfailingly genuine kindness.

Dr. Alfred Gross. At ease during a field trip.

Edward Dana at Bow-
doin

DR. ARTHUR ALLEN WITH HIS CAPTIVE-REARED RUFFED GROUSE

WITH TWO FELLOW GRADUATE STUDENTS, 1932. At right, the author; left, Wilfred Welter; center, John Emlen, who became a distinguished ornithologist at the University of Wisconsin.

ELEANOR AT BELGRADE, 1932

My Parents at Middleton, 1934. At their home after attending a
wedding.

FACULTY AT NEW HAMPSHIRE NATURE CAMP, 1936. Standing, left to right: Jarvis Hadley, Violet Findlay, the author, and Joseph Tidd; seated, Charles Pomerat.

Thornton Burgess at Kent Island

GEORGE SUTTON AT ITHACA, NEW YORK

CHAPTER 16 / *Honeymoon on Cobb Island*

WITH A GREAT FEELING of relief, my deadline met in fulfilling all requirements for my Ph.D. from Cornell, I began the tedious job of clearing out from my corner of McGraw my three-year collection of notebooks, field notes, correspondence, photographs, and lantern slides, as well as packing my personal effects in my room at the Fuertes home. (Mrs. Fuertes was out of town; I had said my farewells to her before she left.) My roadster was piled sky-high by the time I left for Middleton on June 18. I arrived after midnight. Eleanor was still up; she had been expecting me hours earlier.

Now came the rush to get ready for our honeymoon on Cobb Island. I hurried to Wayne to pick up camping equipment. Also I had to buy a light tent for sleeping in warm weather. Green Mansion of my Great Duck Island and Machias Seal Island days was much too cumbersome and designed for cool weather.

Early on June 21 we were off in my roadster, loaded with camera, film, and necessities. Driving all day, we arrived in the evening at Oyster on Cape Charles, Virginia. There we found a friendly fisherman who would take us out to Cobb Island the next afternoon. While we were away, staying on the island, he said I could leave my car beside the driveway that went down to his boat dock where it would be safe.

True to his word, the fisherman at Oyster was waiting for us late the following afternoon. We were soon aboard his fishing smack and headed east across the shallow Broadwater toward Cobb Island, a long, low barrier of dunes on the ocean side of Cape Charles. The one-cylinder motor pounded strenuously, rattling the craft from bow to stern and making conversation virtually impossible. In the distance a thin yellow line appeared on the horizon.

From the fisherman's gestures and bellowed phrases we learned that the line was "Cobb Island . . . eight miles away . . . Coast Guard Station on it . . . couldn't land there without permission . . . would pull in at Captain Cobb's . . . queer old duck . . . owns the island . . . lives alone." Instead of relaxing, I was plagued by the question: Would we be allowed to land, camp, and study birds as we had planned? In the rush of events before starting on our honeymoon, I had neglected to communicate with Captain Cobb. I simply knew that it was an exceedingly attractive spot for coastal birds.

My growing concern was momentarily diverted by eight long-winged birds flying parallel to us to starboard. Striking creatures they were, jet black above and immaculate white below. As they maneuvered liltingly just above the waves, their bodies jerked up and down by strong wing strokes, I could make out their vermilion beaks with the knifelike lower mandibles protruding grotesquely. My first black skimmers! Of all the birds nesting on Cobb Island, they were the ones I wanted most to photograph.

Slowly the island assumed definite character. Near the southern extremity loomed some buildings. Built high on piles so as to escape the tide, they seemed lifted above the island like a mirage. Golden sunlight reflected from their windows. We soon passed the United States Coast Guard Station and approached a frame house flanked by two small bungalows.

It was then that I caught sight of a man standing squarely on both feet, hands on his hips, and motionless. He wore a blue shirt, khaki trousers, and hip boots; his head, though bald, was dignified by a corona of white hair. As our boatman eased his craft toward the landing and killed the motor, I called, "Are you Captain Cobb?" No reply. We jumped out. The man still did not move or speak. Somewhat unnerved by now, I extended my hand, "My name is Pettingill."

"I'm George Cobb, glad to meet you," was the response in a low, pleasant voice. We shook hands, and he nodded graciously to Eleanor. Captain Cobb was the warden posted here by the National Association of Audubon Societies.

I was impressed with his massive build and erect, noticeably stiff posture. Although his tanned face had the deep furrows of a man of sixty, his physique possessed the vigor of one many years younger. His expression, not unkindly, remained immobile and serious.

"We'd like to stay a while," I began cautiously, "to camp and study birds."

At this his face brightened, and I sensed a sudden unbending.

"Do as you wish," he said warmly. "Anyone who likes birds is welcome. Lots of people come to see them."

Much relieved, we unloaded our duffel. The fisherman then poled his craft from the shore. At no time had he exchanged a word or glance with Captain Cobb. Nevertheless, I arranged with the fisherman before he left shore to return and pick us up on July 10.

Still not having taken a step, Captain Cobb said, "You'd better not camp tonight, it's nearly dark."

His words were persuasive, for night was settling down, but the yellow glow in the west still gave some light.

"The upstairs rooms in my house are empty," he continued.

Uneasy lest I hurt his feelings, I tried to explain. "We want to camp—something we've never done together." Had we not wished to appear seasoned to the rigors of the outdoors, I might have told him that my wife had never camped in her life.

"Do as you like," he said. "There's a flat place over there between two dunes where you can pitch your tent. Come with me."

From our campsite on the southern tip of the island we could see the eastern beach rising to the dunes and the marsh stretching westward. Captain Cobb's house was just north of us on piles overlooking the marsh. A wooden ramp extended from his porch to the dunes. The Coast Guard Station was a quarter of a mile away.

In the semidarkness we set up our tent. Meanwhile, Captain Cobb disappeared and returned shortly with a pail and some pieces of iron pipe.

"Drinking water," he said. "My well filled with salt water

during the last storm. Caught this from the roof. It's good."
Just as I thanked him, a breeze rushed by, collapsing the tent.
"Try these for staples," Captain Cobb said, handing me the pipes. "Yours never'll hold in the sand." In no time the tent was up for keeps.
"Sorry we can't offer you a chair," I said, "but how about a cigarette?"
"Never smoke or drink," he replied.
After our uneasy silence, he asked, "You want to see birds?"
We learned that we were just in time. The eggs in the skimmer colony on the beach were hatching; there were many nests of gulls and terns in the marsh.
It was dark when Captain Cobb left. The island was soothingly quiet. Above the light rush of surf on the beach, we heard a few skimmers passing close to shore, their calls suggesting the yelps of beagles in pursuit of unseen prey.
Next morning, as we approached the skimmer colony on the beach, the birds sat peacefully on their nests, all facing into the wind like weather vanes. Even when we were within a few yards of them, they failed to move. But suddenly we passed their limit of tolerance, because into the air they went with a rush of wings and discordant cries. The next moment one resentful bird left the throng and flew toward Eleanor. She screamed, folded her hands over her head, and crumpled in the sand.
"They won't hit you," I assured her; "they're bluffing." Just then another skimmer shot toward me at eye level. Not believing my own words, I ducked as the bird veered sharply upward.
Many birds were soon doing the same thing—shooting downward, veering upward, but never striking. Still confident, but not sure they would not strike, I walked boldly into the colony, followed by my reluctant bride, whereupon some of the skimmers dropped to the ground in seemingly helpless prostration. One rested on its belly with wings limply outstretched; another lay on its side with one wing waving; still another flopped along using its wings as paddles. They were injury feigning, I explained, to distract your attention

from their nests. Frankly, I was surprised to see it in colony-nesting birds.

Nests—mere cups scratched in the sand—were everywhere, often within two or three feet of one another. Many contained white eggs boldly splotched with black and brown. In a few nests there were chicks, the color of sand, squatting tightly, their eyes closed. The sun bore down on us; the sand was painful to touch. Realizing that the eggs and chicks could not long endure exposure to such intense heat, we quickly departed, letting the panic-stricken skimmers return to shade their eggs and young from the burning sun.

That evening Captain Cobb invited us to dinner. When we strolled up the ramp to his house, there were lights in the Coast Guard Station. The air was calm, and from the still unexplored marsh came a medley of bird sounds.

Captain Cobb, fork in one hand and pot holder in the other, greeted us at the door and motioned us into a large unfinished room—kitchen, dining room, and living room in one—plainly furnished but tidy. After we assured him that we had come with appetites, he returned to his oil stove, where oysters sizzled in a pan. In the nearby sink, silvery hogfishes and huge blue crabs still awaited his attention. This was to be a very special meal, of the best the local sea could provide—and it was delicious.

After dinner the captain became voluble, revealing his attitudes and philosophies and, withal, an unexpected sense of humor. Time meant nothing to him. His only timepiece lay somewhere in the marsh where he had flung it in disgust three weeks before. The sun was his clock, he said. Companionship meant little either. He was contemptuous of his only neighbors, the crew at the Coast Guard Station, whom he considerd lazy and careless. He hated to think of a ship in distress calling on them for help and pointed to a bullet hole in his wall made during their "target practice." He liked most of the people who came to see the birds, though he found the women in "trousers" comical. Of the social life enjoyed by his wife on the mainland, a few days a year was all he could bear. What he wanted, he told us, was to stay on his island every day for the rest of his life.

Cobb Island was his home, settled by his grandfather, Nathan Cobb, when it was longer and wider with rich topsoil and many trees and shrubs. It teemed with birds. The family farm grew cabbages "as big as baskets" and turnips "the size of watermelons." Artesian wells supplied water. A hotel accommodated pothunters and sportsmen.

Toward the end of the last century disaster struck. The pothunters all but exterminated the birds and a great storm, accompanied by high tides, destroyed the buildings, filled the wells, uprooted the trees, and washed away the life-giving soil and a third of the island. The family moved to the mainland.

Captain Cobb, a stubborn man, returned and built the present house. Now he was renovating the two bungalows for people coming to see birds. As for the birds, most of the breeding species had recovered from the pothunters. His present struggle was against the mainlanders who came to steal the beach birds' eggs for food. They hated him, even shot at him, but the National Association of Audubon Societies had appointed him deputy warden with authority to enforce bird protection on his and a neighboring island, and *that* he was determined to do, even if he had to shoot in return.

The next day Eleanor and I explored the marsh. She turned up her nose at the musky odors, became entangled in the waist-high grass, jumped out of the way of scurrying fiddler crabs and into a pool of black, sticky mud which smeared her new slacks and sneakers. Although she expressed doubts that any bird could nest in such a place, she followed me gamely.

Overhead a few laughing gulls circled placidly, and from the grass came the sharp cackles of clapper rails. Moving gingerly lest we step into some unseen hole, we finally reached a place where a gull cried out in alarm. Immediately, dozens of gulls together with several Forster's terns flushed from the vegetation and milled over our heads. Occasionally they dove at us, but their attacks were so half-hearted that we ignored them.

The nests of the gulls and terns were clustered here and there on clumps of debris—dead sedge stalks, seaweeds, and driftwood washed in by excessively high tides. In each nest on top of the debris were eggs, usually three. Several were pipped; there would soon be chicks.

The clapper rails we did not see, as they cleverly managed to keep out of sight in the vegetation surrounding us. The nests, however, we found easily, for the grasses over the nests were pulled together and entwined at their tips in a telltale knot. Some of these nests contained as many as fifteen eggs.

In the ensuing eight days I divided my time between the beach and the marsh, using blinds so that I might observe and photograph the birds without their showing fear. Many of the eggs hatched. The weather was perfect, nearly always sunny with a slight breeze. Nights were balmy, moonlit, and delightful.

Early on the morning of July 3, I awoke with the tent slapping against my face. Struggling through its opening, I discovered a guy rope loose. After tightening it, I looked about. Overhead from the northeast sped low, thick clouds, blotting out the rising sun already dimmed by an upper stratum of haze. Dark chasms furrowed the ocean's gray surface. The marsh bore a weird olive color, the beach an intense yellow. My deeply tanned hands and arms were sickly amber.

As I stood, pajama-clad, in the wind, I called sharply to Eleanor. At that moment, with a fresh burst of wind, another guy rope gave way, and Eleanor's sleepy, bewildered face peered out of the tent.

"Get dressed and get out," I shouted, struggling with the guy rope. Her head snapped back like a turtle's.

No doubt Captain Cobb had been watching since dawn, had seen me emerge, and later had watched Eleanor, fully dressed, assume the role of the detached guy rope while I had my turn inside dressing. We were glad to see him coming down the ramp, his pace slow, reassuring.

"Better take down your tent and move your gear to my porch," he advised. "There'll be a high tide out of this. Have breakfast with me."

Minute by minute the wind increased; each gust seemed stronger than the one before. The tent blew down. There was no argument. With the wind tearing at us, we rolled up the tent and carried our duffel up the narrow ramp to the house.

More than once the wind threw us off balance and against the railing which saved us from a tumble into the marsh.

The tide, which, according to Captain Cobb's battered almanac, was due to be high at eleven, reached its normal high soon after we were safely in the house. But what time was that? None of us knew. Our watches had run down, and there was no sun. Captain Cobb guessed eight o'clock. There would be three more hours of rising tide!

As the tide exceeded its normal mark, the ocean seemed to lift up. Great walls of surf rose above the beach, hesitated menacingly, then collapsed in thunderous roars, sending avalanches of water against the protecting dunes. The swelling tide rushed and swirled into the Broadwater. Small ponds appeared in the marsh; the ponds became lakes; the lakes fused into one vast expanse continuous with the Broadwater. Soon the Broadwater crept up to the dunes and under the house. Waves, whipped by the wind, licked at the piles, higher and steadily higher. The ocean sent long tongues of water between the dunes. Our once cozy campsite became a channel. The ramp drifted away. The Coast Guard Station, its piles invisible, seemed afloat. From the boat at the station dock came exhaust fumes indicating that the crew was ready for any emergency.

The plight of the beach-nesting birds was all too apparent. Above the beach a cloud of skimmers hovered momentarily, settled on the sand, hovered again, settled again. Each time they rose, we knew that a wave had swept over their nests, destroying both eggs and young. Above the marsh, now totally flooded, families of clapper rails drifted on the water at the mercy of the gale. Weak swimmers, they floundered helplessly. Parent birds attempted to round up scattered broods by cutting wide circles and giving frantic calls that we could hear above the roar of the storm. One by one the chicks, exhausted, heavily soaked, and already submerged to their heads, were swallowed up by the waves and tidal whirls.

The heaps of debris on which laughing gulls nested now floated like small rafts, often with nests intact and still holding eggs or chicks. While adult gulls fluttered anxiously over them, sometimes attempting to alight, the wind forced the rafts steadily southward away from the island and into the open Broadwater. The mounting waves tore them apart, spilling their live cargo into the sea. We were suddenly distracted from our dismay over the fate of the birds by a muffled crash. A bungalow had dropped on its side. Moments later the waves began slapping under the floor of our house. Captain Cobb still showed neither emotion nor alarm. The collapse of the bungalow, the destruction of the bird colonies, even the floor boards of our house darkened by rising water, evoked no comment from him.

I was, I remember, looking through a window on the oceanside and watching spindrift whipped from the towering waves, when I realized that the surf was breaking over the grass-tufted tops of the highest dunes—our one remaining barrier against the fury of the sea. Suddenly an enormous wave, its force fortunately eased by the dunes, struck the side of the house at floor level, jarring the structure and spraying the windows.

Eleanor gasped. We turned toward Captain Cobb. Instead of the expected evidence of disturbance, I saw one of his rare smiles.

"Tide's turned," he said, pointing to the water flowing eastward out of the Broadwater.

The following morning Cobb Island sparkled under a sunny sky. Gone, however, were the bird colonies. Nature in one great sweep had rubbed out that which she had so generously fostered. The beach where the skimmer colony had been was as smooth and hard as a floor, without sign of eggs or chicks. Beyond the site of the colony several hundred skimmers huddled close together. When we approached, they rose silently in a body and alighted further away. Nowhere in the marsh was there a gull. We heard a few clapper rails and marveled that they had survived.

"Sorry you must go," Captain Cobb said, as we packed that night, confident that the fisherman would realize our plight and come on the morrow. "Come back next year. There'll be more birds than ever."

The fisherman appeared as we had hoped, along with news that did not surprise me: my car had been under water. After landing at Oyster, he helped me find a garage mechanic who drained the oil pan of sea water as well as the old oil. With new oil poured in and my car, inside and out, cleared of tidal debris, I turned the ignition switch. My car started without a cough or whimper.

Thanking the fisherman, besides paying him, for having been so accommodating and for showing awareness of our isolation after the storm, we proceeded to find a nearby lodging and there base ourselves while we searched to acquaint ourselves with Cape Charles land birds during the coming days that we had been denied on Cobb Island. All the southern birds were new to Eleanor and several were new to me, despite my having seen many southern birds in Virginia long before in 1922. We drove home to Middleton in one day, July 12.

Later in August we read how another devastating storm had battered the Atlantic coast. Naturally we thought of Captain Cobb and wondered how he had fared. Weeks later in *Bird-Lore*, the journal of the National Association of Audubon Societies, we were shocked to read:

> George W. Cobb, this Association's warden on Cobb's Island, Virginia, lost his life, on August 23, in the severe storm that lashed the middle Atlantic coast. The meager information received may be all that we will ever learn concerning the fate of this Virginian of well-known pioneer stock, who thus ended his lonely vigils on the wind-swept stretch of dune and marsh which was his ancestral home. Search by airplane and boat has failed, as yet, to reveal his body which, no doubt, rests somewhere among the extensive marshes of the Virginian shores. The storm which took Mr. Cobb's life, we are informed, completely demolished the few buildings on the island, leaving nothing but the drill pole of the United States Coast Guard Station.

Once back in Middleton from Virginia in mid-July, 1933, I set to work developing my photographs taken on Cobb Island. I was particularly pleased with my skimmer pictures even though, because of the storm, they covered only the early stages of nesting.

While we were away, no responses to my job applications had come. The ensuing weeks passed pleasantly enough even though fraught with anxiety. Would I be jobless this fall? Father might have remarked that if I had obtained an M.D. instead of a Ph.D., I would have had nothing to worry about, but if he thought that, he offered no intimation.

Toward the end of August, my dear Grandmother Groves in Belgrade became gravely ill and died on September 4. On the day of the funeral at the Belgrade farm the sky was cloudless, Long Pond was never bluer, and the White Mountains in the distance seemed to shine. Never had I appreciated more the picturesque setting of my birthplace. No longer would I have grandparents to visit. Grandfather would henceforth live with my parents in Middleton.

After the day of the funeral, Eleanor returned to teaching in Swampscott. Then came a stellar day, September 22, with a telegram from President Kenneth Sills of Bowdoin appointing me Teaching Fellow in Biology for the academic year. Elated beyond words, I called Dr. Gross immediately, knowing full well that he was behind my appointment. He urged me to come to Brunswick the next day. It would be Saturday and Eleanor could join me.

CHAPTER 17 / *Bowdoin Teaching Fellow*

 BY THE TIME Eleanor and I arrived in Brunswick, Mrs. Gross had arranged living quarters for us—the second floor, furnished, in a home two blocks away from the Grosses. My job would be to assist Dr. Gross and Dr. Copeland in their laboratories, to help grade papers, and, in the spring semester, to assist Dr. Gross in his ornithology course. Since classes were beginning the following Monday, I must arrive as soon as possible.

Eleanor and I were back in Middleton the same day we left. I spent the next two days packing and was in Brunswick on the job by Tuesday.

Very much on my mind from the start was getting my thesis published. On my second trip to Brunswick from home, I brought it with me for Dr. Gross to peruse and to seek his advice for a publisher. His response, after he had taken into consideration the size of the thesis: "This should become one of the memoirs of the Boston Society of Natural History, just as my heath hen report had become. Take it to the society right away and submit it to the editor, Dr. Clinton V. McCoy, for consideration as a memoir." This I did and in a letter from him, dated October 14, he wrote in part: "Our Publications Committee has viewed with distinct approval your thesis on the American Woodcock, and, if the paper could be reduced to 300 typescript pages or less, we might be able to publish it in the not-too-distant future. . . . " To say that I was pleased is an understatement.

Determined as I was to become an ornithologist like Drs. Gross or Allen, who actually taught ornithology, I realized that I would need a bird skin collection. (I could never have taught night school in ornithology while in Ithaca without borrowing from Dr. Allen's bird skin collection.) Now that I would have spare time when not assisting both professors, I decided to acquire at least some of my collection right in the Brunswick area. Each specimen would be tagged with full data (date when collected, sex, weight, etc.). I would obtain my own tags for the data with my name printed on them. Dr. Copeland agreed to purchase a storage cabinet for keeping the specimens until I needed them later elsewhere. Adhering to my decision, in the months ahead I obtained a desirable variety of bird species for teaching purposes.

When the weather discouraged collecting as it often did in winter, I occupied myself inside with personal projects: writing articles for popular magazines; coloring more lantern slides for lecture purposes; preparing a folder with photographs for printing and distribution about my lectures on Maine's coastal birds and on my trip to Hudson Bay. Writing and lecturing were ways in which I hoped to increase my income.

In the fall of 1933, November 13–16, the American Ornithologists' Union held its semicentennial meeting in New York City at the American Museum of Natural History and I was granted time to attend. I gave two papers: a twenty-five-minute summation of my three years of studying the American woodcock, and a short account of witnessing the destruction of bird nests and young by the vicious storm that had lashed Cobb Island earlier in the year. This being my fifth meeting of the A.O.U., I now felt considerably at ease in this gathering of 266 members, including some of the country's leading professional ornithologists. There were many members I knew now and I had a chance to make the acquaintance of others with whom I had corresponded. George Sutton gave a paper on the birds of the Big Bend country in Texas where he had spent several months. In his regular letters to me I had sensed his growing enthusiasm for ornithological work in the southwestern United States and Mexico.

Christmas in Middleton was, like the ones before, a happy season except this time for the loss of Grandmother Groves. This lent a touch of sadness, but Uncle Bill would not let it prevail; he would think of some foolishness to make everyone laugh. Eleanor and I celebrated our first wedding anniversary by going in to Boston with Father's assistant superintendent and his wife for a lively New Year's Eve party at a well-known hotel.

By good fortune in March of 1934, I lined up for the summer a job of teaching ornithology at the New Hampshire Nature Camp. It came about this way: during the previous summer at the Camp, Dr. Gross had directed its two sessions, each two weeks long, and taught ornithology. Since, during the coming summer, he would be going north on a cruise with Donald B. MacMillan, he asked me if I would like to teach there in his place. Well aware that I would be receptive, he said he would write to Mrs. Laurence J. Webster, the sponsor of the camp, recommending me. Mrs. Webster accepted me and Eleanor and I would show up at the camp in mid-June.

As the academic year of 1933–34 at Bowdoin neared closing, I was invited by the college to give one of my slide lectures in the Moulton Union on May 21. I chose "To Hudson Bay with the Birds"—the first time I had ever given it as a solo performance before a general audience. What would a non-ornithological audience care about birds? Most attending would not know one sparrow from another, least of all a Harris' sparrow. I was nervous about giving it right up to the moment after I had been introduced. (I wrote in my diary that "the Moulton Union was full.")

Everything went well enough, the projection was good, and I thought my comments on each slide well chosen, intelligent, and sufficient. But alas, I was through in thirty-five minutes, saying thank-you, and asking for the lights. Never was an audience more nonplussed, each person looking around, wondering if something had happened. Realizing that my lecture had been shorter than I anticipated and seeing that the audience expected more, I had sense enough to ask if there were any questions. Happily, there were and I gave answers sufficient to fill up an hour. I had learned a lesson: use more slides (twice as many as I had struggled to color), say more about the slides selected, be more in tune with the interests of the audience, and *talk more slowly.*

At the wind-up of the academic year, there were written and oral examinations for biology majors. I was expected to join Drs. Gross and Copeland in questioning them. In many respects my year at Bowdoin (it was understood at the outset that my teaching fellowship was for one year only) was like my undergraduate years at the college, except that Eleanor was with me for weekends and on her vacations, and there were more social occasions, including faculty dinners and receptions. Eleanor was one of the chaperons along with several faculty wives at the Ivy Dance.

After the college closed for the summer, I became better acquainted with Dr. Copeland. We took field trips together. Once we were joined by Arthur H. Norton of the Portland Society of Natural History in searching for sharp-tailed sparrows in some of the nearer coastal marshes. When I visited with Dr. Copeland in his home he suggested that, after I was through teaching at the New Hampshire Nature Camp, I consider taking the four-week course in marine invertebrate zoology at the Marine Biological Laboratory at Woods Hole, Massachusetts, located on the southwestern tip of Cape Cod. By taking the course I would strengthen my application for teaching. He had a summer home at Woods Hole and could be helpful in finding a place for Eleanor and me to stay. I liked his suggestion and said that I would send in my application. I reminded him that Eleanor had taught school on Martha's Vineyard, not far from Woods Hole, and was familiar with— and fond of—that part of the country.

On June 16, I gathered up our belongings in the Brunswick apartment and was on my way to Middleton, the very day that Dr. Gross started sailing north with MacMillan. Eleanor was away attending her class reunion at Wheaton College. She arrived back in Middleton early in the morning of June 17. We packed a lunch and set out for the New Hampshire Nature Camp near North Woodstock, appearing with a little time to spare before dinner.

CHAPTER 18 / New Hampshire Nature Camp, First Summer

THE NEW HAMPSHIRE NATURE CAMP was the concept of Mrs. Laurence J. Webster. She established it in 1932 with the cooperation of the Society for Protection of New Hampshire Forests and approval by the Garden Club of America and several other organizations. A camp was to operate in the summer in a natural setting and employ authorities in field biology to train school teachers about nature. For its site, she chose the Lost River Reservation in Kinsman Notch, where the Moosilaukee River loses itself in caverns under enormous rocks. Above, on the great rocks, were an administration building that overlooked a narrow valley, an assembly hall, and a dining room, while on the slope rising west from the rocks were cabins for the teaching staff and dormitories for students.

At the door of the assembly hall to greet Eleanor and me was Mrs. Webster. A little person, gracious, smiling, and speaking softly, she quickly introduced us to others standing by who would serve on the staff: Charles M. Pomerat, director; Albert S. Carlson, geologist, with his wife; Joseph S. Tidd, botanist; and Violet L. Findlay, expert in methods of teaching field biology. As time for dinner was approaching, Mrs. Webster asked a reservation guide to escort us to our cabin. There Eleanor and I quickly changed and soon joined the staff in the dining room.

After dinner, staff and students gathered in the assembly hall. There were eighteen students, all school teachers and women except one. When I saw the man I couldn't believe my eyes: he had been my high school chemistry teacher, whom I remembered as always teasing me. Said I to myself, "I'll get back at him and have some fun."

Mrs. Webster gave welcoming remarks. Then the students were asked to take their turn standing up, giving their name, and telling where they were from. They were followed by the staff, each member explaining his or her role in the next two weeks.

These formalities completed, Director Pomerat roughly outlined the program for the two-week session. Every day, except the coming Sunday (day off for everybody), there would be field trips which he would lead as general biologist and which would be accompanied by Mr. Carlson as geologist, Mr. Tidd as botanist, and me as ornithologist. Two field trips would take all day: one in the first week to Franconia Notch, and the second in the second week up Mount Washington. The other field trips would be in the mornings only. Most afternoon sessions would be given by Miss Findlay who would teach classroom methods, show various concrete ways of using outdoor material for indoor teaching, and give outlines for each grade level in elementary schools. Each evening there would be a lecture, often preceded by a review of the field trip taken, and a notice of where we would go on the morrow.

Mrs. Webster, I had learned earlier, was first and foremost a bird devotee and went on all the trips. With her it was *birds first*. This Director Pomerat already knew and he made his audience understand that if I saw or heard a bird worth noting, I should call attention to it and expect the entire group to respond. No matter, for example, if Joe Tidd were expounding on some particular plant; ignore him. The plant could wait but the bird would not. This was obviously an advantage to me but an irritant to the person who was interrupted.

The trips selected were to include all significant environments from valley streams and meadows to timberline and alpine regions. The camp itself was ideally situated for birds. From the west slope above the reservation buildings, for instance, one could hear in the early morning five different thrushes—the Swainson's, hermit, veery, wood thrush, and, high up on the slope, the gray-cheeked.

On our first Sunday, the Websters invited Eleanor and me to their lovely summer home in Holderness overlooking Squam Lake. Immediately we could see that the Websters had made a special effort to equip their estate with every means to attract birds. Birdbaths and birdhouses, feeding stations, and flower gardens had been positioned with forethought and care. In their initial efforts they were disappointed in attracting so few ruby-throated hummingbirds despite their flower gardens. Mrs. Webster solved the problem in 1928 from a suggestion she had read about and imporved upon. She "created" flowers by attaching to sticks two-inch-long vials wrapped in bright red ribbons and filled with a solution of one part sugar and two parts water. The "flowers" she scattered generously around the house, resulting in an abundance of hummingbirds. During the course of an hour we saw at least fifty hummingbirds visiting vials here and there along the veranda, some on small clipped shrub branches attached to window frames, others suspended from an overhanging trellis. The vials had to be refilled three or four times a day. I took several photographs of a hummingbird drinking from a vial on a twig held in Mrs. Webster's mouth.

At the nature camp I was again teaching the identity of different birds without the benefit of skins. There was no such thing at the time as a field guide illustrating all species of birds in a comparative manner. For illustrations, my one recourse was to use the *Audubon Bird Cards*, each picturing one species, although they were far from including all local species. I insisted after a trip that the students review all the cards (the names of the birds under the pictures being cut off) and identify the species. Sometimes the futility of using pictures instead of skins was glaringly demonstrated by one student who called an osprey a white-breasted nuthatch, not realizing the difference in size.

The first session was not a week old before I appreciated the congeniality of the staff. Much of its spirit was due to the director, Charlie Pomerat himself, a heavily set man, sandy-haired and pleasant-faced with a rare command of the English language, enhanced by a keen sense of humor and an infectious laugh.

After the first week of the session, Charlie Pomerat and those of us conducting field trips decided to divide the students into two groups, one led by Al Carlson and myself, the other by Charlie and Joe Tidd. In one respect, this arrangement was ideal for it meant fewer students and less subject matter to cover. On the other hand, we instructors had to go over the same ground twice. This division of students did not apply to the all-day trips to Franconia and Mount Washington, on which we all went together. (The Franconia area including the Flume and Profile Lake beneath the Old Man of the Mountains was pleasantly familiar to me after my trip with Miss Wadleigh in 1924.) The ascent of Mount Washington was by cog-railway. Above timberline, with alpine flora abundant, Joe Tidd was in his element. As for birds, the best I could show were white-throated sparrows and slate-colored juncos. For more species, time permitting, I led the students down to timberline where we could hear or see gray-cheeked thrushes and blackpoll warblers.

During each session I gave two evening lectures, one on Hudson Bay and the other on Maine's coastal birds. For clowning on stunt night—the last evening of each session—I resorted to singing old songs such as "Let's All Sing Like the Birdies Sing" and "I'm Only a Bird in a Gilded Cage." Fortunately, I remembered the songs and how well they had gone over when I was a Bowdoin Psi Upsilon initiate in 1926.

Spare time I devoted to nest-hunting, Eleanor helping me, for photographic subject matter. At the beginning of the second session, a young woman student who was equipped with a camera asked if she could take pictures of the birds on any nest I had found. She introduced herself as Helen Gere. Of course, I told her she was welcome to do so. She said she was trying to keep up with her boyfriend who was a masterful bird photographer. Coyly she showed me a photograph of him in a tree, directing his camera down on a hawk's nest. He was Allan D. Cruickshank, soon to be much admired countrywide for his camera work on birds.

On our last Franconia trip, after gazing up at the Old Man on Cannon Mountain, I resolved that the following Sunday, though Eleanor didn't know it yet, she and I were going to climb Cannon Mountain and see what the Old Man looked like close up. In fact, I planned to sit on his forehead. Sunday, July 15, was a clear day; Eleanor was agreeable to my idea and ready. Once we reached the summit, we cautiously scrambled down southward to the Old Man, comprising three ledges. We noted the huge irons preventing the ledge, which formed the forehead, from falling off. Carrying out my idea, I walked out on the forehead, sat down on its edge, and marveled at seeing Profile Lake below, calmly reflecting the sky.

After the stunt night concluding the second session, Charlie Pomerat, the Carlsons, Joe Tidd, Eleanor and I drove down to nearby North Woodstock for a snack. We were in a low mood because our presence was expected the following Monday and Tuesday, July 16 and 17, to host garden club members, taking them on field trips during the day, entertaining them in the evening with lectures—the same old routine. We expected to contend with a mob of women. Only five showed up. I gave my Hudson Bay lecture the second evening, concluding the program for the garden clubbers.

But the evening was not over for us. To our surprise, several of the reservation guides, who had befriended us during the course of four weeks, invited all the staff on a tour of the Lost River caverns, which we knew were below us but had never seen. The guides led us into weakly illuminated caverns and helped us crawl through such crevices as the "Lemon Squeeze." I will never forget hearing Charlie Pomerat's grunts and muffled laughs as he, rather corpulent, coped with some of the passages. Thus, our four weeks at Lost River came to an end.

Eleanor and I were off to Wayne after breakfast the next morning and spent slightly less than two weeks there before taking off for Woods Hole. The great surprise on reaching Wayne was to see that Father had acquired a sailboat. In a short while, the wind suitable, Father and I were aboard, taking turns sailing it. I was grateful for having learned how to sail at Camp Morgan in the summer of 1918. At the end of July Eleanor and I left for Middleton, reaching Auntie Brown's for supper, going afterwards to my parents' home to unpack and repack for Woods Hole where we would spend a month.

We reached Woods Hole late the next day, going directly to the Copelands' where we found young Manton who helped us find our place to stay—a six-room cottage, for rent, completely and handsomely furnished, on the edge of a pond. A dining room, glassed in, overlooked the pond. This was hardly a residence for a student and certainly more than I required, but Eleanor was thrilled. Running through her mind almost surely was the pleasure we would have entertaining. Anyway, we had virtually no other choice for a boarding place, as Manton knew, so we made arrangements to take the cottage. We spent the night at the Copelands' and moved into our luxurious abode the next morning. The course in marine invertebrates at the biological laboratory had already begun.

From the moment we agreed to take the cottage I could foresee, as did Eleanor, the opportunity for hosting relatives and friends, but I had to remind her that I was in Woods Hole to broaden my biological knowledge with yet another course, this one to consist of collecting, studying, and dissecting various marine invertebrates—coelenterates, platyhelminths, arthropods, and others. I strove mightily to concentrate on the course and to a mild extent succeeded, although I was too often sidetracked by social affairs.

The Copelands right away invited us for dinner in their delightful cottage and we soon reciprocated. My parents arrived for a stay as did Auntie Brown, Aunt Millie, and Uncle Bill. We had friends from our college days and Eleanor's friends from Martha's Vineyard. Scarcely an evening went by without depending upon the preferences of our guests: bridge-playing, or movie-going, or attending summer theater, or dancing. In later days when asked how I liked Woods Hole, I replied, "I had a wonderful time and learned more about lobsters than necessary to enjoy eating them."

Eleanor left Woods Hole on September 4 with Uncle Bill; she had a teachers' meeting late that day in Swampscott. I stayed on to finish work in the laboratory and departed on September 6 for Middleton, where I spent two days getting unpacked and reorganized, and developing the photographs I had taken in New Hampshire. Eleanor had much to do also in getting herself reorganized. We were a busy couple.

One matter I attended to promptly was to go in to the Boston Society of Natural History for a conference with Dr. McCoy, who was editing my woodcock thesis, on procedures in preparing it for publication. The work needed reduction and rewriting into a more readable style, as well as to be rendered in typescript for the printer. Furthermore, the references needed not only rechecking but also to be put in consistent form. With over five hundred pages on my hands to reduce and edit for publication, I could foresee many weeks of work ahead—and no teaching job in prospect.

CHAPTER 19 / *Jobless Year*

IN MY DIARY for September 19, 1934, I wrote: "The future never looked more dismal than it does right now." The statement was due in part to a stroke of bad luck. While I was in Woods Hole a letter from a western state university had been mailed to me about a teaching job, expressing interest in my credentials and requesting statements from my sponsors. The letter had gotten mixed in with Father's mail at the sanatorium and had not been forwarded soon enough. By the time my reply with supporting statements had reached its destination, the job was filled. Part of my depression was also due to the lack of responses from teachers' agencies and absence of interest by lecture bureaus in my slide shows.

Reworking my woodcock thesis for publication was now my principal job. At least once a week, I—Eleanor sometimes with me to help, if a Saturday—went to the library, either at the Boston Society of Natural History or in the Museum of Comparative Zoology at Harvard University, to check on the proper form and accuracy of references or to obtain references that were not in the library at Cornell University. Other days for me it was type, type, type. My typewriter was old when I started. Soon I wore it out and had to replace it.

As mid-October approached I had a change of pace coming. The American Ornithologists' Union was meeting in Chicago, October 23–25. Eleanor, getting leave from her teaching, left with me for Chicago on Friday, October 19. We went by way of Ithaca, picking up George Sutton and continuing westward across Ontario. As we drove along, our conversation never lagged. George was excited as his book *Eskimo Year* was about to be published. He told us much about his summer in British Columbia (he would give a paper about the birds there at the coming meeting). We stopped in Ann Arbor, Michigan, to visit with friends, reaching Chicago on October 22 and putting up at the Hotel Stevens. Over 270 members attended the meeting, the largest number ever at an A.O.U. meeting outside of New York, Philadelphia, and Washington. Several sessions were in the Field Museum of Natural History. I gave the lead paper at the Thursday morning session on the food and feeding habits of (what else?) the American woodcock. Not far away the World's Fair was in progress, drawing many members away from the sessions. I must admit to having spent more time at the fair than at the sessions. With George, we started for home late on October 25, going by way of Detroit where I wanted to inquire about a possible job. We reached Ithaca at midday on October 27, leaving George and visiting briefly with Mrs. Fuertes. We were glad to be home the next day after battling miserable weather from Ithaca.

In December, the Massachusetts Department of Education began a series of radio programs, one each week over station WAAB, called "Spotlighting Modern Education," and asked me to give one on ornithology, on the twenty-first. I set to work writing it. Called simply "The Study of Ornithology," it turned out to be eight pages long and dealt with every possible aspect of the subject I could think of. The day before going in to the studio, I practiced reading it repeatedly to my parents, tolerant souls. Eleanor went with me to the studio and sat nearby while I read slowly and precisely (as my parents had urged) before the unresponsive thing in front of me. The next day came a letter from Dr. Gross, my ever-supportive mentor, which read in part: "Your words were well chosen and you put it over perfectly. Your thought of using bird study for the increased leisure which the masses are destined to have is a superb and original idea."

Performing on the radio was a milestone in my life. Another one, less important perhaps, had come earlier on November 14 when I gave a lecture for a fee—all of twenty-five dollars—the first remuneration I had ever received for a lecture. The lecture was on Maine's coastal birds at Academy Hall in Salem. Eleanor projected the slides. This time the audience was not shortchanged as the lecture took over an hour.

Our 1934 Christmas at home in Middleton followed tradition: a gathering of the family on the day itself to exchange
presents. I was showered with gifts, as was Eleanor, every
one of them thoughtful. We celebrated our second wedding
anniversary by going to a movie in the afternoon, then having
friends on the staff at the sanatorium join the two of us with
Father, Mother, and Grandfather Groves for New Year's Eve.
As the radio announced the approach of 1935, I vanished and
quickly appeared with a bouquet of roses I had had hidden in
a closet and gave it to Eleanor, kissing her. This started a bout
of kissing among all in the room. Happy New Year!

The holidays over and Eleanor back teaching in Swampscott, I was again at work on my thesis, which I had begun
calling "my book" on the American woodcock. On January
28, George Sutton's promised frontispiece for the book arrived—a handsome 15 × 17-inch watercolor of a female
woodcock with her brood of four chicks. By early February I
had completed the text, mounted and titled all plates, but my
checking on still more titles in the bibliography yet remained.
This meant repeated trips to the libraries in Boston and Cambridge. The entire revision was completed on February 20.
The next day, Eleanor joined me in delivering the manuscript
and frontispiece to Dr. McCoy at the Boston Society of Natural History; he could not have been more complimentary
about George's watercolor for the frontispiece. Now that
Dr. McCoy had the manuscript, I assumed that when we left
he would soon be editing it for the printer.

The woodcock manuscript was barely off my hands when
I faced a new experience in the weeks ahead. The A. K.
Bloods, a wealthy family in Swampscott, approached Eleanor
about having me tutor their twelve-year-old son, Kim. The
Bloods had withdrawn him from the local public school, where
he was not progressing to their satisfaction, and intended to
enter him in a private day school the following spring. Meanwhile would I tutor him? Eleanor drove me in to Swampscott
to meet the Bloods and decide. I found Kim a sunny youngster, friendly and alert. What the Bloods wanted me to do was
to acquaint him with "the world around him" by taking him

on local tours; assign him relevant books to read at home; and even take him to worthwhile movies. I acquiesced, although I had never tutored anyone.

From the last week of February until the second week of April, I worked with Kim, taking him to numerous colonial homes such as the House of Seven Gables and the Witch House. We visited both the Stoneham and Franklin Park zoos several times, and spent much time at important art museums and collections. When there was a good movie, such as *David Copperfield* or *Great Expectations*, I took him. I found Kim responsive to everything I showed him and always companionable. Unfortunately he broke his foot in late March, prohibiting further tours. As for his homework, from the beginning in late February, I quizzed him at some length on the books I had assigned him, just to make sure that he was following instructions and gaining value.

Beginning on April 8, Mrs. Blood entered Kim in a private school in Cambridge and hired me to chauffeur him daily. This I did until the school closed at the end of May. The time spent amounted to four hours a day of driving, five times a week. My poor old Model A Ford roadster, new in 1930, no longer could take all the chauffeuring—it had come to the end of its days—and consequently (not unhappily) I bought a new Ford two-door sedan on April 23.

During the time while I was tutoring Kim, I had printed on 11 × 8½-inch glossy paper my application for a teaching position in biology (no use mentioning ornithology) with a picture of myself and a summation of my career in sections titled education, teaching experience, and recommendations (that is, from whom these could be obtained), concluding with my address. At the beginning of May, I mailed a copy to an official in every well-known college and university in the country. I also made appointments for interviews, and succeeded, with the heads of all the prominent New England preparatory schools. I was graciously received and "pleaded my case," so to speak. Invariably I was told in effect to be patient, for my credentials were almost certain to win me a position in a college or university.

Amidst this seeming futility, rumor reached me from the alumni office at Bowdoin College that there was a possibility of a vacancy in zoology in the coming year at Westbrook Junior College for women on the northern outskirts of Portland, Maine. Losing no time, I made an appointment with the president, Dr. Milton D. Proctor, for May 23. Yes, he told me, there was a good chance for a job as instructor in zoology if the present incumbent did not return as she had intimated she might not. In every way the interview was pleasant and I felt encouraged. Dr. Proctor was short, rather stout, with a flashing smile. I liked him from the moment I met him.

CHAPTER 20 / *Grand Manan Summer*

ALL ALONG from the time I began tutoring Kim Blood, Eleanor and I were concerned about what we would do in the summer of 1935. Dr. Gross was returning to the New Hampshire Nature Camp. Eventually I decided on making an ornithological survey of the island of Grand Manan, fifteen miles long and seven miles wide, and its outlying smaller islands, collectively called the Grand Manan Archipelago. Lying off the northeast coast of Maine, the islands are politically a part of New Brunswick.

Remembering that Edgar and Alma Russell, whom Edward Dana and I had so enjoyed knowing on Machias Seal Island in 1932, had moved back home to Grand Manan, and remembering their invitation to visit with them if ever we went to Grand Manan, I wrote to Edgar asking if the invitation still held. If so, my wife and I wanted to set up Green Mansion in their backyard and take our meals with them while I spent several weeks searching for birds and photographing some of them. Edgar's reply was prompt and most agreeable. He and Alma looked forward to meeting Eleanor.

On May 29, with my camera and plenty of film, I started for Grand Manan alone. Eleanor would be coming in three weeks as soon as she was through at Swampscott. I stopped in Wayne to pick up Green Mansion, two folding cots, and other paraphernalia, and reached Eastport, Maine, about 10:30 A.M. on May 31, just as the ferry *The Grand Manan* was docking. I had barely time enough to get my car on board and make arrangements with U.S. Customs officials before the ship pulled out in the fog for the dock at North Head, Grand Manan. There, inside the tiny Canadian Customs house for the business of entry, I met Ross Russell for the first time and followed him in his car south to the Russell home in the village of Seal Cove.

Ross Russell, Ronald's older brother, was about eighteen years old. On meeting him at North Head, I noticed at once how well dressed and outgoing in manner he was. When we reached his home came a joyful occasion, my seeing and greeting Ed, Alma, and Ronny again. Before long, with the boys' help, Green Mansion was set up not far back from the Russell house, and the cots were soon readied for use inside with blankets on them. Now for one of those suppers of Alma's that I remembered so well.

On June 4, with directions from Ross, I drove to North Head to meet Allan L. Moses, a life-long resident of Grand Manan who had devoted much of his life to study of the local birdlife. Over the years, as a skilled taxidermist, he had developed a small museum of natural history representing the birds of the region. He welcomed me cordially, offered data from any of his specimens, and expressed willingness to guide me to habitats for different birds.

Despite much fog and many rainy spells during the first twenty days, I covered territory that included all kinds of habitats, and I found many nests. On the night of June 21, Eleanor arrived. Father had driven her into Boston where she had boarded the boat for an overnight sail to St. John, New Brunswick. There she had to wait nearly all day for *The Grand Manan* to North Head where I picked her up after dark. She met the Russells for the first time before we retired to Green Mansion.

The day before Eleanor's arrival, I had received a telegram from Mother indicating that the oral civil service examination for the job of Massachusetts state ornithologist was to be held on June 26 in Boston. The man now on the job in a temporary capacity, I had been told by several well-informed sources, was likely to hold it permanently. The examination was a mere formality, conforming to civil service regulations. Probably true, but I vowed I would take the examination.

Early in the morning of June 24, with Ross as my willing companion, we boarded *The Grand Manan* in my car for Eastport and made it to Middleton about 9:30 in the evening. My parents were impressed with Ross, his attractive appearance and his fine manners. For him this was an adventure. He had never been in the United States and only once in a city, St. John. Everything he saw drew his special attention, even the traffic cops. The next day I took him into Boston for the afternoon show at the Metropolitan Theater, the handsomest of movie palaces. Ross was wide eyed at the glittering interior. He heard the lively music from the great Wurlitzer, and from our seats near the stage, saw the huge orchestra playing loudly in the pit. Then came onstage the long line of thinly clad girls, high kicking as they danced. Finally the featured movie began on an enormous screen. Ross seemed stunned, his face expressionless.

Ross accompanied me into Boston again the next morning, and while I took the oral examination at the State House, he walked through parts of the building open to the public. The examination over, we headed for Grand Manan, stopping briefly to say good-bye to my parents. We slept overnight in my car by the roadside, somewhere near Madison, Maine, and reached Eastport at half-past five in the morning to wait for *The Grand Manan*. We were back at Seal Cove early that afternoon.

I was puzzled by Ross's reaction to what he observed in Boston's Metropolitan Theater. Not a word indicating pleasure or astonishment did he express to his parents or Ronny. He seemed to have been dumbfounded. As for the result of my oral examination, I never heard anything.

While I was away, Eleanor had become intrigued by a family of boreal chickadees nesting in an old woodpecker hole not far from our camp. There were seven young in the nest, about three days old when we examined it, being fed with remarkable frequency by both parents. We decided to devote a day to taking turns counting the number of feeding trips from dawn until dusk. The total was 362 trips or an average of twenty-four trips per hour!

It seemed that staying on Grand Manan for any length of time was impossible: I received on July 5 a letter from President Proctor of Westbrook Junior College, saying that he would like to have me come in and see him as soon as possible. I surmised that it would be important. Again I boarded *The Grand Manan*, this time in the early morning of July 6, Eleanor with me.

We headed south via Belgrade, stopping to check up on Grandfather (he was still on his beloved farm in the summer) and staying overnight in Wayne. We were off to Portland in the morning. By 11:00, I was shaking hands with Dr. Proctor and introducing him to Eleanor. In a short while, Mrs. Proctor appeared in the office, meeting both of us and escorting Eleanor upstairs to the Proctor apartment where all of us would eventually have lunch.

From Dr. Proctor I accepted the position, starting in the fall, as instructor in zoology with salary plus board. I would have an apartment on the main floor of the administration building. This would include Eleanor and meals for her whenever she could be with me. I would be expected on the job September 12.

After a leisurely lunch with the Proctors, we returned to Wayne for the night and, by the late evening of July 9, were in Green Mansion on our cots, exhausted.

One of the outer islands of the Grand Manan Archipelago that I wanted to explore—and by now I had investigated nearly all of them—was Kent Island, site of herring gull and Leach's storm-petrel colonies among the largest on the Atlantic coast. In 1930, J. Sterling Rockefeller had purchased Kent Island as a wildlife sanctuary. In 1935, the same year we were on Grand Manan, Rockefeller gave the island to Bowdoin College for scientific purposes; it was soon to be the location of the Bowdoin Scientific Station.

There were eleven Bowdoin students on Kent Island now, living in a ramshackle building. I prevailed upon Ed Russell to take us there in his boat one day. The students welcomed us graciously, soon gratefully when they saw Eleanor taking over the cooking on a gas stove. Between meals the next day, Eleanor and I explored the island. I fail to remember where and how we bunked that night except that we were uncomfortable. The next morning, after Eleanor had cooked a hearty breakfast for everyone, a couple of the students escorted us aboard their motor craft and delivered us without incident to Seal Cove, Grand Manan.

On July 21, I concluded my survey of the main island, Grand Manan, and all the important outer islands. If there was a good habitat I missed, I doubt it. I had never before found an area to rival this in diversity of birds. Eventually I would bring my data together in "The Bird Life of the Grand Manan Archipelago" to be published in the *Proceedings of the Nova Scotian Institute of Science*. By evening Green Mansion had been taken down and our car packed. We slept that night in the Russell home. Up early and having had our last of Alma's wonderful breakfasts, we bade the Russells heartfelt farewells and drove away.

We stopped briefly in Wayne with my parents, who were vacationing, and also to see Aunt Mame and Uncle Luther, then continued home to Middleton, first checking up on Auntie Brown. After a few days at home, unpacking and taking care of mail, we returned to Wayne at the end of July for three weeks. Going back to Middleton again until it was time to depart for Westbrook Junior College in early September, we stopped to look at our Westbrook "apartment"—just one big room with double bed. We would have, as Dr. Proctor had promised us, a desk and a couple of chairs. Other furnishings we would have to provide.

On August 21, I learned, not unexpectedly, that the man who had been acting Massachusetts state ornithologist when I took the oral examination for the job on June 26 had indeed been permanently appointed.

CHAPTER 21 / *Instructor, Westbrook Junior College*

SEPTEMBER 12, 1935, marked my arrival in Portland to join the faculty of Westbrook Junior College. Founded in 1830 as Westbrook Seminary, offering a liberal education to men and women, in the passing of a hundred years the offering had come to be for young women only. By 1933 it became strictly a junior college for women with a two-year curriculum.

In 1935, freshmen and sophomores numbered about 160, two-thirds of them day students. My job was to teach zoology, physiology, human anatomy, and bacteriology to about fifty students who wanted background for becoming medical secretaries. I had never studied bacteriology, but my assistant, Ruth Sawyer, was trained in the field and would take charge for me.

September 12 simply involved meeting with my assistant and together checking on class materials available or needed, and then going into town with Dr. Proctor to select a desk and a couple of chairs that the college would buy for my room. The time until I gave my first lecture on Monday, September 23, included a faculty meeting; a boresome all-day registration session; my return to Middleton for my typewriter, clothing, bedding, and other necessities; and a brief meeting with my class to give them a list of materials to bring for laboratory work. Eleanor came for the weekend of September 21–22, decided we needed a studio couch, and bought one.

I would meet my classes on Mondays, Tuesdays, Thursdays, and Saturday mornings, requiring nineteen contact hours when counting both hours of lecturing and monitoring laboratories. Meanwhile, I would have ample time for preparing my lectures.

After the first faculty meeting, I became acquainted with

Sumner H. McIntire (Bowdoin, 1933), who had returned as assistant in science and mathematics. He roomed across the hall from me; I was soon calling him Mac. Not only did we like each other at once and often drop into each other's rooms for talk sessions, but I found him an enormous help in advising me on how to handle institutional situations that were perplexing to me, and giving me hints on the quirks of the various personalities of faculty and staff.

I was not long in personally appreciating Westbrook's location in Portland, since the city was the home of many friends including Ed Dana. Ed and I were often in touch with each other by telephone, sometimes for walks or to attend movies. Also, being near Brunswick was a bonus: I could visit readily with Dr. Gross and for an occasional lunch or dinner with him and his family, to attend football games and other college events, and to use the biology department's photographic facilities as well as borrow equipment for use in my classes.

As soon as I was well ahead in preparing lectures, I started writing a short paper on Grand Manan birds for the upcoming meeting of the American Ornithologists' Union in Toronto, October 21–24. I took several trips to Bowdoin to make lantern slides for illustrating it and then sent some of the slides to George Sutton, who had offered to color them. As soon as I completed the paper, I started work on a joint presentation with George on techniques in coloring lantern slides, which he and I would give at the meeting.

On October 21, I drove to Middleton to pick up Eleanor and head for Toronto, where we arrived the next day and put up at the Royal York Hotel. All A.O.U. sessions would be at the Royal Ontario Museum. About 330 members and guests attended the meeting, making it the largest ever held in Canada. I gave my fifteen-minute paper, illustrated by slides, one afternoon, and the following morning, George and I presented "Coloration of Lantern Slides." He talked while I projected a series of slides showing how he had perfected the technique of hand-coloring. Little did we know that there would soon be no need for it. The very next year, 1936, 35-mm Kodachrome appeared on the market, enabling anyone to take slides directly in full color. How I would welcome freedom from the time-consuming task of coloring slides, let alone making the slides themselves! At the meeting I became better acquainted with Karl H. Maslowski, whom I had met briefly in 1932. From Cincinnati and my age, Karl was already engaged in filming wildlife with the intention of making it his livelihood. From him I received strong encouragement for filming wildlife myself. He was using, he said, a remarkably fine 16-mm motion-picture camera, the Cine Kodak Special, which had been introduced in 1933. For filming wildlife this was ideal—sturdy, expertly engineered with a choice of speeds, constructed for through-the-lens viewing, and equipped with excellent lenses of different focal lengths. "As soon as possible," I said to myself, "no more lantern-slide lecturing for me. I will acquire my own Cine Kodak Special when I can afford it and lecture with motion pictures."

Eleanor and I left the Toronto meeting late on Thursday, October 24. By Monday, Eleanor was back on the job at Swampscott and I at Westbrook. While I was away Elizabeth Freese, a special student, had delivered the lectures I had left with her in manuscript.

There were two upcoming dances at Bowdoin that Eleanor chaperoned, I accompanying her. One was an informal gym dance in November and the other a tea dance in early December. The big social affair, however, was Westbrook's formal dance at the Eastland Hotel on Friday, December 13. Dr. and Mrs. Proctor and Eleanor and I were patrons and patronesses.

Eleanor returned to Middleton on Sunday, December 15. The next day at Westbrook there was sudden turmoil because one of the girls had come down with scarlet fever. The day students were sent home, while all the boarding students were quarantined. Fortunately for us all, Dr. Proctor closed the college toward the end of the following day and sent us all home. I packed quickly and started for Middleton.

Along the way I stopped for supper before arriving home in midevening, to the surprise of my parents. After explaining myself, I went on to stay with Eleanor at Auntie Brown's. Alone, Auntie Brown was scared half to death when I walked in on her. It being Eleanor's birthday, she had been invited out to play bridge and would not return until late. Learning that I wanted to surprise Eleanor and spend the night, Auntie was agreeable as well as amused. Having hidden my car, I went upstairs into Eleanor's room and retired. When Eleanor returned, Auntie said simply, "You'll find a surprise upstairs in your bed."

Eleanor continued teaching during the next three days while I loafed. On the third day, December 20, she got through teaching early, and we were soon on our way to Brunswick where she had long ago been invited to chaperon the Psi Upsilon Christmas house party. We called first on the Grosses, who had heard about the outbreak of scarlet fever at Westbrook and warned us that we might not be welcome. It was true; we were not. Furious at not having been advised of this earlier, all we could do was turn around and drive home to Middleton, seething.

Our Christmas vacation that followed was replete with festivities to make up for the disappointment. My family was in high spirits for our traditional Christmas Day. The next day, I dropped in at the Boston Society of Natural History to determine the progress on my woodcock book. Dr. McCoy assured me that it was "about printed" and that I should see proof "soon."

The last day of 1935 was a quiet one. In the evening my parents, Eleanor, and I watched the entertainment at the sanatorium, then returned with some of the staff to join Grandfather Groves in awaiting the new year while giving recognition to our third wedding anniversary. As 1936 arrived amid cheers, hugs, and kisses, in no way did Eleanor and I anticipate the forthcoming year's importance on my way to professional ornithology.

Early in January, Mrs. Webster invited me to have lunch with her in Boston. I hoped that I knew the reason why—and I did. She offered me the same position I had held at the New Hampshire Camp in 1934, as well as the same living conditions for Eleanor and me. I accepted her offer, of course. In the evening, I left for Westbrook with bag and baggage, leaving Eleanor who would soon be back teaching in Swampscott.

January marked the wind-up of the first semester, making

out examinations and grading them with the help of my assistant. The examinations were graded and out of the way when Eleanor arrived at the end of the month for the weekend. On the Saturday, we drove to Wayne with skis aboard to stay with Aunt Mame and Uncle Luther. Skiing was ideal over areas we knew only from our summer visits. On the Sunday afternoon, I drove to Middleton with Eleanor for my break between semesters. She went with me on the evening of February 4 to project my slides while I lectured on Maine's coastal birds to the Manchester (Massachusetts) Women's Club.

Back at Westbrook in early February for the start of the second semester, at the request of a dozen girls taking zoology, I held a no-credit bird class on Saturday mornings. Otherwise there was no change in courses.

February 6 brought the galley proof for my woodcock book. I would need assistance in reading it, one person to follow the manuscript while the other read from the proof, or *vice versa*. Ed volunteered to be the other person when Eleanor was not with me. Thanks to the two of them, I was through with the job in two weeks and went into Boston to deliver the corrected proof to Dr. McCoy before month's end—highly relieved to have it off my hands. Page proof for the book arrived a little over a month later. It would not require much time in reading, being mainly a matter of seeing that corrections from the galley proof had been made. Indeed, it was ready by April 5 when Eleanor took it home with her to turn over to Dr. McCoy.

The evening of April 24 featured a joint concert by the Westbrook Junior College and Bowdoin College Glee Clubs in the ballroom of the Eastland Hotel, preceded by a formal banquet and followed by a dance. Dr. and Mrs. Gross were among the invited guests.

On May 4, my brainchild, the woodcock book, arrived, bound and ready for distribution. Such a gratifying sensation it was for me to leaf through the book, at the same time holding my breath for fear of seeing an overlooked mistake. I postponed a celebration of the book's publication until May 9 when Eleanor, who had come the day before, and I purchased bottles of champagne. After supper, with Ed Dana, we headed for the Grosses in Brunswick to stay overnight. Champagne bottles soon popped as congratulations were given. Then came remarks and reminiscences which grew steadily louder and merrier. Never since have I as much as sipped champagne without thinking of that special night in Brunswick. For the conservation committee of the Longfellow Garden Club, on May 6 I led an early morning bird walk in Baxter's Woods with the assistance of five of my bird students. The next day in *The Portland Press Herald* there appeared a report of the walk with the picture of my father (taken long before), instead of me, as the leader. A fellow physician and close friend of Father's who lived in Portland, on seeing that picture, telephoned me, laughing heartily because he was aware that Father scarcely knew one bird from another.

Like college kids again, Eleanor and I attended part of the Ivy Activities at Bowdoin on May 22. We dined at the Psi U house and danced in the gym to the loud, fast music of Louis Armstrong's big band. I returned to Westbrook early in the morning to take my bird class on its last walk, later returning to pick up Eleanor.

The last days of May and first week of June included the last of my other classes and their final examinations. Then there were inventories to make out and laboratories to clean up. As Commencement approached, first there was the faculty and senior picnic at Tripp Lake, on June 6, the Baccalaureate the next day, and the president's tea. Commencement was in the morning of June 8, followed by a dinner for seniors, faculty, and staff. At the head table were seated, among others, the President and Mrs. Proctor with Mrs. Kenneth C. M. Sills of Brunswick. After the formal dinner, Eleanor and I made the rounds of good-byes, then hurriedly packed and departed for Middleton, glad that my year at Westbrook—although successful—was over.

During our get-togethers earlier in the year, Ed Dana and I had made plans for spending over a week in June—as soon as Westbrook closed and before I would go to the New Hampshire Nature Camp—in the Jones Beach State Bird Sanctuary on Long Island, New York. Here four hundred acres had been set aside for the nesting of over twenty species of birds including the piping plover. In the sanctuary was a large house occupied by a year-round keeper who welcomed visitors.

I spent the morning of June 9 in Middleton unpacking and sorting out my clothes. In the afternoon, Ed arrived and stayed with us overnight. The next morning he and I headed for Long Island in his car, reaching there at four-thirty after ferrying across Long Island Sound. Right away we had trouble finding the sanctuary, so we telephoned the keeper, John Herholdt, who directed us to the Jones Beach Hotel where he would meet us. He led us to the sanctuary but we returned to the hotel for the night, although we would spend subsequent nights in the sanctuary's house.

On returning to the sanctuary in the morning, I was not long in finding a piping plover's nest and setting up my blind near it. The following morning I managed to get a few good shots. In the afternoon Ed and I rode in the sanctuary motorboat to Gilgo Island just offshore, where we found nests of least and common terns. We set up our blinds close to them and left, confident that the birds would accept them.

Saturday, June 13, was a miserable rainy day. We decided it could best be spent by running into New York City, so off we went at midmorning. First we visited the American Museum of Natural History to see the new African Hall, then took in a sky show at the Planetarium. In the afternoon it was Radio City Music Hall for us to enjoy a movie and a glamorous stage show. Rain continued all the next day, quite prohibiting photography.

To our relief the weather cleared on June 16, and we obtained the tern photographs we wanted. In the evening we enjoyed having dinner at Bayside with Charlie Dunbar and his wife Irene, Charlie and I recollecting at length some of our strange experiences with the lighthouse personnel on Great Duck Island in 1928.

Ed and I packed ourselves up a day later and left for Orient Point, the northeastern fluke of Long Island, to find osprey nests. Arriving in the late afternoon, we located a few nests and set up blinds for use in the morning before finding a place to eat and spend the night. The next morning we entered the blinds and obtained a few shots, although the weather was against us and our blinds were not satisfactory for the shots we really wanted. Consequently, we folded up our blinds about noon, catching the ferry to New London,

Connecticut, and reaching Middleton for dinner with Eleanor and my parents.

Ed left for his home the next day while I spent it at home, developing my photographic efforts from Long Island and, with Eleanor, starting to get ready for New Hampshire.

CHAPTER 22 / *New Hampshire Nature Camp, Last Summer*

ELEANOR AND I, after stuffing her roadster full, drove on Sunday, June 21, 1936, to the New Hampshire Nature Camp for me to resume my role as ornithologist, this time at the camp's fifth season. We arrived in the early afternoon. How pleasant it was to see Charlie Pomerat, Miss Findlay, and Joe Tidd again. Mrs. Webster was there to greet us and introduce the new geologist and his wife, Dr. and Mrs. Jarvis B. Hadley. I was delighted to say hello to a couple of students who had been with us for the first session in 1934 and were back for the opening session this year.

We occupied the same cabin. The routine for both sessions was as it had been before, from the organizational meeting the first night to stunt night on the last. Teaching identification of birds was much easier because of a new book, *A Field Guide to the Birds,* by Roger Tory Peterson, but I still was without bird skins and had to rely on the *Audubon Bird Cards* for examinations. Most of the students in both sessions were women school teachers. When I had spare time, as in 1934, I nest-hunted and photographed species whose nests I found for the first time ever.

On July 8, in the second session, I received a letter from a teachers' agency in Boston stating that Dr. Donald J. Cowling, President of Carleton College in Northfield, Minnesota, had a job available in zoology and ornithology and that he would like to meet me in New York. Immediately I made a date by telephone. The following night Eleanor drove me to Plymouth, New Hampshire, where I boarded the train, taking a sleeper to New York.

I arrived in New York early, had breakfast, and met Dr. Cowling as prearranged at nine in the Commodore Hotel. In the lobby I spotted him at once in a white suit, very bald, and with bushy black eyebrows. When I introduced myself and we shook hands, I could not miss his penetrating eyes. During our meeting of nearly two hours he told me about Carleton, that it had extensive grounds, including an arboretum ideal for birds. Indeed, he had been under pressure from a few students for the college to offer a course in ornithology. I had the desirable credentials, he had noted, to give such a course.

As our conversation neared its end, Dr. Cowling said that he was prepared to offer me an assistant professorship in zoology. I would teach not only ornithology but also entomology, and would run three laboratory sections in introductory zoology for the chairman of the department, who lectured in the course. Naturally I expressed keen interest and said that I would gladly accept the position, whereupon Dr. Cowling promised that I would be hearing from him.

After the interview there was still much of the day left before I had to board the night train back to Plymouth. I went to the American Museum of Natural History, where I had lunch with Dr. James P. Chapin, authority on birds of what was then the Belgian Congo, and visited afterwards with Dr. Frank M. Chapman, whose *Handbook of Birds of Eastern North America* was the text in the ornithology course I had taken at Bowdoin College in 1928. I even had time for a show at Radio City Music Hall.

Meeting me at Plymouth, Eleanor was thrilled beyond words when I told her that at last I had been offered the teaching job I had been striving for ever since obtaining my doctorate. It would involve me foremost as an ornithologist. Never happier, we rushed back to the nature camp so that I could catch up with my class.

On Thursday, July 16, I received—joy of joys—confirmation of my appointment at Carleton College. By this time the second session at the nature camp was about over. But whereas I should have been feeling exhilarated over the appointment, I began to feel ill: I was coming down with the grippe. By Saturday I was in bed, running a high temperature. Eleanor gave my final examination and attended stunt night on my behalf. My temperature was still high on Sunday when all students and everyone else had departed except Mrs. Webster, Charlie Pomerat, and Violet Findlay.

On Monday morning, my temperature still high, Eleanor anxiously called my parents in Wayne. They arrived at noon. By then my temperature was about normal but I stayed in bed. Mrs. Webster, Charlie Pomerat, and Miss Findlay, before leaving in the afternoon, came to our cabin to say their farewells. My parents stayed overnight in a nearby cabin. The guides from the reservation helped pack our cars on Tuesday while I looked on. Before long we were bound for Middleton, I with my parents in their car, Eleanor following in her roadster. When by Wednesday I was well, Mother and Father returned to Wayne.

Then Thursday, July 23, at the invitation of Mrs. Webster, we drove back to New Hampshire, this time to her home in Holderness when Dr. Harold E. Edgerton of the Massachusetts Institute of Technology would be there. Having seen photographs of Mrs. Webster feeding ruby-throated hummingbirds from a vial on a twig held in her mouth and realizing how tame the hummingbirds were, Dr. Edgerton had asked Mrs. Webster's permission to come to her home with his stroboscopic high-speed camera to take stop-action pictures of the hummingbirds' wings.

When we arrived, he had his camera set up in the front window before a cluster of vials against a darkened background. As soon as Dr. Edgerton was ready, Mrs. Webster covered over all the other vials around the house. It was not long before three hummingbirds found the uncovered vials, and hovered before them to drink. Dr. Edgerton started the camera, from which came a loud *ziinnnnng*. Although this frightened the birds away, he had exposed the 150 feet of film and secured fifty feet of hummingbird action. The film had sped through the camera at the rate of eight hundred feet per second. Later study of the film, and of others subsequently exposed as the birds became accustomed to the sound of the camera, showed that a hummingbird beats its wings about fifty to fifty-five times per second while hovering and seventy-five times per second when in forward flight.

Early in August, with Dr. Gross's strong encouragement,

I visited the Bowdoin Scientific Station at Kent Island with him and Thornton Burgess. We were picked up by the station's launch, *The Scientist*, at Lubec, Maine, on August 1 and returned August 7. I had time on Kent Island for photography and to obtain additional data for my opus on the Grand Manan Archipelago.

Following the Kent Island trip, Eleanor and I put our minds to work on going to Minnesota, pulling together the necessities we should take, from books to household goods. Eleanor resigned from teaching in Swampscott and sold her roadster. I had already sent Dr. Proctor my resignation from Westbrook. On August 18, we called there for lunch with the Proctors. Both warmly congratulated me on the appointment at Carleton, while I took the opportunity to acknowledge how much I had profited from my experience at Westbrook. We collected some of our things in our room and took them to Middleton, later returning to Westbrook to gather up the last of our belongings.

Finally, by September 3, our trunks had been shipped and our car was literally stuffed. Aunt Millie and Uncle Bill drove out from West Medford to wish us well. The next morning marked our departure. Amid tears we bade Father, Mother, and Auntie Brown good-bye, promising to return for Christmas. In our car, Eleanor beside me, we set out on the long trip to Carleton College in Northfield, Minnesota, for the start of my professional career in ornithology.

Index

Illustrations are indicated by boldface type.